A Western Horseman Book

LEGENDS
VOLUME 2

Outstanding Quarter Horse Stallions and Mares

By Jim Goodhue
Frank Holmes
Phil Livingston
Diane C. Simmons

Edited by Pat Close

LEGENDS
VOLUME 2

Published by
Western Horseman Inc.

3850 North Nevada Ave.
Box 7980
Colorado Springs, CO 80933-7980

Design, Typography, and Production
Western Horseman
Colorado Springs, Colorado

Cover Painting
Orren Mixer

Printing
Publisher's Press
Salt Lake City, Utah

Fifth Printing: November 1996

ISBN 0-911647-30-9

INTRODUCTION

IN THE first *Legends,* published in 1993, I mentioned that we were already planning *Legends Volume 2.* We had made that decision because we could not include all the horses we wanted to in the book. But even if we hadn't already reached that decision, we would have quickly done so after *Legends* went on sale.

It was an immediate, overwhelming success, and the first press run of 10,000 copies quickly sold out. The book went back on press for the second printing within just a few months. This response spurred us into producing *Volume 2* as quickly as possible.

Even though this book is larger (192 pages) than the first book (168 pages), we still had the same problem: We could not include all of the horses and mares on the list for *Volume 2.* This means that there will be a *Volume 3,* which should be ready in 1997.

For this volume, we decided to work with four writers (who are profiled on page 186) instead of just one. Diane Simmons, who authored the first *Legends,* is a respected authority on Quarter running horses, so we asked her to write about the speed horses in this book.

For the performance horses, we turned to Phil Livingston. A lifelong roper, Phil has a wealth of information about the early horses noted for their performance ability. Of course, some of those horses were also tough match-race horses before, or even during, the years they were contested on in the rodeo arena.

No one is more qualified than Jim Goodhue to write about some of the very early horses, such as Traveler and Midnight. Jim worked for the American Quarter Horse Association for 33 years, with the last 22 spent as registrar.

Although Frank Holmes has always been an Appaloosa enthusiast, he has studied Quarter Horses and their bloodlines for years, and can recite pedigrees ad infinitum. He can also identify many of the horses in old pictures in our photograph files. We asked Frank to write about such horses as Oklahoma Star and Oklahoma Star Jr.

Because Frank had been living here in Colorado Springs, he also helped with researching all of the facts and information presented about each horse. This was an enormous job, especially since records of some early horses are often erroneous, misleading, contradictory (or all three), or non-existent.

He also spent hours going through our photo file, searching for photos of the horses profiled in this book, or photos of their descendants.

Just as he did with the first *Legends,* Jim Goodhue proofread every chapter in this book to help make sure all information is correct.

Even though all of us have worked very hard to ensure accuracy in this book, we realize there might be mistakes, especially in the spelling of names. It's difficult, if not impossible, to determine the correct spelling of some of the old-timers' names. If you see any names that you know are spelled incorrectly, please let us know. And if you can identify some of the people in the old pictures, let us know. We can make corrections in the next printing.

Speaking of corrections, I'm pleased to report that, to the best of our knowledge, the first *Legends* had very few mistakes. One of them: In the story about Joe Hancock, we spelled the name of his sire as John Wilkens. The correct spelling is believed to be Wilkins, although it is frequently spelled as Wilkens.

Another: On page 77, the credit for the picture of Chicaro Bill was given to the AQHA. The correct credit: American

Quarter Horse Heritage Center & Museum, Amarillo, Texas.

The date of death for Joe Reed II was also incorrect. This was brought to our attention by Roz Smietanski of Berlin, Wis., who keeps meticulous records of well-known horses. Joe Reed II died in 1962, not 1964, if you want to correct this in your copy of the book.

Ed Roberts also provided the name of the rider on Gay Bar King, in a picture on page 58. The rider is Watt Hardin, who lived in Brenham, Texas. In addition to owning Gay Bar King, Hardin also owned or stood Fourble Joe, King Hankins, and Bill Cody, according to Ed. Ed, of course, is the executive secretary of the American Paint Horse Association.

Except for changing the spelling of Wilkens to Wilkins, these corrections and additional information have been included in the second and subsequent printings of the first volume.

I want to also mention that we received a long and interesting letter from Robert Orin Burges of Skull Valley, Ariz., regarding the breeding of Cowboy P-12. As stated in the book, Cowboy's breeding was somewhat controversial, but Mr. Burges confirmed the breeding and breeder recognized by AQHA; i.e., that Cowboy was by Yellow Jacket and out of Roan Lady, and that he was bred by Edgar Thompson.

Mr. Burges said that Thompson was a close family friend. In his letter, Mr. Burges stated that Cowboy's breeding "has been questioned—unreasonably so, judging by the things I have read—but now it is well accepted that his sire was the Waggoner Ranch's Yellow Jacket . . . and his dam was Roan Lady by Stalks."

His letter also stated: "The sale of Cowboy, by Uncle Ed (Thompson), is not clear regarding how or why he was sold. Uncle Ed had told Dad that he was using him in harness to pull a wagon, and a man offered to buy him and he was sold. This sounds a lot like the Old Fred story and Coke Roberds."

Then, we also received a letter presenting another version of Shue Fly's breeding. As was stated in the book, "Although there is no doubt about Shue Fly's speed on the track, her breeding will forever remain a controversy." Since no one can authenticate the breeding of this great mare, we have decided not to pursue this new version.

As we explained in the first *Legends*, AQHA record-keeping in the early years was not nearly as accurate as it is today. That's why the records of some horses, such as Skipper W, who won three grand championships at halter, do not list any show record. This problem was pointed out and explained in Jim Goodhue's excellent article, "A History of Early AQHA Registration," in the first book.

No doubt the many old photographs in the first volume contributed a great deal to its success. Therefore we tried to get even more pictures for this second volume. That we were successful is due to the cooperation of many people who dug into their files and entrusted us with their valuable old photographs. We are grateful to Art Pollard, Darol Dickinson, Reba Warren, Ray and Joyce Bankston, Walter and Tien Merrick, Sonny Henderson, Hank Wiescamp, Bill Gay, Carrie Herndon, Susie Hutchison, Katy Peake, and others for many of the photographs.

As I have already mentioned, there will be a *Volume 3,* and it's scheduled for release in 1997.

Patricia A. Close, Editor
Western Horseman Inc.

CONTENTS

1 TRAVELER

By Jim Goodhue

**He founded
a great family
of outstanding
running horses.**

MOST HORSE breeders, geneticists, and even bettors whose closest connection is an occasional trip to the racetrack will explain (often at great length) that a great horse comes from great bloodlines. They believe that a superior performer must have close-up ancestors who were excellent individuals and were exceptionally able to pass along their abilities to offspring. Long lists of examples may be cited.

Then there was Traveler! Many horsemen of today might not recognize the name Traveler, but such familiar sires as

Zantanon, Little Joe, King P-234, Ed Echols, Poco Bueno, and Ed Heller all trace back to Traveler.

Traveler appeared in Eastland County of central Texas in the 1890s; that's the earliest that anything definite is known about him. He was believed to have been about 8 to 10 years old at the time. A light sorrel with roan coloring on his flanks, he had a suggestion of roan throughout his coat. He stood about 15.1 and weighed just under 1,100 pounds.

The stoutly built horse was being used

Traveler, as portrayed by Orren Mixer. In painting Traveler, Orren worked from an old photograph of the horse that was over-exposed. That photo gives the impression that Traveler had a large white marking on his forehead. But in reality, he did not, as you will see in the picture of Traveler on page 9, which is a much better picture than the one Orren worked from. This explains the discrepancy in Traveler's facial markings between the painting and the picture.

**Courtesy of
Orren Mixer**

Editor's note:
Because Traveler preceded the AQHA by many years, and his breeding was unknown, we are not including a pedigree chart for him, or a record of his offspring's performance.

to pull a dirt-moving slip or scraper in the construction of a railroad bed. That was not an uncommon procedure during those days before bulldozers and front-end loaders. He carried the mark of the collar used with his harness for the rest of his life.

At the time, Traveler was owned by a man who had come from another state and who was there in Eastland County as a dirt-moving master-contractor. This man used horses who had been shipped from various places. No doubt this is probably what led to one rumor that Traveler had been shipped in from Kentucky.

Some years later, after Traveler had become famous as a race horse, a man named Jim Edwards of Callahan County took notice of the horse. He was a man of means and admired Traveler as an individual. Although he was interested in buying the horse, Edwards was a stickler for good, authenticated bloodlines.

Edwards went to the man who is first known to have owned Traveler—the dirt-moving contractor whose name, now, has disappeared from history. Edwards was told that the horse had come from upstate

New York with a carload of other work horses. Edwards spent years and hundreds of dollars trying to establish Traveler's pedigree. Other than determining that Traveler had been sold by his original owner in New York as a 2-year-old, Edwards got nowhere in the quest and did not buy the horse.

The old colonial Quarter running horses had once been as prominent in New York as they had in other eastern states, and Traveler quite possibly had come from that stock.

One year, the dirt-moving contractor noticed that a subcontractor, called "Triggerfoot" Self had a good-looking mule in his string and offered to make a trade. After some persuasion, Self agreed to take Traveler and part with the mule. Self was finishing up his part of the job, so he drove his new acquisition home. Traveler was hitched with a mule and pulled a wagon, to the small hamlet of Eagle Cove (or Eula), which was near Baird.

7

Buster Brown, by Traveler and out of Fannie Pace, being held by E.H. (Boogie) Leache. Buster gained fame as a polo pony.

Photo Courtesy of the American Quarter Horse Heritage Center & Museum, Amarillo, Texas

George Clegg described Traveler as, "One of the most perfect-looking horses I ever saw."

There's one thing we can be relatively sure about Traveler's early history: He had not been used under saddle. Some of the knowledgeable cowboys and horsemen who knew Traveler at the time he first was being acquainted with a saddle during those days in central Texas agreed that the horse bucked and pitched strenuously before his obvious intelligence calmed him down to accept training.

There lived in Baird a man named Brown Seay whose properties included the Baird Hotel. Seay got wind of Self's new horse and Self's claim that it was a mighty fast horse. (It's not known, however, why Self figured Traveler was a race horse.) Self even bragged to the extent that he was willing to match Traveler against the fast mare Mayflower, a proven quantity on the racetrack.

So Seay sent his friend, the knowledgeable horseman Chris Seale, to look at this wonder. Seale found a mature, well-balanced stallion. He was a little plain-headed, but the other end—with unusually heavy hindquarter muscles—was a sight to

behold. Seay set about to buy Traveler.

There is some difference of opinion these days as to whether Self or Seay owned Traveler by the time the match against Mayflower was held. Regardless of who owned him, however, Traveler won by such a margin that one of the spectators was heard to say that Mayflower's jockey couldn't have thrown a rock and hit the sorrel's dust. It was about then when the sorrel picked up the name of Traveler.

Legend has it that Seay matched his own good runner, Froggie, against Self's Traveler for $500 on each side. The match also included the stipulation that if Froggie won, Seay was $500 richer; but if Traveler won, Self was to take an additional $500 and Froggie, while turning the ownership of Traveler over to Seay. Froggie lost and got a new home, according to this story, and Seay got what he wanted.

But there's another story. George Blakeley, a cowboy who was working for Seale in those days, recollected hearing at that time that Seay acquired Traveler simply by paying $100 for him.

Seay then campaigned Traveler successfully throughout central Texas. Among his victories was a closely contested match with Bob Wilson, a really great runner of the day. Detractors point out that Traveler won only by a neck despite having a definite weight advantage. It seems that the only person who could ride the cantankerous Bob Wilson was Austin Merrick, who weighed in with his tack at 165 pounds. Traveler was easier to handle and was ridden by a lighter jockey. On the other hand, Traveler had a reputation for running just fast enough to win. Perhaps with equal weights, Traveler still might have won by his usual small margin.

Another habit Traveler displayed during his racing career was the way he traveled at the end of a race. No matter how difficult the race, he always returned to the judge's stand with a very distinctive shuffle, almost a singlefoot. He appeared disinclined to waste any more effort once the race was over.

Despite Traveler's age when he began his career, history does not record the loss of any race by Traveler while owned by Seay. The sorrel gained a reputation as having terrific driving power and for being able to break from a score line faster than any other horse in that region.

Because his winning ways made it harder and harder to match any races for him, Traveler was gradually shifted from being a race horse to being the sire of quality foals—both runners and handling horses. Sometime after Traveler's days at Baird, the highly successful speed horse breeder, George Clegg of Alice, in south Texas, described this great horse in writing as, "one of the most perfect-looking horses I ever saw and who sired great running horses from good mares."

Actually, not all of the mares bred to Traveler were "good mares," and some of the lesser ones also produced some outstanding foals. One of the latter was a mare called Fanny, whom Chris Seale found pulling an ice wagon for her owner Tump Pace. Later, Seale called the mare Fanny Pace in Tump's honor. Believed to be a daughter of Gulliver, who was by Missouri Rondo, Fanny Pace did nothing of note until Seale started breeding her to Traveler, while Traveler was still at Baird. Then, her three sons by Traveler made her famous.

The first son was Judge Thomas, foaled

A picture of Traveler, date and location unknown.
Photo Courtesy of the American Quarter Horse Heritage Center & Museum, Amarillo, Texas

in 1897. He was gelded, and is said to have matured at 16 hands. Becoming one of the great sprinters of all time, Judge Thomas won steadily in any company and was campaigned extensively. He capped a notable career by setting a world's record of :40.1 for 3½ furlongs (770 yards) at Butte, Montana. This record reportedly stood for more than a quarter of a century.

Fanny Pace's second colt was foaled in 1898 and was named Judge Welch in honor, apparently, of a bartender at Seay's Baird Hotel. The population of Baird felt

Possum, first known as King, was by Traveler and out of Jenny, by Sykes Rondo. Possum was bred by Will and Dow Shely, and owned by Dick Herring and Bill Bowman (at the halter) before being sold to J.J. Kennedy and taken to Arizona. He established his own strain of horses in the Southwest, and among his descendants were Red Cloud, Mark, Tony, and Joe Bailey (of Gonzalez) P-4. Possum was foaled in 1904 and died in 1925.

Photo Courtesy of the American Quarter Horse Heritage Center & Museum, Amarillo, Texas

that this second colt was as good a runner as Judge Thomas, but he was not raced at recognized tracks and did not gain the reputation of his older brother. Unlike his gelded brother, however, Judge Welch carried on the family tradition as a sire.

Ella Moore Seale, daughter of Chris Seale, has recalled that Judge Welch was one of the most prolific of Traveler's sons in the Baird area, where he sired a great many good sons and daughters. She remembered riding some of them. Among others, she listed an outstanding son known as The Virginian. This black stallion was bred by E. H. (Boogie) Leache, who was famed for the quality of the polo mounts he shipped back east.

George Blakeley, the Seale Ranch cowboy, verified the quality of those Judge Thomas foals. He reported that Chris

Seale, who partnered with Brown Seay in their horse breeding operation, didn't get a lot of foals by Traveler, but raised a large number by Judge Thomas. Blakeley said that he broke 30 or 40 of the Judge Thomas youngsters, as well as many sired by Traveler. He said that when these horses weren't being raced, they were top ranch horses. They had good dispositions, were fast learners, and were easy handlers.

It has been written that all three of Fanny Pace's foals were gelded. This may be so, but it would seem that Judge Thomas served as a sire for several years first.

Fanny Pace's third Traveler colt, known to the Seale family as Jack Tolliver, was to become internationally renowned. He was foaled in 1903. Fanny Pace died while this foal was young and he was raised as an orphan in his own small pasture and barn.

When Jack Tolliver was about 2 years old, he was sold to Boogie Leache. Leache changed the bright sorrel's name to Buster Brown and shipped him to Virginia, where he earned an impressive reputation. By 1908, a leading horse breeders' publication called *Bit And Spur* specified that Buster Brown was the world's greatest polo pony. It was reported that he had a terrific grasp of the sport, tremendous speed, and unequalled endurance. It was even claimed that he could be turned loose on a polo field with his reins tied on his neck and that he still would "play the ball" better than many tournament-grade polo players.

Buster Brown also was exhibited as a trick or high-school horse with his own crowd-pleasing act. On at least one occasion, he was shipped to England to display his talents.

Most of Traveler's sons from this era were gelded. However, his daughters and granddaughters filled the broodmare bands around Baird to the extent that Traveler was sold.

Traveler spent the next few years at the Sweetwater, Tex., ranch of the Trammell family and on the Gardner Ranch at Big Lake, Texas. Both of these establishments were famed as Quarter running horse nurseries, but virtually nothing is known about any foals sired by Traveler during that period, except for a few horses being used for breeding purposes. The best known of these were Chulo Mundo, John Gardner, Three Finger Jack, and Bulger. Perhaps the small number of outstanding foals during these years was the cause, but for some reason Traveler was sold.

Then Traveler became the property of Jack Cunningham of Comanche, Tex., who, in turn, sold him to Will and Dow Shely. These were two former Texas Rangers whose father had come from Kentucky with a thorough knowledge of horses. It was on their Palo Huerco Ranch near Alfred, Tex., that Traveler was crossed with the "good" mares. The Shely brothers truly complemented each other in their breeding of horses. Dow, who is said to be the one who actually located and bought Traveler, operated a business in San Antonio and kept an eye out for good horses. Will ran the ranch at Alfred and made their horse production work.

Before buying Traveler, the Shelys had accumulated a quality group of Rondo mares in their broodmare band. Most of these were purchased from the Wilson County ranches of Crawford Sykes and Joe Mangum. This included Jenny, a daughter of Sykes Rondo out of the great producer May Mangum, a daughter of Anthony. From the six fillies and four colts May Mangum produced by Sykes Rondo were such other well-known names as Dogie Beasley, Nellie, Mamie Sykes, and Blue Eyes.

When bred to Traveler, Jenny produced the legendary horses Little Joe in 1904 and Possum (originally called King, and sometimes King Cardwell) in 1905. During this same period, Traveler sired Texas Chief, who was out of The Halletsville Mare; Captain Joe, out of Mamie Crowder; and El Rey, out of Black Bess.

George Clegg, one of the 20th century's most notable breeders of running Quarter Horses, moved to Alfred in 1904 and thought that he had never seen a more beautiful sight than the Shelys' Traveler foals. The following year, Clegg bought the yearling Little Joe. The only person ever to race Little Joe, Clegg wrote that Little Joe could run a quarter of a mile in 22 seconds flat from a 20-foot score.

Clegg campaigned Little Joe at age 2 and then took on comers of all ages when Little Joe was 3. One notable match against an older horse was the one he won over Carrie Nation. This mare had won extensively in Illinois before John Wilkens of San Antonio brought her to Texas where she had continued to win impressively.

The only race Little Joe lost was against Ace Of Hearts after Little Joe had "run off" from the score and went the distance of the track before the actual race was started. The losing margin was about a head. Ace Of Hearts' owner turned down a rematch.

Clegg used Little Joe for breeding purposes until he had built up a good band of fillies. He then sold him to Ott Adams of

Most of Traveler's sons from this era were gelded. However, his daughters and granddaughters filled the broodmare bands around Baird to the extent that Traveler was sold.

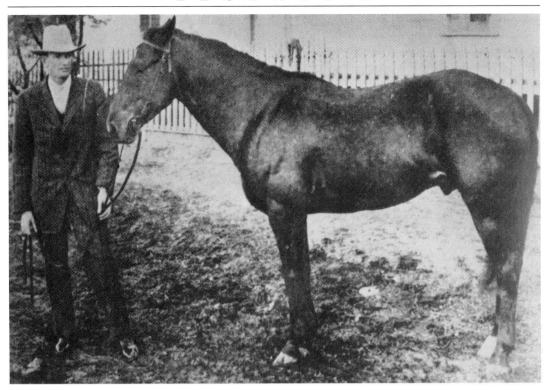

Little Joe, foaled in 1904 and a full brother to Possum, was Ott Adams' principal sire for years, and was considered by some horsemen to be Traveler's greatest son. Just a few of Little Joe's greatest sons included Zantanon, Joe Moore, Cotton Eyed Joe, and Grano de Oro.

Photo Courtesy of the American Quarter Horse Heritage Center & Museum, Amarillo, Texas

Alice, Tex., in about 1910. Little Joe was never raced again. By this time he had matured at about 14.3 and weighed around 1,100 pounds.

At stud, Little Joe consistently turned out such top-quality foals as Zantanon (the so-called Man o' War of Mexico), Joe Moore, Grano de Oro, Lady of the Lake, Old Poco Bueno (grandsire of the more famous Poco Bueno of modern time), Adalina, Balmy Days, Pancho Villa, and Cotton Eyed Joe.

In 1926, Adams was suffering the common problem of horsemen—a cash flow deficiency—and sold Little Joe to O.W. Cardwell of Junction, Texas. Cardwell, an avid polo player and respected horseman, once wrote that Little Joe was considered by most horsemen to be "the most ideal sire of the century."

Little Joe's life ended there in the hill country when he was shot by his owner. Cardwell stated that the old horse had

crippled himself and had to be destroyed. However, a neighbor claimed that the quick-tempered Cardwell had shot the stallion when he refused to cover a mare.

Whatever the reason for the shooting, we do know that Adams, who had continued to miss Little Joe, later went to the Cardwell Ranch and gathered the bones of the great horse. He buried the remains back at Alice under a huge mesquite tree where Little Joe had dozed in the shade many times. Later, Adams buried Joe Moore next to his sire.

Possum, the other fabled son of Jenny and Traveler, went another route. Possum first was sold to Dick Herring of Devine, Texas. When campaigning the successful runner began to take too much of his time, Herring sold the horse to his brother-in-law, W.H. Bowman, who continued to win races with him under the name of King.

The reputation of Possum spread even to Arizona and came to the attention of James J. Kennedy of Bonita. Kennedy was so anxious to improve the luck of his racing stable that he sent for the sprinter and paid a big price for him—a price that was reputed to include a whole herd of other horses.

Once Kennedy had his new star in Arizona, he changed the name from King to Possum. Perhaps he was afraid that other people also may have heard of King's Texas reputation and felt he would be easier to match under the name of Possum.

Kennedy hired top trainer Berry Gardner to race Possum. Unfortunately, it was not to be. On the way to his first match, being led behind a wagon, Possum stepped into a very deep mud hole and injured his left hind leg. It was not a permanent injury, but Possum could never run again with his usual speed.

Possum soon became the leading sire of Quarter Horses in Arizona. Among his famous foals were Guinea Pig, Red Cloud, Brown Possum (who earned the AQHA foundation number P-15), Rita Del, Kitty Parker, and Little King. His grand-get included Joe Bailey (the one given foundation sire number P-4 by the AQHA), Mark, and Tony.

When the American Quarter Racing Association tallied its records for racing in the 1940s, it was found that no other tail-male family had produced as many Register of Merit runners as the Traveler family, and all of them had descended from either Little Joe or Possum. Through Little Joe had come Miss Panama, Squaw H, Stella Moore, Monita, Miss South Saint Mary's, Hank H, Ben Jay, Ed Heller, Hill Country, Miss Billy Van, Billy Van Dorn, and others. Possum contributed, among others, Flicka F, Wayward Joe, Blueberry Hill II, Hoddy, Little Joe Jr., Liberty Girl, Johanna, Idleen, and Ariel Lady.

The family managed to produce more than its share of noted using horses, too. Zantanon sired such famous sires of performance ability as the immortal King P-234 (featured in *Legends 1*), San Siemon, and Ed Echols. Subsequent generations of Zantanon's family include Poco Bueno, King Fritz, Poco Lena, Royal King, King's Pistol,

Joe Barrett, Poco Tivio, Poco Champ, Poco Pine, and Poco Stampede. One can check almost any show arena for a current update on his performing descendants.

Other branches of Traveler's family also did their share for the rodeo and show performance arenas, as well as ranches. You can ask almost any Arizona cowboy about the good using horses who trace back to Possum, and they will be glad to list some great ones.

While at the Gardner Ranch, Traveler himself sired what many considered the greatest steer roping horse of all time. This was a gelding named Skunk, who became Joe Gardner's personal mount.

When the Shely brothers held their dispersal in 1914, much of their Traveler bloodline moved to the famous Burnett and Waggoner ranches in north Texas. There, it helped make both organizations leading breeders of ranch and performance horses.

George Clegg and Will Shely's daughter have both reported that Traveler died on the Palo Huerco ranch, about 1912. This brought to an end the life of a horse who seemed to come from nowhere and then made Quarter Horse history. He stood on his own and made his reputation without the aid of a known family tree.

If the theorists are right, though, Traveler must have had exceptional ancestors, even if we don't know who they were. As a superior race horse, a noted sire, and founder of an outstanding family, Traveler must be considered a great horse.

2 OLD JOE BAILEY

By Jim Goodhue

Old Joe Bailey sired a group of individuals of such quality that he came to be recognized as the progenitor of a distinct family of Quarter Horses.

THERE ONCE was a U.S. senator named Joseph W. Bailey who was very popular in Texas. As a consequence, several good horses were named in his honor in those days of unregulated naming before the formation of the American Quarter Horse Association. There were so many of these horses that it eventually became necessary to add modifiers to their names to keep them straight: Gonzales Joe Bailey, Nixon's Joe Bailey, and Weatherford Joe Bailey, for instance.

The horse known to us today as Old Joe Bailey was the Weatherford Joe Bailey.

Robert M. Denhardt, Quarter Horse historian and an early secretary of the AQHA, once stated that Old Joe Bailey was the most important Joe Bailey.

Old Joe Bailey, a bay horse, was foaled in 1907 and lived until 1934. He was bred by Dick Baker of Weatherford, Texas.

The sire of Old Joe Bailey was Eureka, who stood on the Couts Ranch at Weatherford. Owned by Colonel Bob Couts, the ranch was a successful breeding operation, and the owner had the means to buy the best stock. In 1906, Eureka was the Couts Ranch premier stallion.

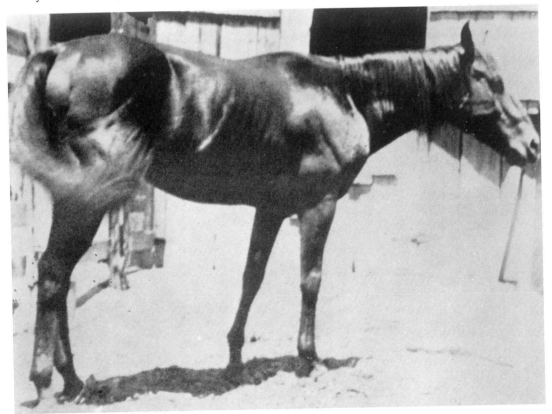

Old Joe Bailey, also known as Weatherford Joe Bailey, was foaled in 1907.

Photo Courtesy of the American Quarter Horse Heritage Center & Museum, Amarillo, Texas

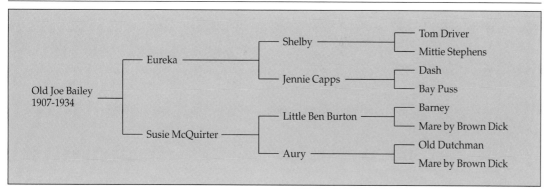

Buckskin Joe was a linebred grandson of Old Joe Bailey. Foaled in 1939, he was by Fred Bailey, by Old Joe Bailey, and out of Maudy, also by Old Joe Bailey. Buckskin Joe's biggest claim to fame came in 1945 when he was sold for $25,000, an unbelievable price in those days. The seller was Ramon Wood of Henrietta, Tex., and the buyer, Morris S. Clark of Sheridan, Wyoming.

Bred by E. Shelby Stanfield of Thorp Springs, Tex., Eureka was sired by Shelby, by Tom Driver, and was out of the noted producer Jennie Capps, by Dash, by Little Jeff Davis. Jennie Capps also was the dam of Pid Hart, Anti-Pro, Red Seal, and Stepping On It.

Eureka was one of the best-known short-horse runners in central Texas at the turn of the century. It is said that he held track records at the Texas State Fair in Dallas for both 440 yards and at 3½ furlongs. His career was so successful that the time came when he was handicapped with excessive weights. This brought his racing days to an end, and he was sold, eventually coming into the ownership of Colonel Couts to be used as a sire.

The remuda of the Couts Ranch was widely known for its quality. This reputation was enhanced as Eureka began to sire horses with speed and horses with conspicuous cow-working ability. In 1906, Dick Baker sent a mare to Eureka named Susie (or Suzie) McQuirter. A good performer as well as a well-bred individual, Susie McQuirter had the necessary qualifications for a broodmare. Bred by Webb Christian of Big Spring, Tex., she was sired by Little Ben Burton (also known as Old Ben Burton), by Barney, by Steeldust. She was out of Aury, who was sired by Old Dutchman (a son of the original Old Rondo), and was out of a mare by Brown Dick.

Today, the names in the pedigree of Old Joe Bailey seem obscured by the mists of time, but at the end of the last century, these names were synonymous with top quality. Going on farther back, it has been calculated that Old Joe Bailey traced seven times to Steeldust, six times to Shiloh, and

Editor's Note: *Because Old Joe Bailey preceded the AQHA by many years, there is no official record of his offspring's performance.*

Pretty Pam, sired by Buckskin Joe, was a great-granddaughter of Old Joe Bailey. This mare was the 1954 AQHA Honor Roll Halter Horse, and was owned and shown by Bob Sutherland of Kansas City, Missouri.

Photo by Clarence Coil / Stewart's Photo

twice to the Billy family. Those were the horses who started dynasties that even now are heralded as the foundations of the Quarter Horse breed.

Old Joe Bailey, on the other hand, did not have the spectacular career that his antecedents and his descendants indicate should have been his, had he had the opportunity. Not asked for any demonstrations of performance, he was simply put to stud without fanfare. The 27 years of his life were those same years in which automobiles and airplanes made their appearances around the country and grabbed the imagination of the general public. Whether being raced or merely carrying passengers, cars and planes had much more glamour than a stallion being allowed to quietly live out his life in central Texas.

At the same time, the U.S. government's Remount Service had an intensive program to encourage breeders of horses to mate their mares with Thoroughbred stallions. Also, a conflict that grew into World War I did its part to tear a hole in the years of Old Joe Bailey's productivity.

During his lifetime, however, Old Joe Bailey was bred to hundreds, or maybe thousands, of mares. Standing at public service with no reservations as to the quality of his mates, he managed to sire a group of individuals of such quality that he came to be recognized as the progenitor of a distinct family of Quarter Horses.

Even with the cards stacked against him, Old Joe Bailey sired some horses who gained fame in various areas. Old Joe Bailey sired many top rodeo horses, but the star among them was Stranger, the mount of professional rodeo champion Mike Hastings and reputed to be the greatest bulldogging horse of all time.

Among Old Joe Bailey's foals who did race was the exceptionally fast-breaking quarter-miler Roan Peggy. Other noted runners were Peggy Ray, Peggy Parker, Topaz, and Ben. One such speedster, named Dan, became a fine sire in his

16

Although Old Joe Bailey died almost a decade before the AQHA was beginning to build its reputation and momentum, 23 of his foals lived long enough and proved sufficiently worthy to be issued registration certificates.

Miss Nancy Bailey was by Royal King and out of Nancy Bailey, a daughter of Old Joe Bailey. With owner-rider Bob Burton of Arlington, Tex., in the saddle, Miss Nancy Bailey was among the top money-winners in the National Cutting Horse Association in the 1950s. **Photo By James Cathey**

Gold King Bailey was by Hank H. and out of Beauty Bailey, by Old Joe Bailey. He was foaled in 1945, was rated AA on the track, sired 9 AQHA Champions, and was a leading maternal grandsire of racing Register of Merit qualifiers. He was also the paternal grandsire of Pacific Bailey, AAAT and AQHA Champion, owned by Guy Ray Rutland of Independence, Kansas. Pacific Bailey was a tremendous sire.

own right. Dan's daughter Queen H was the dam of Squaw H and Hank H, both successful race horses and capable progenitors. Dan also sired Jimmie Allred, another excellent source of speed in the early history of the AQHA.

The stories about Old Joe Bailey and his offspring had spread enough, however, that when the well-known W.T. Waggoner of Vernon, Tex., was looking for a stallion prospect, a colt named Yellow Wolf was recommended to him. Yellow Wolf, a young son of Old Joe Bailey, was a dun with a black mane and tail.

Waggoner not only appreciated Yellow Wolf's color, he saw so much potential in the youngster that he quickly acquired him. Then, typically of Waggoner, he also bought Yellow Wolf's dam, Old Mary, who was again in foal to Old Joe Bailey. The resulting colt was Yellow Bear. The

offspring of these two sons of Old Joe Bailey, particularly their daughters used as broodmares, became the foundations of top using-horse remudas throughout the Quarter Horse world.

Breeder Dick Baker sold Old Joe Bailey when he was a relatively young horse, and the unheralded stallion came into the hands of Bud Parker, also of Weatherford, who kept him throughout most of his life. The Quarter Horse world owes Parker a considerable debt of gratitude for preserving the blood of some excellent Quarter Horses in those days when they were so unappreciated. He is the one who recognized the worthiness of Old Joe Bailey, his good race mare Old Mary (another daughter of Little Ben), and many others during those days, and made their blood and qualities available to present generations of Quarter Horse enthusiasts.

Parker owned Old Joe Bailey until the spring of 1928, when he was purchased by C. D. Swearington of Eastland, Texas. The following year, Old Joe Bailey was purchased by Jack Tindall and son, who sold him in 1931 to Bus Whiteside of Sipe Springs, Texas. Old Joe Bailey died on the Whiteside Ranch in 1934.

Although Old Joe Bailey died almost a decade before the AQHA was beginning to build its reputation and momentum, 23 of his foals lived long enough and proved sufficiently worthy to be issued registration certificates. None of them were still in their prime when the association began keeping records on races and shows, and the horses who competed in them.

While at the Whiteside Ranch, Old Joe Bailey sired the registered stallion Fred Bailey, known on the ranch as Chief, and the mare Maudy Bailey. When these two were bred, the resultant foal was Buckskin Joe. A leading show horse in that era, Buckskin Joe achieved the ultimate when named grand champion stallion of the 1945 Southwest Livestock Exposition at Fort Worth. That was the biggest and best Quarter Horse show in those years, and the best ranches and stables sent their best horses. Despite the fact that he subsequently was sold for the unheard-of-price of $25,000, Buckskin Joe continued to be used for cutting and calf roping.

Maudy Bailey also was the dam of the performance Register of Merit qualifier, Joe Tom Bailey. The sire of Joe Tom Bailey was the versatile Thoroughbred stallion Band Time. This combination also produced a stallion who won 17 straight matched races while in the ownership of Dr. Minton T. Ramsey of Abilene, Texas.

Old Joe Bailey was bred to his own granddaughter, a mare by Yellow Wolf, to produce a registered daughter named Beauty Bailey. She was bred by O. C. Holcomb of Eastland. When Beauty Bailey was bred to Hank H., the previously mentioned grandson of Dan (by Old Joe Bailey), she produced two racing Register of Merit qualifiers, Gold King Bailey and Beauty Bailey II. Gold King Bailey continued the line by becoming a leading sire of race horses.

Earl Albin of Comanche, Tex., earned a widespread reputation as a judge, exhibitor, and breeder of cutting horses. He once wrote that while Old Joe Bailey was improving the quality of horses in central Texas, even though large numbers of his get are unknown to us today, the roll call of his known get and their offspring is enough to place him among the Quarter Horse immortals.

Albin was in a good position to have firsthand knowledge of these horses' quality and ability. When his great cutting horse stallion, Royal King, was bred to Nancy Bailey, a daughter of Old Joe Bailey, she produced the spectacular cutting mare Miss Nancy Bailey. Competing in the relatively early days of the National Cutting Horse Association, Miss Nancy Bailey earned $38,084. She was among the top five NCHA money-earners for the years 1952, 1953, 1955, and 1957.

AQHA records show her to be the high-point cutting horse for 1952 and 1953. In that association, she won the awards of Superior Cutting Horse and Performance Register of Merit qualifier.

Other Performance Register of Merit qualifiers out of daughters of Old Joe Bailey include Jiggs Bailey, Romeo Dexter, and Red Bubbles.

Old Joe Bailey never appeared on the racetrack or in the show ring or in a rodeo arena, but all those fields of competition owe a big debt to this stallion who quietly passed along the traits that are so much appreciated in Quarter Horses.

3 GONZALES JOE BAILEY

By Phil Livingston

Gonzales Joe Bailey was designated as one of the 19 AQHA foundation sires.

THROUGH THE 1930s and 1940s, a common statement from south Texas horsemen was, "If you want a good colt, breed your mare to that old horse at Gonzales." They were referring to the Joe Bailey who sent so many good sons and daughters to the match racetracks, the dusty rodeo arenas, and the working ranches of the area.

While no one knows exactly, it is estimated that during his long career at stud, the blaze-faced chestnut stallion was responsible for at least 1,500 live foals. Since that figure includes foals for some

20 years before the formation of the American Quarter Horse Association in 1941, only a small portion of his blood came into the AQHA studbook in the first generation.

He lived for about 7 years following the establishment of the AQHA and many of his later offspring became well known. Some of them made an indelible mark on organized Quarter racing of the time and in the show ring. Gonzales Joe Bailey was designated as one of the 19 foundation sires by the fledgling AQHA in 1941, and

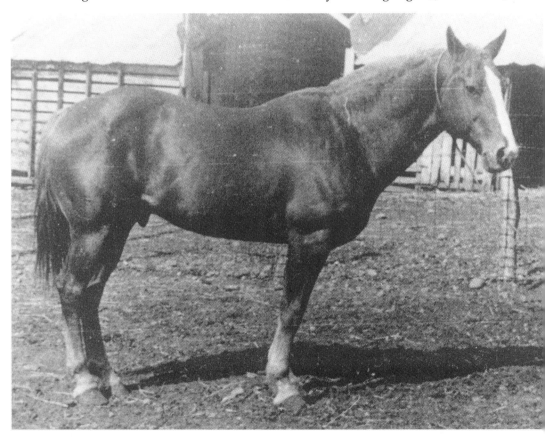

Gonzales Joe Bailey P-4. This photograph was probably taken in 1941 at the time he was inspected for AQHA registration by Bob Denhardt and Jim Minnick. It clearly shows the horse's overall balance, good feet and legs, and the heavy muscling that characterized his get.

Photo Courtesy of Phil Livingston

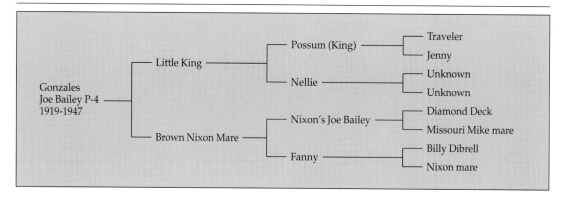

Gonzales Joe Bailey P-4 1919-1947
- Little King
  - Possum (King)
    - Traveler
    - Jenny
  - Nellie
    - Unknown
    - Unknown
- Brown Nixon Mare
  - Nixon's Joe Bailey
    - Diamond Deck
    - Missouri Mike mare
  - Fanny
    - Billy Dibrell
    - Nixon mare

therefore received the number P-4.

In the early years of the 20th century, there were three well-known Quarter Horse stallions in Texas named for the controversial, but popular, Joe Bailey, a U.S. Congressman and later a senator from Gainesville. The trio of stallions did as much for the Quarter Horse as their namesake did for his home district.

According to an article in the July 1947 *Quarter Horse*, the first of the Joe Baileys was foaled in or about 1900. In either 1902 or 1903, Tom Stephenson and H. Kimble Woods went to Missouri and purchased two young stallions, full brothers, sired by Diamond Deck, who was by Cold Deck and out of a Missouri Mike mare. One of these young stallions, a dark chestnut who eventually matured into a powerfully built animal of 15.1 or 15.2 hands, was sold to Dr. J.W. Nixon and named Joe Bailey after the aforementioned legislator who was in his political prime.

When the horse was 3 or 4, he was sent to the John P. Nixon Ranch in Medina County. From all reports, he was not too well broke. Only one attempt to race him was made, at Hondo, Tex., as his owners gave up after the horse repeatedly threw the jockey. His pedigree, however, made him a popular sire with south Texas horsemen. He was kept at the ranch and bred to the Nixon mares, mostly of Billy stock going back to Old Billy, the W.B. "Billy" Fleming horse. This Joe Bailey became known as Nixon's Joe Bailey, and he contributed strongly to the pedigree of the third Joe Bailey, who became known as Gonzales Joe Bailey.

The second Joe Bailey was Joe Bailey of Weatherford, known today as Old Joe Bailey. He is discussed in the previous chapter.

The third of the Joe Baileys was foaled in 1919 on the ranch of Dr. J.W. Nixon. The

Halter and Performance Record: None.

Progeny Record:

Foal Crops: 18	Performance Registers of Merit: 1
Foals Registered: 257	Race Money Earned: $1,418
Performance Point-Earners: 1	Race Registers of Merit: 7
Performance Points Earned: 1	Race Starters: 15
Leading Race Money-Earner: Flicka F ($767)	

ranch was located west of Gonzales, near Belmont where Billy Fleming had bred his "Billy horses" who were so well known in Texas during the 1880s and 1890s. Fleming's original stallion, Old Billy, was by Shiloh and out of Ram Cat, by Steeldust.

Gonzales Joe Bailey was named after his maternal grandsire, Nixon's Joe Bailey. Gonzales Joe Bailey was to spend his life near the little town on the Guadalupe River and become one of the most significant sires of his time. And the name of the town where he was foaled was usually added as a prefix to his name to distinguish him from Weatherford Joe Bailey. Gonzales Joe Bailey was Quarter Horse royalty if there ever was, since he was blood kin to all the top Quarter running horses in south Texas during the early 1900s. His sire was Little King, by Possum. (Possum causes confusion because he was first known as King when he was raced in Texas. When he was sold into Arizona, where he earned a reputation as a sire, his name was changed to Possum. And he was also sometimes referred to as King Cardwell.)

Possum was by Traveler, who established Dow and Will Sheley of Alfred, Tex., as premier Quarter Horse breeders

Gonzales Joe Bailey as an old horse. His clean legs, with the chestnut coloring fading into white below the knees and socks, can easily be seen in this photo. Holding him is J.B. Ellis, his co-owner and handler for 20 years.

Photo Courtesy of Phil Livingston

Although this isn't a good picture, it's worthy of using because it depicts Bob Denhardt aboard Gonzales Joe Bailey. Denhardt remarked after the ride, "I doubt if I have ever ridden a faster horse." **Photo Courtesy of Phil Livingston**

shortly after the turn of the century.

The bottom side of Gonzales Joe Bailey's pedigree was also solid speed. His dam was known only as the Brown Nixon Mare and was described by the Nixon family as "a very nice mare." Her sire was Nixon's Joe Bailey, purchased by Dr. Nixon when the horse was taken to south Texas as a

2-year-old. Nixon's Joe Bailey was by Diamond Deck, by Old Cold Deck.

The Brown Nixon Mare was out of a mare known as Fanny. She was by Billy Dibrell (sometimes spelled as Dibbell), by Anthony, by Old Billy (the Fleming horse). Dr. J.W. Nixon was a long-time Texas breeder of top horses, having received his first Quarter mare when he was a child in either 1864 or 1865. He raised good horses his entire life and passed the interest, and the bloodline, on to his children.

According to an August 1963 article in *The Quarter Horse Journal*, by Bob Denhardt, Gonzales Joe Bailey matured into a solidly built chestnut stallion who stood just 15 hands and weighed 1,150 pounds. He had a white blaze that stretched from just below the poll to the nostrils. His legs below the knees and hocks were roan, shading to almost white at the hoofs.

He had exceptionally good legs and feet, with dense, flat bone and clean, hairless fetlocks—as free from feathers as if they had been clipped. His withers were high and the shoulders well laid back. He was deep through the heart and had a tremendously powerful rear end and good muscling both inside and outside of the gaskins. Joe Bailey was not excessively wide between the front legs, and he had a

Nixon's Joe Bailey, the sire of Joe Bailey of Gonzales, was originally from Missouri and was sired by Diamond Deck, by Old Cold Deck.

Photo Courtesy of Phil Livingston

good, but not exceptional, head. All in all, he was a horse built to use as well as run.

He passed on the conformation and coloring to his offspring to the degree that a Gonzales Joe Bailey could be easily identified. Old-time horseman N.Y. "Jack" Plume, of Yoakum, grew up some 30 miles south of Gonzales during the 1930s, owned a few of the Joe Baileys, and looked at a bunch more of them. He commented, "The Gonzales Joe Baileys were of good, blocky, Quarter Horse type; with most of them light sorrel with a mealy mouth (muzzle shading of almost white) and the legs the same way; light manes and tails and white markings on the face. When I was growing up, a lot of the ranch and rodeo horses in this country were by him, and you could tell 'em at a glance."

While the pedigree of Gonzales Joe Bailey reads "speed," there is no record of where and when he raced . . . but he evidently did. An excerpt from an article in *The Quarter Horse* (June 1947) reads: "And though a horse of excellent performance on his own account—he was a 23-second horse on oval tracks—it was as a breeder that he earned his fame."

Bob Denhardt verified Gonzales Joe

This good picture of Gonzales Joe Bailey appeared in the September-October, 1947 issue of Western Horseman *magazine.*

Bailey's speed. He had the opportunity to ride the horse when he inspected him for registration in 1941. In *The Quarter Horse Journal* of August 1963, Bob commented:

"He had a tremendous start. When we (Joe and I) were much younger, I rode him. The wind whistled in my ears and my eyes were watering when I dismounted. I doubt if I have ever ridden a faster horse. I have been on many horses, and felt them leave a chute after a calf or goat, but none left with the absolute abruptness of Joe Bailey, and none had

23

Little Joe Jr., the best known and most prolific son of Gonzales Joe Bailey. This photograph was widely used during the early years of the AQHA as an ideal representative of the breed. It also greatly enhanced Little Joe Jr.'s reputation.

Photo Courtesy of Phil Livingston

Ellis and Dickinson bought Gonzales Joe Bailey as an investment and as a breeding horse. At $10 per mare, it didn't take long to pay for their new stallion.

the same sensation of sheer speed."

Gonzales Joe Bailey's races must have been under the ownership of Dr. J.W. Nixon and were probably at such south Texas tracks as Cuero, Eagle Pass, Skidmore, Columbus, and Kingsville. During the 1920s and 1930s, these small-town racetracks were the proving grounds for the Quarter Horse. Gonzales Joe Bailey may have also participated in the match races that Texans of the time were so fond of. Undoubtedly, the chestnut stallion upheld the reputation of the Traveler family at enough of these affairs to interest mare owners in breeding to him.

In 1927, Dr. Nixon decided to sell or trade the horse. No comments have come down through history as to why the decision was made. As an 8-year-old, this Joe Bailey was taken to Gonzales where he

was traded to Orange Thomas for a breeding jack. The trade was made with no boot money changing hands on either side, which gives an indication of the value placed on a Quarter Horse stallion, and on a good jack, at the time. Perhaps the swap took place during one of the monthly trade days found in small towns, or maybe Dr. Nixon had decided to go into the mule business.

Thomas was a trader, and he wasted no time in turning his new horse into cash. Joe Bailey was sold to brothers-in-law J.B. Ellis and C.E. Dickinson of Gonzales for $225. That was a hefty sum for any Quarter stallion in November of 1927. Once home with the Ellis-Dickinson partnership, Gonzales Joe Bailey made it a 20-year stay and brought into existence a family of terrific using horses.

Ellis and Dickinson bought Gonzales Joe Bailey as an investment and as a breeding horse. At $10 per mare, it didn't take long to pay for their new stallion. At first, only local horsemen brought their mares to Joe. Then, his owners began to send the stallion on a circuit of the surrounding towns every spring. One of them either rode or led Joe to the various ranches where mares would be waiting. Later on, a pickup and homemade trailer were acquired, and the trips were made in relative ease. A lot of mares could be bred each year in that way.

L.T. "Buster" Burns Jr. of Yoakum was in the horse business at the time; track stars that he owned or raised included Chicaro Bill and Arizona Girl, as well as a number of polo ponies ridden by such players as Tommy Hitchcock. Burns remembered, "They used to pull that ol' stud around in a slat-sided, homemade trailer. That's the only way they could have bred all the mares they did. You couldn't go to a ropin' or a race meet without seein' a whole herd of Joe Bailey colts . . . and they could all run a little," which is horsemen-speak for blazing speed.

One of the first Gonzales Joe Baileys to make a name in the AQHA record books was Little Joe Jr. He was a horse who could do it all: win at halter, racing, and rodeo. Foaled in 1937, Little Joe Jr. was bred by Preston Johnson of Rosanky, who took his good mare Dumpy, by Little Dick, to Gonzales Joe Bailey in 1936. His idea was to raise a rope horse, but the results were so good that Johnson was talked into selling him. Larry Baumer of Utopia and W.E. Richardson of Concan bought him at 10 months of age for the high price of $150.

Little Joe Jr. went into training at the Boerne track when he was old enough, and soon showed that he could run in the best of company. Early in 1941, Little Joe Jr. went up against Clabber, Nobodies Friend, and Balmy L at Eagle Pass in a race that has become one of the classics in Quarter Horse history. Clabber came out on top, but Little Joe Jr. pushed him to the limit and was barely defeated. Later that year, Baumer took Little Joe Jr. to Tucson, where he quickly showed his ability to sprint down the track at Hacienda Moltacqua.

In writing about Little Joe Jr. in a 1942 issue of *Racing Quarter Horses*, published by the Southern Arizona Horse Breeders Association, Melville H. Haskell said, "As a race horse, Little Joe Jr. rates well toward the top. He runs every jump of the way from the gate to a full quarter. Finished second to Clabber in the 1941

Spencer, by Gonzales Joe Bailey and out of Cricket Fleming, was owned by Helen Michaelis of Eagle Pass, Texas. Helen was an acknowledged authority on bloodlines, and served as the second secretary of the AQHA. This photo appeared in the AQHA Studbook No. 3, and is reproduced courtesy of AQHA.

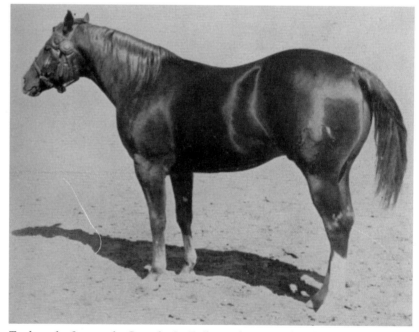

Toad was by Spencer, by Gonzales Joe Bailey, and was out of the famous race mare, Goldie McCue. Toad was a grand champion at halter and became a good sire. This photo appeared in the AQHA Studbook No. 3, and is reproduced courtesy of AQHA.

25

Figure 5 Ranch Quarter Horses

BACCHUS No. 1227
Stud fee for 1946 season—$50.00
A few of this horse's 1945 foals for sale for November delivery

J. D. COWSERT • JUNCTION, TEXAS

This ad for Bacchus, a good son of Gonzales Joe Bailey, appeared in AQHA Studbook No. 3, and is reproduced here courtesy of the AQHA.

World's Championship and, in 1941, he won two stallion races (beating Joe Tom, Chicaro, Bartender, and Shadow), and was second in a free-for-all behind Don Manners, beating Blueberry Hill."

Little Joe Jr. was not only picked among the top 20 competing at Hacienda Moltacqua during 1941, 1942, and 1943, but his time for the ⅛-mile was excelled only by Chicaro and Redman. His time was better than that of Shue Fly, Joe Reed II, Nobodies Friend, Pay Dirt, Domino, and Prissy. He was listed as covering the quarter in :23.2. The AQHA awarded him one of the first Registers of Merit for his performance on the track.

At the big Tucson horse show in 1942, Little Joe Jr. received the judge's nod as the grand champion cow horse stallion, proving that he had the kind of conformation that horsemen were looking for. Photographs of Little Joe Jr. were widely circu-

lated in various publications as an example of what a top quality Quarter Horse stallion should look like. This helped to spread his fame, as well as that of his sire.

Any stallion with Little Joe Jr.'s looks, breeding, championship ribbons at halter, and his racing record was not long for the racetrack. And so Little Joe Jr. was purchased by the Diamond 2 Cattle Company of Kirkland, Ariz., and retired to stud. He sired 180 AQHA-registered foals out of 24 crops. Forty of those went to the track, where they earned $34,469, 24 ROMs in racing, and 1 Superior race award. His leading money-earner was Mousie's Little Bay, out of Mousie, with winnings of $5,610.

Probably his best son was Joe Jimmy, out of Brownie High, who outran the sensational Miss Panama, among other horses. Little Joe Jr. also sired 9 AQHA halter winners, who earned 55 points, and 8 performance point-earners with 89 points. The latter included Dooly M, who earned both a performance ROM and a Superior in cutting.

Other Joe Bailey of Gonzales offspring who achieved recognition on the short tracks included Blueberry Hill, who could cover a quarter in :23 and went 350 yards in :11.4 at Hacienda Moltacqua; Image Joe; Little Foot; Little Joe II; Little Johnnie; Sally Rand; Sleepy Joe; Sleepy Lou; Commando, who not only could run but also earned an ROM in performance; Flicka F, who set a new track record of :12.5 seconds for 220 yards; Joe Bailey's Image; Pokey Joe; and Boiling Joe Bailey.

In the early days of the breed, the racetrack was *the* proving ground, and the name stallions and mares all demonstrated their ability to sprint. The get of Joe Bailey of Gonzales were no exception; they all showed that they had the speed to either race or catch a calf. The conformation went along with the run as far as horsemen were concerned.

Other top Joe Bailey of Gonzales horses were: Menton Northington's Little King, who was sold to the Mullendore Cross Bell Ranch for a big price; Conformation, a daughter who won numerous ribbons before ending up in R.L. Underwood's broodmare band; Little Joker, the O'Conner Ranch stallion who sired so many good using horses along the Gulf Coast;

Joker Joe was a chestnut son of Gonzales Joe Bailey, foaled in 1938 and owned by the Spanish Springs and Double Diamond ranches, Reno, Nevada.

Bacchus, owned by J.D. Cowsert of Junction, the sire of the well-known Hoddy P-5982; Spencer and Teddy Bear, used by Helen Michaelis; Hot Shot, owned by Jack Frost; Anton Joe Bailey, who carried the colors of Anton Jerseck of Halletsville; Joker Joe, owned by the Spanish Springs Ranch and Double Diamond Ranch of Reno, Nev.; and the good mare, Maggie Bailey.

For years, Joe Bailey was credited as the sire of the sensational Painted Joe, since the spotted speedster was also from the Gonzales area. Even Melville Haskell listed the pedigree that way in *Racing Quarter Horses*, which he published for the Southern Arizona Horse Breeders Association in the 1940s. It wasn't until 1965, when the American Paint Horse Association was formed, that new evidence proved that the horse was sired by Rondo Joe, by Grano de Oro, by Little Joe, by Traveler.

Joe Bailey sired so many horses who could run well that it was natural to assume that any exceptional individual coming out of the area around Gonzales was his offspring.

The grandsons and granddaughters of Gonzales Joe Bailey were literally legion, both registered and unregistered. For a quarter of a century after Joe's death, south Texas abounded with good-minded, solidly built, sorrel and light chestnut horses who shaded to almost white below the knees. These were horses who could catch a calf in money-winning time, win a match race, or go to the pasture in that little jog trot that covers so much country quickly. They were Joe Baileys and the men who rode them were proud of the fact.

According to the June 1947 *Quarter Horse*, Joe Bailey of Gonzales died quietly when he was just 2 days short of turning 28. He had come home from a short breeding campaign at a ranch near Gonzales, between Luling and Lockhart. During the night of May 2, he became ill, went down, and got stuck on his back in a break he had kicked in the stall wall. Mr. Ellis, at whose ranch Old Joe had lived for 2 decades, heard the noise, went to the barn, and got the horse up. He lived through the next day, but late that night, he died.

27

4

LUCKY BLANTON

By Phil Livingston

This chestnut stallion was a top rope horse—and sire of rope horses.

This picture of Lucky Blanton was taken sometime during the years when he was owned by Tom Mattart. The chestnut stallion was renowned for his dense bone, muscling, and powerful hindquarters.

Photo Courtesy of Phil Livingston

IF YOU were a calf or team roper in California, Arizona, Nevada, or Oregon during the late 1940s and into the 1950s and the 1960s, you just weren't mounted if you weren't straddlin' a Lucky Blanton. The chestnut stallion, owned by Tom Mattart of Salinas, Calif., was a top rope horse himself, and probably put as many good rodeo hands ahorseback as any other stallion in the country.

As just one example, 13 of the ropers entered at the huge 1954 Salinas Rodeo were contesting on Lucky Blantons. All of those horses were about the same in height and conformation, demonstrating ol' Lucky's ability to stamp his get.

Foaled in 1936, Lucky Blanton was bred by Burns Blanton of Bowie, Ariz., who produced so many good cowboy horses on his southern Arizona ranch. Lucky Blanton's sire was Mark, a sorrel son of Red Cloud, who was by the well-known Possum (aka King), by Traveler. Mark's dam, Maga, was also by Possum,

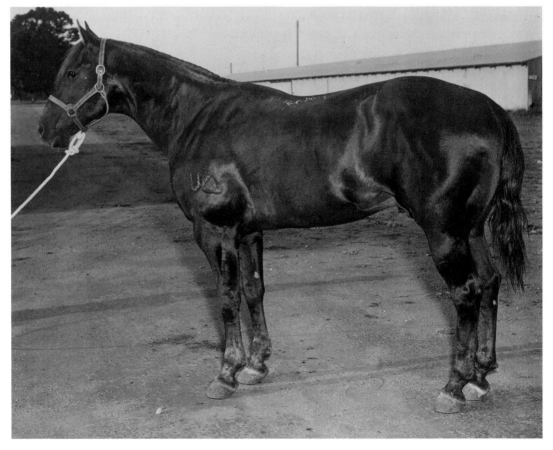

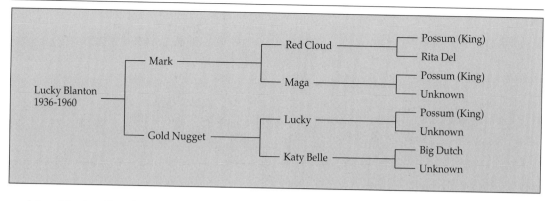

```
                                                    ┌─── Possum (King)
                                      ┌─── Red Cloud ─┤
                                      │               └─── Rita Del
                     ┌─── Mark ───────┤
                     │                │               ┌─── Possum (King)
                     │                └─── Maga ───────┤
 Lucky Blanton ──────┤                                └─── Unknown
 1936-1960           │
                     │                                ┌─── Possum (King)
                     │                ┌─── Lucky ──────┤
                     │                │                └─── Unknown
                     └─── Gold Nugget ┤
                                      │                ┌─── Big Dutch
                                      └─── Katy Belle ─┤
                                                       └─── Unknown
```

making Mark a line-bred Traveler.

Mark was a proven sire of top ranch and rodeo mounts. Arizona roper Fred Darnell's good calf and heel horse Carrot and the Paint called Jiggs, on whom Jim Brister won the 1947 R.C.A. World Champion Team Roping title, were two of them. Mark was also a great rope horse himself.

Carl Arnold, from Buckeye, Ariz., used Mark in every type of rodeo roping event and won a bundle on him. In his six matched single steer ropings with Bob Crosby, Arnold won five of them riding Mark.

This sorrel stallion went on to sire 103 AQHA-registered foals in 22 crops. Since they were in such demand as cowboy horses, only a few found their way to the show ring or the racetrack. But they certainly made a name for themselves in the rodeo arena.

Mark's best success as a sire resulted when he was bred to a number of Gill Cattle Company mares. The Gills, who ranched in California and Arizona, were renowned for having good horses.

Mark's grandsire, Possum (aka King), was brought to Arizona from south Texas when he was only 4, but he already had the reputation as a speedy straightaway match race horse. One of his triumphs was outrunning the celebrated Yellow Jacket at Kyle, Tex., in 1911. This feat almost cleaned out the "sports" in the area, since according to the legend, over $100,000 changed hands after that race.

Possum was bred by Dow and Will

Halter and Performance Record: None.

Progeny Record:

Foal Crops: 23
Foals Registered: 196
Halter Point-Earners: 9
Halter Points Earned: 19
Performance Point-Earners: 8
Leading Race Money-Earner: Washo Queen ($18,881)

Performance Points Earned: 9
Race Money Earned: $25,390
Race Registers of Merit: 3
Race Starters: 18

Shely of Alice, Tex., who sold him as a suckling colt to "Uncle Dick" Herring. Possum's dam, Jenny, died soon afterwards, and Herring raised the colt as a dogie. Later, after he was broke to saddle, it was discovered that he was a running fool, and it wasn't long before it became difficult to match him. At this time, the colt was known as King.

Jim Hocket bought King from Herring, and then traded him to James J. Kennedy in 1912 for a reported 100 horses. Kennedy took King to Arizona and changed his name to Possum to avoid confusion with another race horse he owned with the same name.

Crossed on Kennedy's mares, many of them half-Thoroughbred daughters of the imported Bay King (TB), Possum produced a string of real doin' horses. Many

Mark was the sire of Lucky Blanton. He was owned by Carl Arnold of Buckeye, Ariz., who is shown here tuning Mark for single steer roping by logging him. Carl used Mark in every type of rodeo roping event, and won a bundle of cash on him.

Photo by Richard Schaus; Courtesy of Phil Livingston

of the colts were shipped to the East where they were used as polo ponies. Three of his better-known sons who stayed in Arizona were Red Cloud, Baby King, and Guinea Pig. All made notable contributions to the quality of local saddle stock. Possum, incidentally, died in 1924.

Red Cloud, considered to be the best of Possum's sons, spent most of his life on Mark DuBois KY Ranch near Bonita, Arizona. There he sired Mark, Pee Wee (who sired Clay Carr's dependable calf and heel horse KY Charlie), and a host of other good using horses.

Lucky Blanton's dam, Gold Nugget, was by Lucky, by Possum, further intensifying the Traveler line and compounding the speed. Burns Blanton's breeding program was built by concentrating Traveler blood and this meant line breeding, something he did throughout his long career as a horseman.

Jimmy Blanton, Burns' son, was just 12 years old when he broke Lucky Blanton to saddle. That meant lots of work on the 14-section ranch— making circles, cutting out

cattle, and dragging calves to the branding fire. He was also match raced occasionally against the neighbors' horses and showed that he could run a pretty good lick.

In a conversation some years ago, Arizona horseman Tom Finley told about one race: "One time Burns Blanton and Mr. McKinney (who owned Red Joe of Arizona, by Joe Reed P-3) got to jawing about their horses. The whole deal was about who had the fastest horse. The only way to find out was to match them, and that's what they did. There was no starting gate, so they just marked off a line in the dirt for a lap-and-tap start. Red Joe was completely lathered by the time he got into place, so they decided to let him rest for 20 minutes before they took him back to the score.

"Lucky had the advantage since he was always a quiet, calm horse," continued Finley. "If I remember right, after the two horses got tapped off, they finished in a dead heat at 330 yards.

"Lucky Blanton was sort of an orange-colored sorrel, real smooth muscled with exceptionally heavy hindquarters," said Finley. "As I remember, he stood about 15.1, weighed about 1,250 pounds, and was an athletic-looking horse. You could

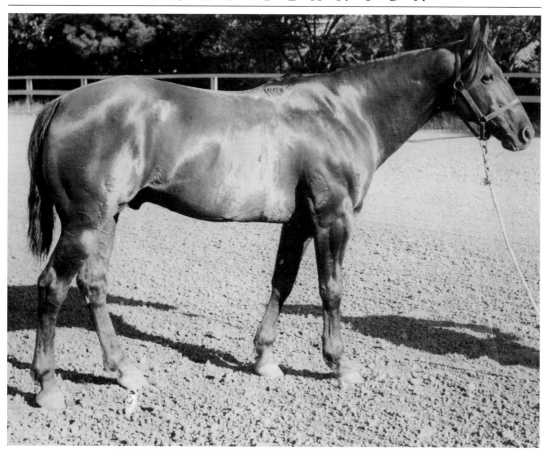

Carrot, another son of Mark, had the same functional conformation and strong bone that Lucky Blanton did. Carrot was owned and contested on by Fred Darnell, Apache, Arizona.

Photo Courtesy of Phil Livingston

recognize Lucky Blanton offspring as soon as you saw them coming down the road."

In 1942, Tom Mattart, a Salinas, Calif., rancher and roper, was in Arizona, met Burns Blanton, and saw the then 6-year-old Lucky Blanton for the first time. He liked what he saw and bought the speedy chestnut stallion.

While he was at the Blanton ranch, Mattart also purchased 10 or 11 broodmares, including Faithful, by Hard Tack; Sweetheart, by Hard Tack; Little Sister C., by Red Joe of Arizona; Betsy, by Red Cloud; Loya, by Mark; Miss Pee Wee, by Pee Wee; and Lady Mack. When bred to Lucky Blanton, these mares helped to establish Mattart's reputation with the California cowboys as a breeder of good horses.

Once Mattart had his new stallion in California, he tuned the horse's roping skills and introduced him to professional rodeo. For 6 of the 17 years that Tom Mattart owned Lucky Blanton, the horse was a fixture in California arenas, competing in calf roping, heading, heeling, and steer stopping. Mattart didn't pass up an occasional match race either, and won his share.

At Pleasanton one year, Lucky Blanton was matched against Perry Ivory's horse The Pig, a horse who had outrun many of California's speediest, including the well-known Colonel Clyde, by My Texas Dandy, whom he daylighted.

Tom Mattart's wife, Phyllis, rode the stallion occasionally on the ranch, and often talked about his gentleness and quiet dispostion. She once commented, "It's all been said before, about how hard he ran and how hard he stopped . . . his powerful forearm and hip muscling . . . but when you stood next to Lucky, you were aware of the mighty *plus* quality that makes a

31

A group of Lucky Blanton daughters that were owned by Perry Cotton of Visalia, California. They all show the uniformly powerful hindquarters of their sire. When Cotton had his dispersal sale in 1962, 14 own daughters of Lucky Blanton sold for a total of $38,400, an impressive figure for that time.

Photo Courtesy of Phil Livingston

great horse. Perhaps it's intelligence combined with ability. It's hard to know, impossible to define."

When Lucky was 12, Mattart permanently retired him to stud at the Salinas ranch. Over the years, Lucky was to sire 196 AQHA-registered foals out of 23 crops. While Lucky Blanton was a popular sire, the majority of his offspring stayed on ranches or were used in the rodeo arena. Only a few were shown in horse show events either in AQHA or AHSA (American Horse Shows Association) shows. And his offspring who were shown in horse show classes usually competed in open events, such as the hackamore and reined cow horse events. These were not AQHA events, and that's another reason Lucky Blanton's AQHA sire record reflects so few performance and halter winners.

One of his better show horses was Nevada King, out of Nevada Queen, who was shown very successfully by Marten Clark of Soledad, California. Fol-

lowing his show career, Nevada King headed the broodmare band at Fresno State College for several years, where he passed on his heritage of speed, performance, and conformation.

Eighteen Lucky Blanton foals went to the racetracks, where they won 37 races and earned $25,390. Included in this group were three sons of Faithful: Big Sandy, Mattart's Buster Brown, and Lucky Mac. Another was General Agent, out of Sweetheart, who went on to be an outstanding calf and team roping horse for Everett Muzzio of Fresno.

Washo Queen, out of Nevada Queen, was Lucky Blanton's leading race horse. She earned $18,881, and an AQHA Superior and ROM in racing. In 1957, Washo Queen sprinted to third place in the 400-yard Bay Meadows Handicap in San Francisco.

One of the first Lucky Blantons to demonstrate versatility was Mattart's Buster Brown. Foaled in 1940, this brown gelding was out of Faithful, by Hard Tack, making him a line-bred Traveler. He earned $5,406 and a AA rating on the track, equaled the track record for 220 yards at Kansas City with :12.70 for 220 yards, and earned his ROM in racing. He later became an outstanding calf and team

Lucky Bet, a 1943 mare by Lucky Blanton and out of Betsy, by Red Cloud, was one of the top halter mares in her time. At the 1950 Prescott, Ariz., Quarter Horse show, she was the grand champion mare. She was owned by Lyle Christie of Coalinga, Calif., and shown by Charlie Araujo.

roping mount for Tom Mattart. Buster's speed in catching cattle over the long roping scores then in use made him popular.

Buster Brown's full brother, Lucky Mac, was foaled in 1941. This brown stallion was bred by Burns Blanton and owned by New Mexico roper Roy Wilmeth. Lucky Mac went to the racetrack, where he excelled, before starting his roping training. He sired a few good colts, but was kicked by a mare and injured before he could establish his reputation as a sire. Wilmeth gelded him and used him as a rope horse for years.

In 1943 the Lucky Blanton-Faithful combination produced Lucky Tom. Jim Rodriguez Sr., of Watsonville, Calif., successfully roped on this sorrel stallion for a number of years before eventually selling him to the Parker Ranch in Hawaii. Chuck Sheppard, 1946 R.C.A. World Champion Team Roper, also roped off Lucky Tom a number of times at the big Salinas Rodeo, winning money every time.

To the California ropers of the 1950s, the best-known Lucky Blanton-Faithful cross was Lucky Tack C., called Eight-Six around the roping chutes. He was bred by

Louis Coelho (who eventually traded Tom Mattart out of Faithful) and was foaled in 1947. Lucky Tack C. was sold to Sam Edmonson, who roped off him during 1953, 1954, and 1956. He received the nickname of Eight-Six as a young horse when Frank Ferreira roped a set of heels off his stout back at the Redding rodeo in the then unusual time of :8.6 seconds. Edmonson used Eight-Six to head on, but the horse would hunt a set of heels, jerk a calf down and get back on the rope, and haze a 'dogging steer with equal ease.

Another good son of Lucky Blanton who excelled in the rodeo arena was Skeet Shooter. Better known as Buck, he was out of Leftalone, by Hard Tack. This 1950, blaze-faced dun gelding was owned by Chuck and Phyllis Bryant of Shafter, California. A top head horse who carried

Chuck to many team roping wins, including at least one trip to the National Finals Rodeo when it was held at Los Angeles, he was also tough around the barrels with Phyllis in the saddle. He frequently won money in both events at a rodeo.

Pleased with the performance of Buck, the Bryants purchased a Lucky Blanton granddaughter, Blanton's Ribbon, in 1963 and roped and ran barrels on her. Bred by Burns Blanton, this 1958 dun was sired by Red Ribbon Blanton, a grandson of Lucky Blanton, and was out of Eureka Blanton, by Lucky Blanton. A capable mare, Blanton's Ribbon carried Phyllis to a third-place finish in the 1964 California barrel racing standings, and won lots of cash in the team roping.

Another son of Lucky Blanton who earned respect in the roping arena was Scotty H, out of Check Out, by Pay Check, by Hard Tack. He was owned first by E.V. Dorsey, and then by Marvin Myers of Golconda, Nevada. Still another was Skipper Bill, out of Boots, by Dammit, owned by Simon Hogue and ridden to lots of calf roping money by Billy Hogue and Gordon Davis.

In 1957 and 1958, Lucky Blanton was leased by Spencer Childers to stand at his Fresno ranch. That gave horsemen in the San Joaquin Valley an opportunity to take their mares to the prepotent sire. Among his foals produced, there was the 1959 blue roan stallion, Blue Blanton, out of Corn Cob, by Lee Moore. Childers retained Blue Blanton as a stallion, while also using him as a rope horse. Blue Blanton joined a high-powered stallion battery that included Bunny's Bar Boy and Tiny Charger, both AAA on the track.

Lucky Blanton also sired a number of good mares who excelled in performance and as producers. Among them was Lucky Bet, a 1943 sorrel mare out of Betsy, by Red

Cloud. She was one of the top halter mares of her era and was shown by the legendary Charlie Araujo.

Betsy Luck was another daughter of Betsy. Foaled in 1944, she produced Lucky Betsy, by Jimmy Reed.

Dusky Ruth was out of Bajita Fifi, by Hard Tack. When she was bred to Driftwood, she produced Dusky Peake, a bay stallion owned and roped on by John Bacon of Los Olivos.

Another Lucky Blanton daughter was Lucky Choice, out of Knock Knoc, by Woo (TB). She was purchased in foal to War Chant in a 1960 breeders sale by Vernon McPhillips for $8,000.

Lucky Split was perhaps Lucky Blanton's best producing daughter. Out of Bonita Adair, by Tom Adair, this 1954 bay mare was bred by W.M. Sullivan of Soledad, California. A good performance mare, she was honored by the Working Cow Horse Breeders of Yuba-Sutter Counties Inc. when they included her in their Cow Horse Hall of Fame. This group also documented her achievements in an impressive leather-bound book that also includes her sire, Lucky Blanton. Two of her outstanding foals were the AAA running horses Loretta Bar and Redwood Blossom, both sired by Lucky Bar (TB).

Two of Lucky Split's offspring who excelled in performance were Happy Chance and Triple Go Bar. They were shown successfully to many major wins in hackamore and reined cow horse competition at the big open shows in California—the Cow Palace in San Francisco, Monterey, Salinas, and the state fair. These events were sanctioned by the California Reined Cow Horse Association, not by the AQHA.

Two more great performers produced by Lucky Split were Burnt Girl, by Burnt Spur, and Doc's Abe, by Doc Bar. Burnt Girl was a CRCHA hackamore champion, while Doc's Abe was a bridle horse sweepstakes winner at the Cow Palace.

A number of California breeders utilized Lucky Blanton daughters in their broodmare bands. Included among them were Spencer Childers, the Sessions Ranch, Rancho Jabali, Bill Dana, California State Polytechnical College, and Perry Cotton.

Cotton, who ranched in Visalia, assembled an exceptional group of Lucky Blanton daughters. When he crossed those daughters on different stallions, the resulting progeny established Cotton as one of the area's premier breeders in the 1950s. When he dispersed his horses in 1962, buyers snapped up the Lucky Blanton mares at premium prices.

Lucky Blanton's athletic ability, speed, and disposition carried on beyond the first generation, and he became a successful broodmare sire. In addition to his grand-get already mentioned, he was the grand-sire of, among others, Blanton's Ribbon, a top barrel and team roping horse; the AQHA Champions Miss Poco Possum, Penny Blanton, Lucky Wood, Babe's Gray, and Poco Targette; and the AAA race horses Luap Nosbod, Irish Lad, Minnaca-duzza, and Pistachio Bar.

In the spring of 1957, according to an August 1965 *Quarter Horse Journal* article written by Emma Jeanne Judkins, Jim and Bob Clyde of Heber City, Utah, came through California on a mare buying trip. They purchased, among others, Lady Goldust, by Lucky Blanton. After owning this good mare, they were so impressed that they decided they needed to own her sire. Two years later, on Febuary 5, 1959, the deal was finally completed and the Clyde brothers purchased Lucky Blanton from Tom Mattart and moved him to Utah. He was 23 years old at the time.

During the 1959 breeding season, 18 mares were brought to Lucky Blanton, and 14 of them dropped foals the follow-ing spring. But during the winter of 1959-60, Lucky Blanton grew steadily weaker, reportedly because of rheumatism. He finally reached the point where he needed help to get to his feet. The following spring, 1960, he was able to breed only one mare, Heart 87, owned by Sterl Creer of Spanish Fork, Utah. This resulted in a fine filly in

Lucky Bob Blanton was a maternal grandson of Lucky Blanton; he was by Joker, and out of Nina Chiquita, by Lucky Blanton. He was owned and shown by G.B. Oliver Jr. of Alamogordo, New Mexico. This picture was taken at the 1950 New Mexico State Fair, where Lucky Bob Blanton was grand champion palomino stock-type stallion. Lucky Bob Blanton went on to sire Flying Bobette. When that mare was bred to Jack-straw (TB), she produced Fly Straw and Straw Flight, both rated AAAT.

1961. Named Barbara Blanton, she was Lucky's last foal.

In April of 1960 the chestnut stallion with excellent conformation, quick speed, athletic ability, and the prepotency to pass his traits on to succeeding genera-tions of horses was humanely put to sleep. He was buried on the ranch of Blaine Moore near Henefer, Utah.

In his career at stud, Lucky Blanton probably sired more top rope horses than any other Quarter Horse stallion living at the time.

5 PETER McCUE

By Frank Holmes

His name is still one of the most recognizable in Quarter Horse history.

WHILE TIME and numbers have diluted the influence that Peter McCue once had on the Quarter Horse breed, they can never totally erase it. He remains, many years after his death, one of the absolute fountainheads of the breed.

The story of Peter McCue begins before the turn of the century, near the town of Petersburg, located in west-central Illinois. This was the land of Abraham Lincoln. From the mid-1800s through the first decade of the 20th century, it was also where a prosperous farmer by the name of Samuel Watkins raised cattle, crops, and good horses.

In 1894, there were two top-notch stal-lions at Watkins' Long Grove Stock Farm. One was Duke of the Highlands, a Thor-oughbred, and the other was Dan Tucker, a descendant of Cold Deck and Steel Dust. In 1895, 17 Watkins-owned mares had foals, with 15 being credited to Duke of the Highlands and 2 to Dan Tucker.

One of the mares, a Thoroughbred by the name of Nora M., foaled a colt on February 23, 1895, who was subsequently named Peter McCue. As was true of so many horses in the early days, there is confusion regarding Peter McCue's pedi-gree. In Watkins' ledger, he was listed as having been sired by Duke of the High-lands, and he was registered as a Thor-

A photograph of Peter McCue and Milo Burlin-game taken around 1911 in Cheyenne, Oklahoma.

Photo Courtesy of Walter Merrick

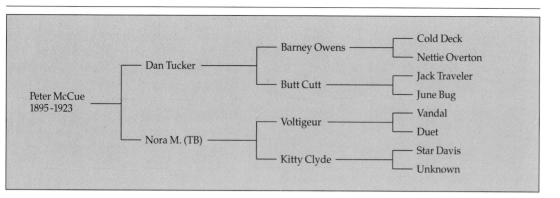

```
                                          ┌─── Cold Deck
                       ┌─── Barney Owens ──┤
                       │                   └─── Nettie Overton
          ┌─ Dan Tucker┤
          │            │                   ┌─── Jack Traveler
          │            └─── Butt Cutt ──────┤
Peter McCue┤                               └─── June Bug
1895-1923  │
          │                                ┌─── Vandal
          │            ┌─── Voltigeur ──────┤
          └─ Nora M. (TB)                  └─── Duet
                       │
                       │                   ┌─── Star Davis
                       └─── Kitty Clyde ────┤
                                           └─── Unknown
```

oughbred in the *American Stud Book*.

But, in a brief note that appeared in the March 10, 1945, issue of *The Blood Horse*, it was stated that Peter McCue's sire in the *American Stud Book* was listed as Rathnerod (TB).

Yet, repeated testimony given later by friends and the family of Sam Watkins, definitively established Peter McCue's sire as being Dan Tucker. And, AQHA recognizes Dan Tucker as Peter McCue's sire.

The discrepancy, while controversial for years, was easily explained and lay rooted in the basic economics of the time. Then, as now, good running horses were in demand and Samuel Watkins had the reputation of breeding some of the best. At most race meets, however, only registered Thoroughbreds were allowed to compete. In registering Peter McCue as a son of Duke of the Highlands, Watkins was simply following a practice that was in widespread use by horse breeders of that era. In doing so, his sole aim was to give Peter McCue the opportunity to prove his mettle on the racetrack.

When Peter McCue was a 2-year-old, he was broke by Dick Hornback, a local horseman. Watkins then allowed a nephew, Charles Watkins, to put the horse in race training. He was campaigned heavily in 1897 and recorded eight wins at distances from ½ mile to 4½ furlongs. His races were run at places such as Forsyth, Ind.; St. Louis, Mo.; Ingalls Park, Ill.; Detroit, Mich.; and Windsor, Ontario.

Milo Burlingame, of Cheyenne, Okla., rode Peter McCue to several of his racing wins and, in an interview printed in the September 1948 issue of *The Quarter Horse* (the official publication of the old National Quarter Horse Breeders Association), he reminisced about his experiences:

"I first met Peter McCue in St. Louis. I had only ridden one or two races until the owners came and engaged me to ride

An early-day ad for Peter McCue that was reproduced in AQHA's studbook No. 1. It is reproduced here courtesy of AQHA.

Harmon Baker, as pictured in AQHA's Studbook No. 1, was one of the Peter McCue's greatest sons. He was owned by William Anson.

**Photo Courtesy of the American Quarter Horse
Heritage Center & Museum, Amarillo, Texas**

Tom Caudill and Peter McCue in a photograph taken around 1911. Caudill was the man who handled the horse for Milo Burlingame, and stood him at his livery stable. Note the injury to Peter McCue's left front pastern that ended his racing career.

Editor's Note: *Because Peter McCue preceded the AQHA by many years, there is no official performance record for him, or record of his offspring's performance.*

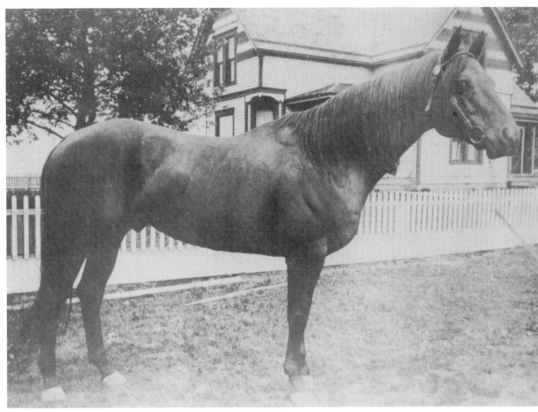

This photograph of Peter McCue was taken in either 1901 or 1902, in Illinois, when the horse was 6 or 7 years old.

This photograph was taken in 1917 in Fort Worth and depicts what is believed to have been the first Quarter Horse show ever held. Peter McCue's son, Harmon Baker, was named grand champion stallion. Even though the AQHA was not formed until 1940, early-day horses noted for their speed at short distances were often referred to as quarter-of-a-mile running horses, or Quarter Horses.

Peter McCue. I never saw him raced with horses that could make him straighten his neck out. There were 2,500 horses stabled at St. Louis in that meet, and after Peter McCue had run two races, it was common knowledge that he was by far the best and fastest there. I was just a kid then, but swore I would own that horse some day."

With no horse at the St. Louis meet seemingly capable of pushing Peter McCue to his limit, there was no chance to see exactly how fast he could cover a quarter of a mile. One morning, his trainer decided to run him wide open against the watch, with Milo Burlingame up.

"Those were the days before gates," recalled Burlingame. "We went to the track

at daylight, and there were five watches put on him, all clicking from flags, two at the start and three at the finish.

"Well, I broke from an 18-foot score and really pushed him out. It was the closest to flying I ever felt. When I got back, the five watches had been brought together. As I got off, I saw them all with his time, just as they were snapped. Two were under 21 seconds and three were exactly 21 seconds. All five watch-holders were experienced race timers and handicappers, and knowing the horses of his day and their

39

Jack McCue, another great son of Peter McCue, appeared on the cover of the November 1947 issue of The Quarter Horse. Foaled in 1914, Jack McCue died in 1939. He was a noted race horse and sire. His blood figured prominently in the breeding programs of such noted breeders as J.W. Shoemaker and Hank Wiescamp.

While in Illinois, Peter McCue sired three of his most famous sons— Harmon Baker, Hickory Bill, and John Wilkins.

The
QUARTER HORSE

Vol. 2 - No. 8   KNOX CITY, TEXAS   NOVEMBER - 1947

Subscription price: $2 per year   All contents copyrighted 1947   Single copies 25c

Official Publication of

THE NATIONAL QUARTER HORSE BREEDERS ASSOCIATION

R. J. (Rusty) Bradley, Jr., *President*   Ed Bateman, Sr., *Editor*   J. M. Huffington, *Sec'y-Treas.*

New Mexico Cowboys Back His Family Strain

JACK McCUE—This Son of Peter McCue Endowed His Get With Superb Qualities and Fine Speed — Read His Story In This Issue

Entered as Second Class matter at the postoffice at Knox City, Texas, under Act of March 3, 1879. Published monthly. Business address of The QUARTER HORSE is Box 547, Knox City, Texas; Telephone 3102. While exercising reasonable care, the publishers will not be responsible for the safe return of unsolicited manuscripts or photographs sent in for publication. STAFF: DALE GRAHAM, Associate Editor; Photographers, Tommy Thompson, 112 S. Washington, San Angelo, Texas, specialist in livestock photography and photo-finish; BILLIE WILCOX, Box 333, Olympia, Washington, specialist in photo-finish. Editorial contributors, DANA STONER, Houston; NELSON C. NYE, Tucson, Ariz.; MRS. LUTHER BULLOCK, Texola, Oklahoma. The National Quarter Horse Breeders Association hereby gives notice that it reserves the right in case of any dispute over subscription rates and changes in said rates, made with or without notice, to return any sum already paid in, or proffered it, for subscribing to The QUARTER HORSE. ADVERTISING RATES: full page $60; half page $30; one-third page $20; inch rate $2.00, with minimum size of 4 inches. Standard breeder ad on yearly contract only. $6 per month or $66 per year. No classified ads accepted. Engravings 65 to 85 screen. Copy deadline, receipt of same in QUARTER HORSE office by 25th of month preceding publication. Contracts: rate open only and subject to change by notification after any date of issue.

times, I can say quite honestly that I believe the watches of that morning were correct. I feel sure it would be under 22 seconds from a gate in our day."

In addition to his starts on recognized tracks, Peter McCue, as a 2-year-old, ran scores of races on the fair circuit. This heavy use reportedly displeased Sam

Watkins, with some justification it would seem, for Peter McCue suffered a broken left fore pastern as a 3-year-old. He was put in a sling for 9 months and, contrary to some published reports, was never raced again.

With some difficulty, Watkins got his horse back from his nephew and retired him to stud. By this time, Peter McCue had matured into quite a horse. He was a dark bay in color, with no white on his head or legs. He stood 16 hands and weighed more than 1,400 pounds. He had a good head, with prominent jaws. His back was on the long side and his hip a bit short. Conformation faults not withstanding, he was readily accepted as a breeding stallion by midwestern horsemen.

While in Illinois, Peter McCue sired three of his most famous sons—Harmon Baker, Hickory Bill, and John Wilkins. All three were foaled on the Watkins farm; John Wilkins in 1906 and the other two in 1907.

Harmon Baker was out of Nona P., a daughter of Duke of the Highlands. Nona P. was out of a mare by the name of Molly D., who was, in turn, out of Nora M., the dam of Peter McCue.

Owned for most of his life by Billy Anson of Cristoval, Tex., Harmon Baker excelled both as a race horse and a sire. Four of his better-known sons were Dodger, Jazz, Harmon Baker Jr., and New Mexico Little Joe.

Hickory Bill was out of Lucretia M., and was sold in 1911 to a man named John Wilkins, who lived in San Antonio. This horse eventually wound up in the hands of the well-known south Texas horseman, George Clegg. While owned by Clegg, Hickory Bill sired Old Sorrel, the eventual cornerstone sire of the King Ranch line of horses.

The horse named John Wilkins was out of a Thoroughbred mare named Katie Wawekus. This stallion spent most of his life on some of the most famous Quarter Horse breeding ranches in Texas. While in that area, he sired the immortal Joe Hancock and many other fine horses.

In 1901 or 1902, Peter McCue was leased to a Mr. Michaels who lived near Lincoln, Illinois. Several years later Peter was sold to the same John Wilkins who would purchase Hickory Bill.

Milo Burlingame had kept track of Peter McCue and, in 1911, he wrote to Wilkins and asked if he would consider selling him. Wilkins wrote back that he had used him about as long as he could and reportedly priced him for $10,000. Burlingame never even went to look at the horse; he just sent a man to pick him up.

Again from the September 1948 issue of

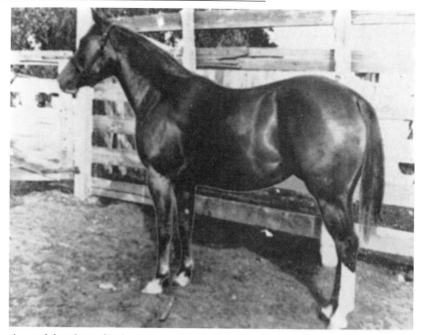

A noted daughter of Jack McCue was Jackie McCue, the dam of Little Meow, Jack Casement's great race mare. This photograph appears in AQHA's Studbook No. 3 and is reproduced courtesy of AQHA.

Chief P-5 was another good son of Peter McCue. He was bred and owned for his entire life by W. Claud Stinson of Hammon, Okla., who is holding the horse in this photograph taken in the 1940s. When Chief was 24 years old (in 1941), Stinson showed him in halter at the Elk City, Okla., Quarter Horse show, and the horse placed first in his class. One of Chief's daughters was Bay Lucy; when she was bred to Oklahoma Star, she produced Nowata Star, the sire of Star Duster.

Orren Mixer's painting of Peter McCue illustrated this show bill for the 1957 Peter McCue Memorial Horse Show in Cheyenne, Oklahoma.

PETER McCUE MEMORIAL HORSE SHOW

AQHA APPROVED

CHEYENNE, OKLAHOMA

APRIL 19, 1957

OPEN TO THE WORLD

HALTER CLASSES

STALLIONS:

1. Aged Stallions		Ribbon
2. Three year old Stallions		Ribbon
3. Two year old Stallions		Ribbon
4. Yearling Stallions		Ribbon
5. Stallion Foals		Ribbon
Grand Champion Stallion		Trophy

MARES:

6. Aged Mares		Ribbon
7. Three year old Mares		Ribbon
8. Two year old Mares		Ribbon
9. Yearling Mares		Ribbon
10. Filly Foals		Ribbon
Grand Champion Mare		Trophy

MISCELLANEOUS

11. Mare and Foal		Ribbon
12. Produce of Dam (2 colts from one mare)		Ribbon
13. Get of Sire (3 colts sired by one horse, need not be owned by one exhibitor)		Ribbon
14. Gelding (age 1-2)		Ribbon
15. Gelding (Any Age)		Ribbon
Grand Champion		Trophy

WORKING CLASSES

16. Roping Contest	50—25—15—10%
17. Cutting Contest	50—25—15—10%
18. Reining	50—25—15—10%
All Round Champion	Trophy

OPEN:

Barrel Bending — Ladies
Jackpot Calf Roping

Trophies will be awarded by the American Quarter Horse Association to the Grand Champion mare, stallion, and gelding. All entry fees in working classes will be split 50—25—15—10%. Six ribbons with Rosettes will be awarded in each class. Entry fee for working classes, $10.00. Feed will be available on grounds.

For Information and Entry Blanks, Write:

J. W. CHALFANT — Cheyenne, Oklahoma

MARCH, 1957

33

The Quarter Horse, Burlingame reminisces about Peter McCue.

"Where I made my mistake with him," he explained, "I should have allowed him to breed only extra-good mares. But I had lots of good friends and I would tell them to go breed to him. My first intentions were to get about five top Thoroughbred mares to breed, knowing he was registered as a Thoroughbred, and I could register those colts and get an animal that would run from a half a mile to 5½ fur-

This is the original Buck Thomas—the Thorough-bred gelding by Peter McCue. Buck was considered one of the fastest horses of his time for a half-mile. Watching Buck Thomas run at Denver is what inspired Si Dawson and Coke Roberds to go after Peter McCue. This picture was taken at Gordon, Neb., in 1911. The rider is identified only as "Mizzou."

longs and beat most anybody's horse.

"I didn't follow this out, except with John Wilkins (the horse) out of Big Alice. I honestly believe he was the greatest son of Peter McCue."

This John Wilkins, however, is not the same John Wilkins who was bred and foaled in Illinois. The John Wilkins to whom Burlingame refers was a chestnut son of Peter McCue, foaled in 1912, and out of a mare called Big Alice. Burlingame bred him and named him. But his name was later changed to John Wilkes when he was owned by Matt Renfro of Fort Sumner, New Mexico.

Even if it did not unfold as Burlingame had originally planned, Peter McCue's tenure as a breeding horse in the Southwest was a productive one.

In addition to John Wilkins (John Wilkes), some of the better-known horses he sired during this stage of his life were Jack McCue, A.D. Reed, Chief P-5, Badger, and the famous race mare, Carrie Nation,

who once held the world's record for ⅝ths of a mile.

Peter McCue remained under the ownership of Milo Burlingame until 1916, when he was purchased by Si Dawson of Hayden, Colorado. Dawson, along with his friend and neighbor, Coke Roberds, had become interested in Peter McCue after seeing a gelded son of his named Buck Thomas burn up the racetracks at Denver.

Dawson was inclined to go in search of a top son of Peter McCue, but Roberds lobbied in favor of buying the old horse himself. Both Dawson and Roberds were serious horse breeders. After corresponding with John Wilkins, George Clegg, and William Anson regarding their sons of Peter McCue, Si Dawson made a trip to personally check the stallion out.

43

This is the Buck Thomas bred by Coke Roberds, and originally referred to as Buck Thomas II, but the "II" was eventually dropped. He was by Peter McCue and out of Stockings, by Old Fred. This picture was taken in 1925 at Cody, Neb., and the handler is Clint Anderson, whose father bought Buck Thomas from Roberds. The horse was later sold to the Waggoner ranch in north Texas, where he became the maternal grandsire of Pretty Buck.

Mary McCue, a great daughter of Peter McCue and out of an Old Fred mare, was purchased at the Si Dawson dispersal sale by Marshall Peavy. A tremendous race mare, she is pictured here with Dan Sykes in the irons. She was the dam of Ding Bob, a foundation sire who contributed greatly to the breeding programs of Peavy and Quentin Semotan. **Photo Courtesy of Marsha Witte**

He liked what he saw and gave Burlingame $5,000 for the 21-year-old horse. He then arranged to have him shipped by rail to Colorado.

Three years later, Dawson signed a contract to manage a huge cattle ranch in Brazil. The ranch covered some 250,000 acres and was called Fazenda Morungave. While celebrating Thanksgiving dinner on the ranch with friends, Dawson's appendix ruptured and he died December 3, 1919, at the age of 49.

When he went to Brazil, Dawson left Peter McCue and about 35 mares with Coke Roberds. After Dawson's death, all but Peter McCue were dispersed in a sale. Peter McCue was given to Roberds, under whose care he remained until his death in 1923 at the age of 28. For the last 2 years of Peter's life, Roberds supplemented him with cow's milk and always maintained that it contributed to his longevity.

During the Dawson-Roberds portion of his life, Peter McCue was every bit as productive as he had been in Illinois and on the southern plains. It was during this period of his life that he sired Sheik P-11 and Buck Thomas (the stallion). This was also when he sired Roberds' race mare Squaw, who won 49 of 50 starts, and Marshall Peavy's race mare Mary McCue,

Sheik P-11, a well-known son of Peter McCue, out of Pet, by Old Fred. Bred by Coke Roberds and foaled in 1918, he was used by Marshall Peavy for 5 years and then sold to the Matador Land and Cattle Company in Texas, where he sired many outstanding ranch horses. Sheik was the paternal grandsire of Nick Shoemaker, the sire of Skipper W. Sheik was given back to Roberds when he was 27 or 28 years old, and that's when this picture was taken.

whom Peavy purchased at the Dawson dispersal sale. Old Red Bird P-14, who was sired by Buck Thomas and was out of a Peter McCue mare, was foaled during this time period, as were such top race and breeding horses as Peter McCue II, Mistress McCue, and Biddy McCue.

When put into breeding production themselves, the sons and daughters of Peter McCue spread his blood like wildfire. Such foundation Quarter Horse sires as Old Sorrel, Wimpy P-1, Peppy, Bert, Joe Hancock, Ding Bob, Midnight, Midnight Jr, Grey Badger II, Pretty Boy, Pretty Buck, Blackburn, Nowata Star, Poco Bueno, King Fritz, Cowboy P-12, Plaudit, Nick S, Skipper W, Jessie James, King's Pistol, and a host of others are all descendants of Peter McCue.

Among the more prominent modern Quarter Horse sires, Coy's Bonanza, Blondy's Dude, Two Eyed Jack, Zan Parr Bar, and Rugged Lark trace, or traced, to Peter McCue.

And the list goes on . . . and on . . . and on.

In a poetic tribute to this great horse, penned years ago, J.A. Estes probably described Peter McCue's influence most succinctly when he wrote, "Though he never learned to subtract or divide, he was mighty good when he multiplied."

Squaw was a daughter of Peter McCue out of an Old Fred mare. One of the fastest mares of her time (late 1920s or early '30s), she won 49 of 50 starts. Owned by Coke Roberds for her entire life, she was never registered. Squaw was the dam of Mountain Maid, who produced Ute Chief (by Smoky T.), one of Roberds' last great sires.

Photo Courtesy of the American Quarter Horse Heritage Center & Museum, Amarillo, Texas

45

6 MIDNIGHT

By Jim Goodhue

He passed his speed and working ability to succeeding generations.

THE NAME Midnight conjures up the blackness of a coal mine in the middle of the night, but for the most famous Midnight in Quarter Horse history, there must have been a full moon involved. He was a flea-bitten gray at maturity and before his death at an advanced age, he was almost snow white.

The colt, born looking black enough to earn the name of Midnight, was foaled early in May 1916. This event took place on the Cooper ranch 5 miles south of Roosevelt, in western Oklahoma. That ranch was the realm of the well-known horsemen Jess, Al, Keller, and Bill Cooper. Keller was the one who first saw the handsome colt as he stood and nursed. From his earliest days, Midnight showed signs of the conformation and spirit that were to distinguish him at his prime. At

Midnight, as an aged horse, when his knees were starting to buckle.

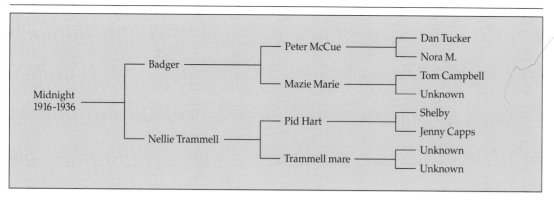

```
                                        ┌─── Dan Tucker
                       ┌─── Peter McCue ─┤
                       │                 └─── Nora M.
          ┌─── Badger ─┤
          │            │                 ┌─── Tom Campbell
          │            └─── Mazie Marie ─┤
Midnight ─┤                              └─── Unknown
1916-1936 │
          │                              ┌─── Shelby
          │                 ┌─── Pid Hart ┤
          │                 │            └─── Jenny Capps
          └─── Nellie Trammell ┤
                              │             ┌─── Unknown
                              └─── Trammell mare ┤
                                                └─── Unknown
```

maturity, he stood 15.2 and weighed about 1,150 pounds.

The name of Midnight's sire is officially recognized as Badger; but he was sometimes referred to as Grey Badger, and for a time even went by the name of Midnight. The dam of the colt was a club-footed mare called Nellie Trammell, owned by Jess Cooper. Jess had bought her from John Parvell of Elk City, Oklahoma.

Despite her affliction, Nellie Trammell won a number of races when her owner had been able to match the races on soft ground. Keller Cooper remembered, though, that "she would buck you off about half the time."

She was sired by Pid Hart, a son of Shelby, by Tom Driver, by Steel Dust. Pid Hart, one of the most noted race horses of his day, was out of Jenny Capps, a great-granddaughter of Shiloh.

Nellie Trammell had already produced a great race horse called Roger Mills, who, despite her name, was a mare. Because Roger Mills was by a stallion whom Jess considered to be a common saddle horse, he decided to breed her dam, Nellie Trammel, to a stallion he considered to be outstanding. He selected Badger.

On the theory that a chain is only as strong as its weakest link, Badger was a very strong link. He was a link between his sire, the immortal Peter McCue, and his amazing son, the legendary Midnight.

Because of Badger's limited breeding career, little is known of this horse today; but at the match-race tracks of his day, he was a formidable competitor at 220 yards to a quarter of a mile. He, too, was bred by John Parvell. Roy Cochran of Cordell, Okla., bought Badger in the fall of his 3-year-old year and started his race training under the name of Midnight. By the following summer, the gray colt had a rep-

Another picture of Midnight, probably taken when he was younger.

utation for being very quiet on the score, a particularly important trait in short distance racing. He had been so successful that Cochran was having difficulty matching any more races. So, he sold him to brush-track trainer and jockey Reed Armstrong of Foss, Oklahoma.

Armstrong, the one who changed the promising youngster's name from Midnight to Badger, proceeded to take the colt on a wider range of match-race venues, and the pair consistently won races from 220 yards to a quarter of a mile.

The breeding career of this stout runner, however, was more erratic. From Nellie Trammell, he got Midnight, but his only other foals were a daughter or two who were undistinguished.

The time came when Armstrong, also,

Editor's note:
Because Midnight preceded the AQHA by many years, there is no official performance record for him, or record of his offspring's performance.

47

Jole Blon S, foaled in 1947, was sired by Chubby, by Midnight, and was out of Dundee, a granddaughter of Silver King. Jole Blon was an outstanding halter mare and produced several good horses when bred to Bill Cody, including Win-fred Cody, an AQHA Champion. The handler shown here is Doyle Saul.

Photo by Gressett

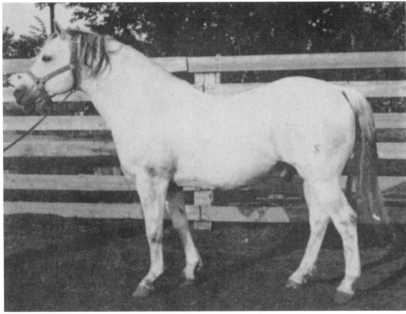

Dan Waggoner, a gray stallion foaled in 1930, was by Waggoner's Rainy Day and out of a mare by Midnight. His second dam was a daughter of Yellow Wolf. This picture appeared in the AQHA Studbook No. 5, and is reproduced courtesy of AQHA.

was unable to match any more races for this powerful sprinter, so he sold him to a farmer. The value of former match-race horses being what it was in those days, the farmer gelded Badger and used him for a plowhorse.

Meanwhile, Jess Cooper traded Badger and Nellie Trammel's son, Midnight, to his brothers, Al and Bill. They broke him at 2 and began his race training. Soon, needing a test to see just how much speed he had, they ran him against his experienced half-sister, Roger Mills. Despite carrying about 200 pounds, including a heavy stock saddle, Midnight won going away.

About 1919, Article, a sprinter with a solid reputation, was shipped from Cuba to run against one of the good runners owned by the Waggoner Ranch of Vernon, Texas. For reasons unknown today, that race was never held, so the Coopers took a daring step. They knew what they had in their stable, so they matched the virtually unknown Midnight against Article for $500 a side in a race to be run at Lawton, Oklahoma. Midnight won from start to finish.

When Reed Armstrong heard about the youngster by his former bread-winner, he

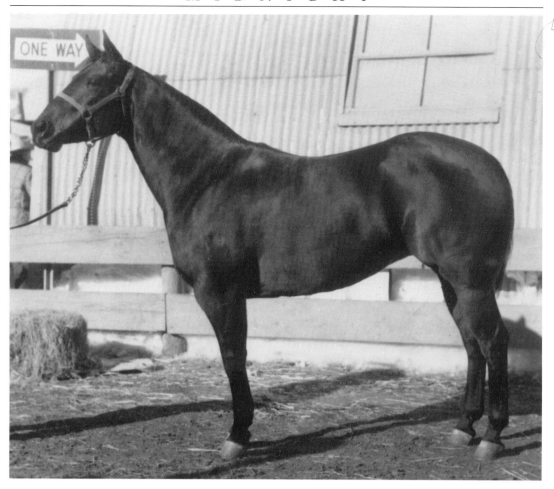

Irene 40, a terrific halter mare in the 1950s, was a great-granddaughter of Midnight. She was foaled in 1953, and was by Chuck Wagon W, by Chubby, by Midnight, and was out of Miss Wardlaw 39.

talked the Coopers into a 220-yard race at Elk City against A.D. Reed. This was another horse known to have plenty of speed; he was owned by Armstrong and J. Harrel. With Bill Cooper on Midnight and Armstrong on A.D. Reed, the race proved to be another victory for Midnight. It is said that in another race at about the same time, he ran ⅜ths of a mile in :33.0.

With wins such as this, the Coopers experienced the old problem. They couldn't find any competitors for this young champion, so they sold him to Red Whaley, a Texas cowboy. Whaley was a man with an inspired idea.

Whaley knew that the Waggoner Ranch had a policy of trying to buy any horse who defeated one of their top runners. This not only eliminated competition, it brought to Vernon some excellent horses who had a potential for improving the ranch's breeding program.

Whaley also knew that there was not much future in trying to campaign a horse who had scared off the owners of most of the available competition, so he was interested in making a sale at a good price. He trailered Midnight to Vernon and wrangled a match against one of the Waggoner speedsters.

The plan went like clockwork. Midnight won the race; the ranch made an offer; and Midnight had a new home.

The Waggoners raced Midnight for several years at distances up to ⅜ths of a mile while turning him out with their mares during breeding season. During this time, he sired such outstanding horses as Chubby, Waggoner, and Rainy Day.

Chubby, a powerfully muscled bay foaled in 1924, was out of Fourth Of July, by Bobby Lowe, a son of Eureka. He stood 14.2 and weighed about 1,100 pounds in his prime.

Chubby, too, made his mark at match-race tracks. It is claimed that he won 20 out of 21 starts—losing his last race while being ridden by a strange jockey. He was

The plan went like clockwork. Midnight won the race; the ranch made an offer; and Midnight had a new home.

49

Fritzi M, sired by Waggoner, by Midnight, stood grand champion mare at the 1953 Colorado Springs Quarter Horse show. She was out of FL Flaxie, by Peter McCue Jr.

This picture of Midnight with his last owner, Aubra Bowers of Allison, Tex., appeared in the March 1948 issue of The Quarter Horse. *The caption says this was the final picture taken of Midnight, and was made 4 months before his death. It quotes Bowers as saying: "I tried to hide his buckled knees in this picture, to keep him from looking so bad."*

known for a very fast break.

Following his race career, Chubby was put to work on the ranch. During most of his adult life, Chubby was owned by J.C. Hooper and his sons of Plainview, Texas. His owners found him to be very capable in cutting and roping.

He also was found to be an excellent breeding horse. His offspring included many horses who were tops in their day. Though most of Chubby's later foals gained their reputations in the show ring, three qualified for a Register of Merit in racing. Many of his earlier foals demonstrated speed in matched races and passed that speed on to their foals.

Chubby sired such well-known horses as Manitobian, the halter and performance winner Chubby W, the top halter mare Jole Blon S, Dutch Boy, Chubby III, and Bob Steel. In addition, his daughters went on to make him particularly prized as a sire of broodmares.

Waggoner, foaled in 1930, was another gray horse. His dam was one of the many good daughters of Yellow Wolf bred on the Waggoner Ranch. Yellow Wolf, one of the premier horses of his generation, was sired by Old Joe Bailey, by Eureka, a son of Shelby.

As a weanling, Waggoner was purchased by B.B. Van Vacter of Mangum, Oklahoma. Though registered later as Waggoner, he was known for most of his life as One Eyed Waggoner because of an early injury that caused him to lose one eye. Even though the skin grew completely over that eye socket, it did not keep him from being a handsome horse, even at an advanced age.

Van Vacter paid $35 for Waggoner in those early days of the Great Depression. He kept the horse long enough to get six crops of foals before selling him. He later came under the ownership of Duwain E. Hughes, San Angelo, Tex., a member of the first board of directors of the American Quarter Horse Association. By the time Waggoner was registered, however, he was owned by V.B. Likins' Flying L Ranch near Davis, Oklahoma.

Waggoner's reputation was made as a sire. Some of the excellent individuals he sired were Silk McCue, Sage Hen, and Bud-weiser. After the AQHA began keeping performance records, more luster was added to his name. One of the best was Gray Lady Burk, an early AQHA Champion and 1953's top point-earner in reining. Another was Roan Midnight, a good runner and sire of race winners. His progeny also included Roan Wolf, C C A's Sugar, Roan Alice L, and the versatile By Wag.

Though foaled in this time period (1923, to be exact), Rainy Day was bred by the Coopers rather than the Waggoner Ranch. He was out of Old Allie, by Peter McCue. Old Allie, out of a mare named Flaxie O'Neal, also produced another noted son in Oklahoma Shy, a son of A.D. Reed. At various times, he also was known as Kid McCue and as Billy The Kid.

Rainy Day eventually came under the ownership of the S.B. Burnett Estate, which had ranches in King, Carson, and Hutchinson counties of Texas. From the Burnett mares, he sired a large number of top ranch horses. At the same time, an unusually large number of the leading professional rodeo calf ropers were mounted on Rainy Day's progeny.

Despite the quality of these horses and others, the Waggoner Ranch management apparently decided that Midnight did not cross well on their mares. So, when he got too old for racing, he was sold to the JA Ranch out of Clarendon, Texas. This was the ranch that had been founded by Charles Goodnight, the pioneer rancher of the Texas Panhandle.

Midnight then roamed with a band of mares in the rugged Palo Duro Canyon country. The ranch's primary objective was to produce ranch horses for its extensive holdings.

One old cowboy from the JA remembered that the Midnight horses were fast and quite smart. The result, according to him, was that on many cold mornings the Midnights turned their considerable capabilities to bucking and the cowboys wished for mounts who weren't quite so talented.

Some JA hands admired the old horse and his offspring. One of the JA cowboys at the time Midnight was moved from the Waggoner Ranch to the JA Ranch was Aubra (Aubrey) Bowers. He appreciated the speed and brains passed on by the old stallion. An ambitious cowman, Bowers bought his own 11-section ranch south of Allison, Tex., just in time for oil to be discovered under its surface.

Bowers had seen that the old horse's knees had begun to buckle while navigating the rugged terrain of the JA, and with his newly found revenue, he bought Midnight and a band of good mares. By this time, Midnight was rather feeble and his front legs were so crooked that it was difficult for him to stand.

By giving the stallion particularly good care, Bowers got two crops of foals from Midnight before the old-timer died. Bowers later reported that all of the resulting foals had lots of speed and were good for cow work and roping.

During this period, Kenneth "Skip" Montgomery, also of Allison, owned the good mare Salty. She was one of three excellent daughters sired by Billy The Tough in his one season at stud. Salty was out of Peachie, by Joy. Billy The Tough was sired by the speedy A.D. Reed.

When bred to Midnight, Salty produced one of his most renowned sons—a black foal who stayed black. His name appears in the pedigrees of many prominent horses as Midnight Jr. Both as a race horse and as a sire of speedsters, Midnight Jr. did his part to embellish the legend of Midnight.

Badly crippled with rheumatism, Midnight died in July 1936. The gallant old campaigner was mourned by a widespread group of horsemen who knew his worth, which has been proven repeatedly throughout succeeding generations.

7 MIDNIGHT JR

By Jim Goodhue

He was a superior individual as a race horse and as a sire.

WHEN A horse carries "Jr" at the end of his name, he often doesn't live up to the reputation of his sire. But one horse who actually increased his family's distinction was Midnight Jr, a superior individual as a race horse and as a sire.

Midnight Jr is credited with putting the great breeder Walter Merrick into the business of racing. Merrick bought Midnight Jr for $300, a price that was considered steep in 1938. After breaking the black colt, the new owner put him back in the capable hands of the young trainer-jockey who had bred Midnight Jr. This was Kenneth "Skip" Montgomery.

This trio accomplished the feat of winning 16 match races from 16 starts. This was during the 2-year period when he was raced by Merrick. Although never asked to go a full quarter of a mile, Midnight Jr

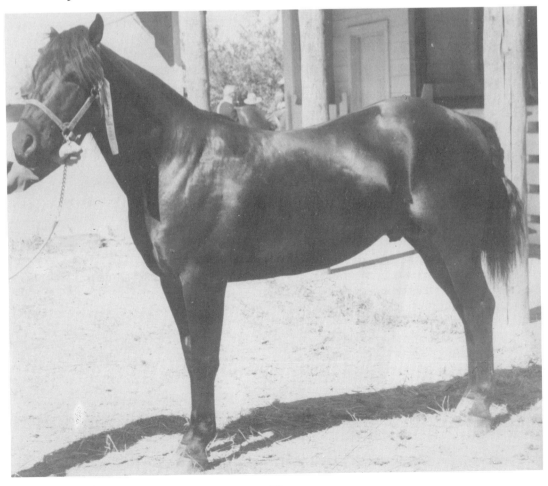

Midnight Jr as a 3-year-old.

Photo by C.E. Redman, Courtesy of Walter Merrick

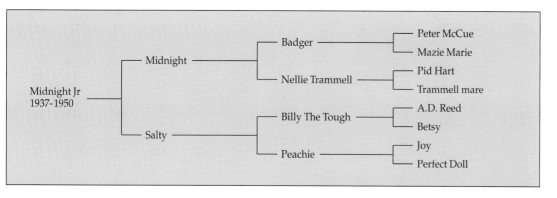

usually led from start to finish.

Midnight Jr was conspicuously bridle-wise and calm at the start of those lap-and-tap sprints. Some of this could be attributed to his naturally good disposition, plus the fact that he was well trained and capable as a calf-roping horse. In those days of matching a race with as much advantage as possible, including misleading the other owner as to your horse's abilities, Merrick was a master. A proficient roper, Merrick would haul Midnight Jr to a fair or rodeo where they were not well known. After the pair competed in the calf-roping event, Merrick would modestly admit that he was willing to pit his roping mount against any horse around whose owner thought he might have a race horse. It usually worked—to the advantage of Merrick and Midnight Jr.

Despite some rough times as a young cowboy during those Depression days, Merrick was as willing to put his money where his mouth was on the outcome of a race as he had been in buying the unknown quantity who had come to be known as Midnight Jr. He had begun to accumulate a bankroll.

Skip Montgomery got involved in this chapter of Quarter Horse history because he owned a good mare named Salty. He has stated that Salty, the dam of Midnight Jr, was never broke to saddle. But because he had faith in the young, 14.2-hand mare who weighed about a thousand pounds, he started breeding her to the best stallions available.

Salty was one of three outstanding mares sired by a horse called Billy The Tough during the one season he was at stud. It is said that since this young stallion showed so much unrealized speed and ability, and because he was difficult to handle, he was gelded so that his mind could be kept on business. After that, he proved himself both as a race horse and a roping horse.

Halter and Performance Record: None.

Progeny Record:

Foal Crops: 13	Performance Points Earned: 24
Foals Registered: 163	Performance Registers of Merit: 3
Halter Point-Earners: 3	Race Money Earned: $7,572
Halter Points Earned: 13	Race Registers of Merit: 6
Performance Point-Earners: 3	Race Starters: 21
Leading Race Money-Earner: Lewis' Miss Prissy ($5,363)	

Billy The Tough had every right to be a runner, since he was a son of the speedy A.D. Reed, one of the major rivals of the great Midnight. A.D. Reed was a son of the brilliantly fast Peter McCue and was out of a mare called Good Enough, by Ned Harper.

Salty's dam was Peachie, a daughter of Joy, by Jeff (from the Printer line), and was out of Perfect Doll, by Pid Hart. Peachie's second dam was from that famous Quarter Horse nursery, the Trammell and Newman Ranch—as was the dam of Billy The Tough.

Montgomery was working for Aubra (Aubrey) Bowers when Bowers brought the old, rheumatic Midnight to his ranch at Allison, Texas. There, Midnight received the kind of care that made it possible for him to be in relative comfort during his last two breeding seasons.

Salty's first foal was Midnight's last. Foaled June 5, 1937, the foal was named Midnight Jr. As the coal black colt began to fill out and grow, Montgomery and his brother, Lindsey, began to make plans to race and to rope on the promising newcomer.

Those plans went awry, however, when Skip went to work for a few months on a California ranch and left Midnight Jr in

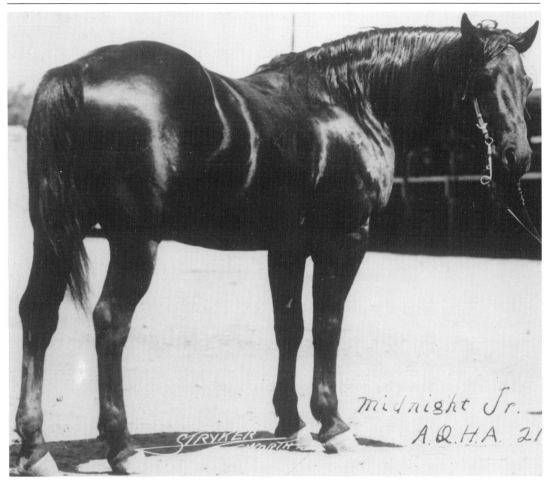

Midnight Jr as an aged horse.

Photo by Stryker, Courtesy of Walter Merrick

Although this photo has water spots on it, it's a good picture of Midnight Jr. Walter Merrick says, "This is a picture of me and my son, Jimmy Wayne, the day I sold and delivered Midnight Jr to Mr. H.S. Bissell in Las Cruces, New Mexico."
Photo Courtesy of Walter Merrick

the care of Lindsey, who was the horse trader in the family. Lindsey also thought he knew a good price for a yearling when he heard it. So when Merrick offered $300 for Midnight Jr and persisted, Lindsey took his money.

Then came the 2 years in which Midnight Jr made his mark as a race horse and made it possible for Merrick to go from farming some very sandy acres south of Allison to a ranch of his own near Crawford, Oklahoma.

Even though Merrick was the trainer of Midnight Jr, his wife, Christien (best known as "Tien," and also sometimes called "Tina,") played a key role. She was in charge of conditioning the black stallion when he was a 2-year-old. As she said, "We used to race Midnight Jr on Sundays, but during the week Walter was busy earning a living, so I exercised him." She explains that although she did ride in those days, she was no race-horse exercise rider. So she "ponied" Midnight Jr from their Buick. "I put a halter and lead rope on him, and led him with my arm sticking out the window.

"I'd lead him up to the top of a hill where we had an oval. I would start him at a slow

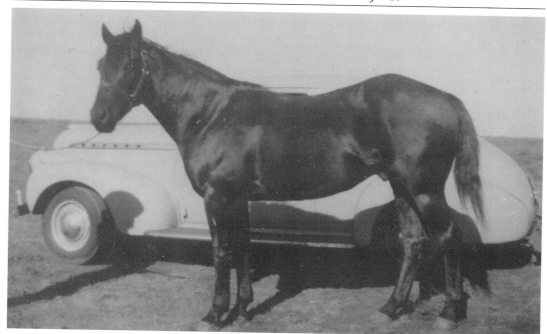

Midnight Jr as a young horse. Tien Merrick used to "pony" the black stallion from the window of the Merricks' Buick.

Photo Courtesy of Walter Merrick

trot, then go faster and faster. Coming back down the hill would be a real horse race with him, but I never had to turn him loose . . . although I nearly crashed through the corral gate a time or two."

Some of the first residents of the Merricks' new spread were five quality mares. One was a daughter of Joe Hancock named Joan, and one was another of the short crop sired by Billy The Tough. Her name was Grey Annie.

When crossed with Midnight Jr, those mares produced the kind of foals that added to Quarter Horse lore. Though these foals by Midnight Jr arrived a few years before the AQHA began recognizing and keeping records, the official files do show a part of his capabilities as a sire.

According to AQHA files, Midnight Jr had 163 foals registered. From 21 starters, he had 11 winners of some 26 races. His top official money earner in those days of small purses was the filly named Lewis' Miss Prissy, with a respectable $5,363. She later produced two racing Register of Merit qualifiers and one foal who earned a performance Register of Merit.

Three of Midnight Jr's foals earned points in working events and all three qualified for the performance Register of Merit. To round out the record, he sired three halter point-earners.

One of his racing Register of Merit qualifiers was the renowned Grey Badger II, out of Grey Annie. Although he won both of his only two AQHA-recognized races, Grey Badger II earned most of his fame

Here's another picture of Midnight Jr, taken when he was in New Mexico. Merrick describes it as follows: "This is R.B. Felmer, a friend of mine who was in the service and stationed at Las Cruces. He always admired this horse (Midnight Jr). So he went to the Corralitos Ranch and asked to have his picture taken on him."

Photo Courtesy of Walter Merrick

in match races, where he was the leading 220-yard specialist of the 1940s. As a progenitor, he added sparkle to both racetracks and working arenas.

When Joan was bred to Midnight Jr, she capped her broodmare career by producing a filly known to history as Hot

55

of runners. Bred again to Leo, she produced the stakes-placed Johnny Do It. Crossed with Top Deck (TB), Hot Heels was the dam of the good producer Mary Sunshine, a Register of Merit runner herself.

Midnight Jr sired other good mares, too, who made him a leading broodmare sire. From 96 starters, those daughters produced 2 winners of 16 stake races and a total of 49 winners of 196 races. His daughters also were dams of 21 qualifiers for the show Register of Merit, 45 performance point-earners, 37 halter point-earners, and 4 AQHA Champions.

In 1941, Merrick's band of horses had a lot of Midnight Jr blood, so he reluctantly sold the horse to H.S. Bissell. The new owner took Midnight Jr to his Corralitos Ranch, located 15 miles west of Las Cruces, New Mexico.

Although Bissell was primarily interested in raising working horses from his new stallion, he did send the black horse to Tucson for one race. It was Midnight Jr's first race from a starting gate, and he didn't like it. He was unplaced.

Returned to Corralitos, Midnight Jr spent his days working cattle and breeding mares. In addition to the owner's desire to raise using horses, Bissell's daughter, Dorothy Cox, and her husband, Ed, had ambitions to get some more sprinters. So, Midnight Jr was bred to a variety of mares. Most of the mares bred to him at that time were from the old-line New Mexico and Arizona Quarter Horse families, such as daughters of Pankey's Lucky by Apache Kid. But he also was offered some half-Thoroughbred mares. From both crosses, he got good working horses, and horses who contributed to short-horse racing history.

Much of the reputation, but not all, that Midnight Jr acquired during this period came from daughters who went on to add their own decorations to the family tree. Their foals excelled in both racing and at shows.

For instance, the Camelot Square A Ranch gathered several of Midnight Jr's daughters for their broodmare band in addition to some top geldings they trained and showed successfully. Located at San Luis Rey, Calif. (about 35 miles north of San Diego), this ranch was noted for turning out good performance horses.

The Camelot Square A's mares by Midnight Jr produced such foals as AQHA

Salty, the dam of Midnight Jr. When this picture was taken, circa 1948, she was 16 years old and had produced 12 foals. Two of them were Salty Chief, a well-known Burnett Ranch sire, and Revenue, a leading sire.

Quarter To Midnight was a bay gelding, foaled in 1946, bred by H.S. Bissell. He was by Midnight Jr and out of Myrna Loy, and was a full brother to Belle Of Midnight.

Heels. Though a good individual in her own right, Hot Heels is best known as an amazing producer.

Hot Heels, when bred to Leo, foaled Mona Leta, a multiple stakes winner, a multiple track record holder, and the 1952 Champion Quarter Running 3-Year-Old Filly. When bred to Three Bars (TB), Hot Heels came up with Bob's Folly, a winner of many important stakes races, a multiple track record holder, and an important sire

Champion Camelot Easter, the 1964 high-point working cow horse, and AQHA Champion Camelot Helen. The Camelot mares were also the dams of these other performance Register of Merit earners: Camelot Jewel, Camelot Broom, Camelot Whisp, and Camelot Minute, as well as the racing Register of Merit qualifier Camelot Lucy.

Of course, outside mares were still being attracted to Midnight Jr's court. Among others, Art Penhall of Clinton, Okla., hauled his good homebred daughter of Joe Reed, Nellie Bly Penhall, out to New Mexico. He was rewarded with a nice filly who was named Patter Lou.

An attractive individual, Patter Lou became another dependable broodmare. When bred to Depth Charge (TB), she produced the track record holder Hustle Charge. When bred to Dee Dee, she was the dam of racing Register of Merit qualifiers Patricia Dee, Patter Dee, Ruff, and Necona Dee. When crossed with the Thoroughbred stallion Equa Charge, Patter Lou added Honey Darlin', who qualified for the performance Register of Merit while becoming the nation's seventh high-point horse in jumping for 1968.

The short-horse racing industry profited considerably when the astute horseman James V.A. Carter took some of those Midnight Jr mares (mostly out of broodmares from the old Quarter Horse lines) home to Oregon with him.

One such mare was Carter's Midnight Star, out of Willie, a granddaughter of Old Lucky. Carter's Midnight Star produced two racing Register of Merit qualifiers and a daughter named Miss Night Star. From eight foals, Miss Night Star produced five racing Register of Merit qualifiers, including a stakes winner, Whirlaway Star, who set three track records.

Carter really hit the jackpot, though, with a Midnight Jr mare named Belle Of Midnight, who was out of Myrna Loy, by Pankey's Lucky. Belle Of Midnight became the dam of Midnight Bar, a racing Register of Merit qualifier, who also was the AQHA high-point pole bending Horse in 1961; Barbecue, the high-point pole bending stallion of 1962; Jordan Red, another performance Register of Merit horse; and four other racing Register of Merit qualifiers: I'm Prohibition, Cat's Bell Boy, Barred's Belle, and Miss Night Bar. It was Miss Night Bar, a daughter of

Bob's Folly, an outstanding race horse and sire who had a speed index of 100, was a maternal grandson of Midnight Jr. Sired by Three Bars (TB), he was out of Hot Heels, who was by Midnight Jr.

Barred, who changed the course of racing history. From 14 foals, she produced 13 racing Register of Merit qualifiers. These included the stakes winning Miss Jet Deck, by Moon Deck, and her full brother, the immortal Jet Deck. Several others included Three Jets, by Rocket Bar (TB), and Jet Moon, Jet Too, and Lightning Jet, all by Moon Deck.

When Walter Merrick got back into the picture by breeding the speedy Lena's Bar (TB) to Jet Deck, Merrick got the future All American Futurity winner Easy Jet. When Easy Jet sired the All American winner Easy Date, Merrick became the second person to have bred two All American winners.

During the years that Midnight Jr lived on the Corralitos Ranch, his owner repeatedly turned down offers of big money to sell him. Bissell was not interested in selling the horse at any price.

In 1949, however, Bissell closed down his ranching operations and contacted Merrick. They reached an agreement whereby the great horse would be returned to the care of Merrick for the rest of his life, but he was not to be sold.

Midnight Jr went back to Crawford, Okla., in October of that year. He had a heart attack during the next breeding season while covering a mare and died. The legacy of his descendants was his best monument.

8 GREY BADGER II

By Jim Goodhue

He was a sizzling speed horse with legs of iron.

IN HIS heyday, Grey Badger II resembled nothing so much as a silver machine efficiently doing its task. His job was simply demolishing almost every horse matched against him. He was the gauge against which the fastest 220-yard horses of the 1940s were tried.

Grey Badger II was foaled May 5, 1941. His sire was Midnight Jr and his dam was Grey Annie, by Billy The Tough. Since Midnight Jr was out of a Billy The Tough mare, that made Grey Badger II double-bred Billy The Tough, who was aptly named.

True to his breeding, Grey Badger II was a playful colt, and that playfulness got a little rough when it came time to break and train him. He bucked off his breeder, Walter Merrick, and a few other members of the Merrick family before he was considered broke enough to race. Even then, it was judged prudent to use the very experienced trainer-jockey Kenneth "Skip" Montgomery for his first match race.

Montgomery was familiar with Grey Badger II's family, since he had bred Midnight Jr and had ridden that horse throughout his successful career. He knew from painful personal experience the his-

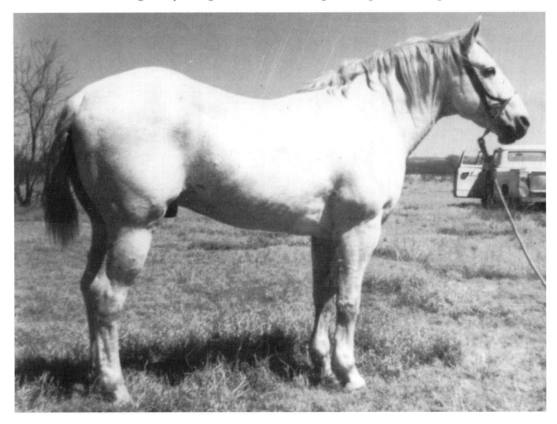

A 1958 picture of Grey Badger II when he was 18 years old and on the Triangle Ranch in Texas.

Photo Courtesy of Walter Merrick

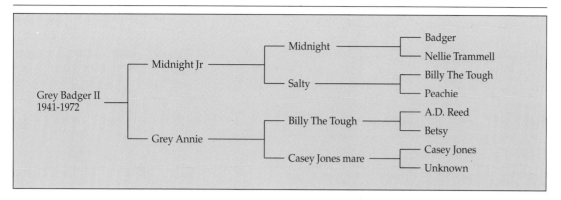

Grey Badger II
1941-1972
├─ Midnight Jr
│   ├─ Midnight
│   │   ├─ Badger
│   │   └─ Nellie Trammell
│   └─ Salty
│   ├─ Billy The Tough
│   └─ Peachie
└─ Grey Annie
    ├─ Billy The Tough
    │   ├─ A.D. Reed
    │   └─ Betsy
    └─ Casey Jones mare
        ├─ Casey Jones
        └─ Unknown

tory of Billy The Tough. Montgomery was one of those who got tired of being unloaded by the powerful horse, and he helped make the decision to geld Billy The Tough after only one breeding season. He was well aware that Grey Badger II had two crosses to Billy The Tough.

The stud books of the AQHA indicate that Grey Badger II was purchased at an early age from Merrick by Chick Crisp, who registered him with the association. Crisp owned a livestock auction at Sayre, Oklahoma.

When the gray colt was old enough, Crisp turned him back over to Merrick for training, and at least part of that training consisted of being used to work cattle on the Merrick ranch. It made a world of difference.

It has been suggested that Crisp would occasionally let his high spirits take over from his better judgment, such as when he later scheduled the first match race for his gray colt.

Grey Badger II's first race was scheduled to be run at Sayre, Okla., in 1943 against an experienced and capable mare called Black Bottom. Crisp is the one who matched this apparently hopeless race for the youngster. Yet despite the playful tendencies and greenness of their young horse, Grey Badger II's camp agreed to stakes of $1,000 a side. It is said that there was an escape clause built into the race that stipulated that if either horse bucked, the bets were called off.

Neither horse bucked. Grey Badger II handled the lap-and-tap start with the aplomb of an old campaigner, outran the mare easily, and began his racing career with a $1,000 deposit.

Another race quickly was matched for a few weeks later at Woodward, Okla., on the Fourth of July. This race, however, was to be from a starting gate. That was the infernal machine that had been the neme-

Halter and Performance Record: Racing Register of Merit.

Progeny Record:

AQHA Champions: 3	Performance Points Earned: 312.5
Foal Crops: 28	Performance Registers of Merit: 15
Foals Registered: 250	Race Money Earned: $19,390
Halter Point-Earners: 18	Race Registers of Merit: 11
Halter Points Earned: 146	Race Starters: 37
Performance Point-Earners: 23	
Leading Race Money-Earner: Sumrall's Bay Badger ($7,494)	

Grey Badger II in his racing days, with Wayne Cox in the irons. Cox was the son of Oscar Cox. **Photo Courtesy of Walter Merrick**

Walter Merrick with Grey Annie, the dam of Grey Badger II.

Photo Courtesy of Walter Merrick

This picture of Grey Badger II was taken in his younger days, when he was still a dark gray. **Photo Courtesy of Walter Merrick**

sis of Grey Badger II's sire, Midnight Jr, in his only race out of a gate. The day before the big race, however, Merrick and Montgomery trailered Grey Badger II to a track with a starting gate. They worked against an older horse who knew his way in and out of a gate. Although it was Badger's first such lesson, the budding star learned quickly and well.

The following day, Badger broke ahead of his competition, a mare called Queenie, and steadily pulled away from her until crossing the finish line. He added another $1,000 to his bank account.

With a few races under his belt, Grey

Badger II calmed down considerably. This change in attitude even helped Merrick, who was still training the 14.2-hand gray for Crisp, match some additional races. His relaxed and easygoing attitude before a race convinced a number of match-horse owners and other bettors that he was too much of a deadhead to be a runner. They were wrong and had to pay for the learning experience.

One such experience happened in September 1944 when a group of horsemen from Pampa, Tex., agreed to match their good sprinter, called Pee Wee, against Grey Badger II. The race was to be held at Cheyenne, Oklahoma. A Joe Moore-bred horse originally from south Texas, Pee Wee had a history of being an exceptional gate horse. Pee Wee's backers were confident that he would prove too tough for Grey Badger II to handle, and they backed up their opinion with cold, hard cash.

Grey Badger's fans, on the other hand, felt just as sure that he would emerge victorious, so the Texans had no trouble in getting their bets covered.

The town of Cheyenne had only one bank and it had opened for business on the morning of the race with $56,000 in cash in its vaults. By noon, Grey Badger's supporters had drawn every cent of their savings out to back their favorite.

Pee Wee broke on top, but Grey Badger II quickly took the lead and won easily. From that day on, the event became known as "the race that broke the bank," at least temporarily, because the bank had to shut down until after the race.

Grey Badger continued to beat both local champions and some horses with

Wilcox Precision Race Camera, Inc.   FORT DUNCAN RACE TRACK — Eagle Pass, Texas

Horse *Grey Badger*   Owner *Oscar Cox Willie Shrum*   Trainer *owners*

Jockey *R. Kennedy*   Distance *220 yds*   Time *.12 4/10*   Date *Oct 27 1945*

widespread reputations. One memorable race took place on the old fairgrounds track at Kingfisher, Oklahoma.

This was a colorful race, as well as an exciting one. Our silver hero was matched against two mares—the bright sorrel Redsailes and a pretty little golden buckskin mare, whose name has been forgotten. Redsailes came up from Texas with a notable reputation behind her. She was a daughter of the famous speed sire, My Texas Dandy, and she had done her share in earning him his celebrity.

At the race in question, Grey Badger II broke just inches in front of Redsailes. They held that position like two pit bulldogs locked onto each other's throats the entire 220 yards and at the finish line they seemed to be separated by the same margin they had established at the break. The buckskin mare finished a few lengths back.

Just like his sire, Grey Badger II also had to travel to find new competitors. He was hauled down to Eagle Pass, on the banks of the Rio Grande, to defeat the good sprinter, Nettie Hill; and then up to the Texas Panhandle to defeat Squaw H at

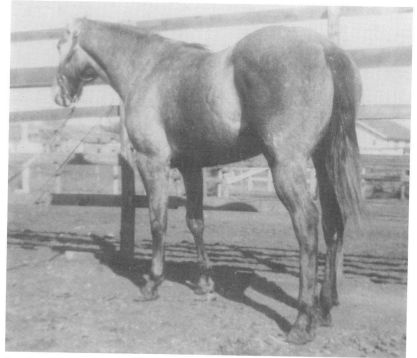

Marching Feet, whose name was later changed to Bonnie Blue, was a full sister to Grey Badger II.

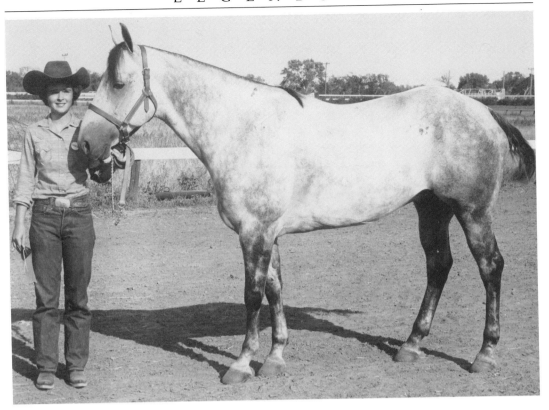

Wyoming Badger was a 1947 gelding by Grey Badger II and out of Flaxie W. He was an AQHA Champion and the 1958 high-point gelding in AQHA barrel racing.

Amarillo. After Montgomery decided it was time to hang up his tack, the honor of riding the silver bullet went to such capable jockeys as Pete Durfey and Rex Drake.

Drake, one of the most successful match jockeys, was smart as well as athletic. In those days, a race from a starting gate began when the starter pulled a long rope that triggered the gates. While riding Grey Badger II, Drake formed the habit of looking over his shoulder and keeping an eye on that rope. He knew that Merrick, who was standing behind the gate, would spank the horse at the right moment and, thus, the break usually went in their favor.

Among other horses beaten by Grey Badger II were Black Out, a Ronald Mason-bred speedster sired by Beggar Boy (TB), and a mare of Earl Craig's called Lucky Lady.

Walter Merrick, who has owned and raced some of the best-known horses in Quarter Horse history, has indicated that Grey Badger II may have been the best match-race horse ever in his stable. Ed Burke, the renowned California racing secretary who helped shape pari-mutuel wagering on Quarter Horses into the industry it is today, once told me that he felt Merrick's success as a trainer was primarily

based on the fact that "he can read a condition book." In other words, he knew when and where his horses had the best chance of winning. Possibly Merrick's experiences in matching Grey Badger II honed his expertise in reading condition books.

The records show that Crisp sold the successful runner to Oscar Cox and Willie Shrum of Lawton, Okla., in October 1945. It was in this ownership that Grey Badger II suffered one of his more notable defeats. It was in a match against the ill-tempered Paint stallion, Painted Joe, handled by the crafty match-race master "Rabbit" Goodrich, and a horse called Gray Eagle. Grey Badger II acted up at the beginning of the race and lost all chance. But he still finished just a half-length behind the winner.

During those years, Grey Badger II was literally "open to the world" and he usually brought home the paycheck. It is said, though, that the person who made the most money from Grey Badger II's races was not an owner. It was a dentist from Sayre who was not only a loyal fan of the gray speedster, but who also was willing to back him with liberal amounts of cash.

Colorado horseman L.R. "Pat" Thompson, who has trained, owned, and bred some of his own well-known horses, worked for Merrick in those days. One of the first horses he got to work with was

Grey Badger II. Thompson, who had the opportunity to see Billy The Tough says, "He (Billy The Tough) was as good-looking a horse as I have ever seen." He felt that Grey Badger II, the double-bred descendant, strongly resembled the old horse.

Thompson also says, "Grey Badger II and his offspring had legs like iron. They were tough enough, as well as fast enough, to hold up well whether they were race horses or roping horses." The gray stallion's legs and speed lasted long enough that, eventually, he was raced against his own foals, such as the very classy Badger's Grey Lady.

A stakes-placed filly, Badger's Grey Lady set five track records at distances from 250 to 440 yards. She won or placed in 26 of her 36 starts, and earned $2,012. She was out of another one of Earl Craig's mares, one called Red Lady.

Grey Badger II's leading money-earner in recognized races during those days of small purses was, however, Sumrall's Bay Badger. He won the New Mexico Breeders' Derby and ran second in the Ruidoso Stallion Stakes.

From 37 starters in races recognized by the AQHA, Grey Badger II got 15 winners. Eleven of them qualified for the racing Register of Merit.

In show arenas, his offspring built an equally good reputation. He sired 15 performance Register of Merit qualifiers, 18 halter point-earners, and 3 AQHA Champions.

Those performers include such horses as Wyoming Badger, an AQHA Champion who was the AQHA high-point barrel racing gelding of 1958; Figa Hancock, an AQHA Champion and 1956 AQHA high-point horse in western riding; and the AQHA Champion Quinine Kid.

Today, Grey Badger II's popularity and influence on the breed probably lie more in the show ring than on the racetrack. This is largely through his son, Grey Badger III. Oscar Cox bred a Thoroughbred mare named Mary Greenock, by Greenock, to Grey Badger II and got Grey Badger III. The younger horse ran well enough to qualify for the racing Register of Merit, but his main claim to fame came as a fine breeding individual.

When bred to Grey Badger III, a Tom L. Burnett Estate mare named Lady Hancock produced Triangle Tookie, who went on to become a leading producer of AQHA

Champions. One of those AQHA Champions was Two Eyed Jack, bred by H.H. Mass of McHenry, Illinois. As a sire, Two Eyed Jack became a legend, himself. He was owned by Howard Pitzer.

Another daughter of Grey Badger III was Sugar Badger, owned by R.H. Fulton and Company of Lubbock, Texas. When bred to Mr San Peppy, Sugar Badger produced Peppy San Badger, an all-time great as a cutting horse who has become another very influential sire in the Quarter Horse breed.

Peppy San Badger, frequently referred to as "Little Peppy," earned $172,710 while winning the 1977 National Cutting Horse Association Futurity, the 1978 NCHA Derby, and many other cutting horse events. He was the second leading money-earner of 1980 in NCHA contests. He earned the NCHA Bronze, Silver, Gold, and Platinum awards, and was named to the NCHA Hall of Fame.

As a sire, Peppy San Badger continues to be a leader. The AQHA files show him to be the sire of three world champions and forty-nine performance Register of Merit qualifiers in open events. He also sired six Register of Merit qualifiers in amateur performance and two in youth events. His offspring have earned points in both open and amateur events.

Going back to the source of all these accomplishments, one finds that Walter Merrick reacquired Grey Badger II from Oscar Cox and Willie Shrum in the late 1940s. Some years before, he had sold Salty Chief (a son of Chief P-5 and Salty, the dam of Midnight Jr) to the Burnett ranches. Salty Chief had proven successful enough that the Burnetts wanted more of the same blood. In November 1949, Grey Badger II was sold to the Tom L. Burnett Estate.

Merrick remembers: "I sold Grey Badger II to Miss Ann Burnett in 1949, and she used him extensively on their ranch mares. He sired some very outstanding ranch horses. The Burnett horses still carry a lot of Grey Badger II breeding.

It is believed that Grey Badger II died on the Triangle Ranch owned by Miss Ann Burnett, in 1972.

By the time of his death, his descendants already had begun to prove themselves worthy heirs of his considerable reputation.

9 SKIPPER W

By Frank Holmes

"If I had to point to one single thing that was most responsible for Skipper W's success as a breeding horse, I would have to say that it was due to the family of mares that I bred him to."

ONE OF THE most universally recognized names in the annals of the American Quarter Horse is that of Skipper W. This sorrel stallion was foaled in the spring of 1945 on the Alamosa, Colo., ranch of H.J. "Hank" Wiescamp.

At the time of Skipper W's birth, Wiescamp had already been raising horses for 20 years. Initially, his program was set up to produce polo ponies and cavalry mounts by crossing middle-of-the-road Thoroughbred stallions with Quarter-type mares—"Steeldust horses" as they were called then.

By the time the AQHA was formed in 1940, however, Wiescamp had made the decision to concentrate on the Old Fred family of horses that had been popularized by Coke Roberds of Hayden, Colorado.

"I admired Coke as one of the outstanding breeders of all time," says Wiescamp in recalling the reasoning behind the change of direction in his breeding program. "In size and type, the Old Freds were not all that different from the horses I had been raising, but they had a lot more color and chrome. They were also a family of horses that you could linebreed success-

Here's the most frequently used photo of Skipper W. George Mueller, who worked for Hank for years, is at the halter.

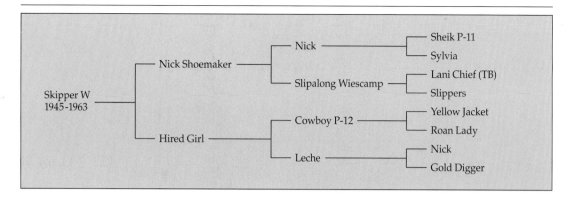

```
                                            ┌─── Sheik P-11
                            ┌─── Nick ───────┤
                            │                └─── Sylvia
            Nick Shoemaker ─┤
          ┌─────────────────┤                ┌─── Lani Chief (TB)
          │                 └─ Slipalong ────┤
 Skipper W│                   Wiescamp       └─── Slippers
 1945-1963┤
          │                                  ┌─── Yellow Jacket
          │                 ┌─ Cowboy P-12 ──┤
          └─── Hired Girl ───┤                └─── Roan Lady
                            │                ┌─── Nick
                            └─── Leche ──────┤
                                             └─── Gold Digger
```

fully in order to set your type and uniformity, and that was what I wanted to do."

To head his new breeding program, Hank purchased a 4-year-old stallion named Nick Shoemaker from Warren Shoemaker of Watrous, N.M., in 1943. This 15-1, 1,300-pound palomino was sired by Nick, who was by Sheik P-11 and out of Sylvia. Sheik was sired by Peter McCue and was out of Pet, by Old Fred.

Nick Shoemaker's dam was subsequently purchased by Wiescamp and registered as Slipalong Wiescamp. She was by Lani Chief, a Thoroughbred, and out of Slippers, who was by Jiggs, by Fred Litz, by Old Fred.

By the time that he purchased Nick Shoemaker, Wiescamp had already accumulated an outstanding set of Old Fred-bred mares. He obtained them primarily from the Philmont and Ghost ranches in New Mexico.

Included in a group of mares who came from the Ghost Ranch in 1939 was a yearling palomino filly sired by Cowboy P-12 and out of Leche, by Nick. Registered as Hired Girl, she was placed in Nick Shoemaker's band of mares in 1944. The following spring she foaled a sorrel colt who was subsequently named Skipper W.

When asked how he came to choose that particular name for the promising youngster, Hank relays the following story:

"I had another good stud colt born around the same time as Skipper. He was a palomino sired by Gold Mount and out of Slipalong Wiescamp. That was also the year that the good movie, *Showboat*, came out and I named the little yellow colt after that picture.

"Anyway, I had Hired Girl up in a corral and, after she foaled, I told a fellow who was working for me to disinfect the navel on the colt. After the man did that, the colt

Halter and Performance Record: None.

Progeny Record:

AQHA Champions: 13	Performance Registers of Merit: 18
Foal Crops: 18	Race Money Earned: $2,424
Foals Registered: 132	Race Registers of Merit: 4
Halter Point-Earners: 58	Race Starters: 10
Halter Points Earned: 1,392	Superior Halter Awards: 7
Performance Point-Earners: 27	Superior Performance Awards: 1
Performance Points Earned: 586.5	
Leading Race Money-Earner: Skip Hi ($1,014)	

This is a rarely seen photo showing a three-quarter front view of Skipper W.
Photo by Darol Dickinson, Courtesy of Bill Gay

An unknown photographer took this picture of Skipper W.

"'I've got a showboat, and every boat needs a skipper, so that's what I'm going to name him—Skipper.' I added the W for Wiescamp."

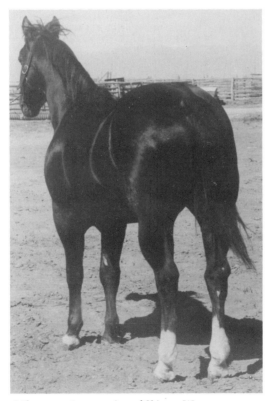

A three-quarter rear view of Skipper W.

got up and turned around and kicked him, 'cause it smarted.

"I said to that fellow, 'Look at that, he already knows he's the boss! I've got a showboat, and every boat needs a skipper, so that's what I'm going to name him—Skipper.' I added the W for Wiescamp."

For the first year or so of Skipper W's life, it seemed doubtful that he was even going to remain on the Wiescamp ranch. Hank remembers:

"I priced Hired Girl for $150 before Skipper was born and didn't get any takers. Then, when he was a weaner, I priced him to Gus Roberson from Gunnison for $500. He asked, 'Ain't that an awful lot for a gelding? I want to make him a rope horse, and I'd have to geld him.'

"'Well, don't buy him then,' I said. 'It doesn't make any difference to me.'

"You can see what would have happened to him if Gus would have bought him—he would have just made a ranch gelding out of him.

"Then, when Skipper was a yearling, Herman Snyder from Pendleton, Ore., stopped in here one day. He was looking for a stud prospect, and wanted to know what I'd take for him. I said $1,500, and he thought that was a little steep. So he went down to Warren Shoemaker's and bought Music Mount, and Skipper stayed right here."

When Skipper W was a coming 2-year-old, Hank turned him over to George Mueller, a top all-around hand, to break. In the December 1982 issue of *The Quarter Horse Journal*, in an article about Skipper W authored by Richard Chamberlain, Mueller made the following observations about his early experiences with the young stallion:

"I drove Skipper about 3 or 4 days; drove him in a little corral, and then just got on him. And the first time I got on him, I just turned this colt around, clucked to him, and just kind of spanked him with the rein a little bit. And the colt took to it and just walked off. That's the way he was. The colt never hopped up, he never done nothing.

"Now, when I first started him, he was just a little ol' heavy-muscled colt, kind of awkward and one thing and another. But the colt learned to handle himself real good, and the longer I went with him, the better he got. I never tried to put a fine rein or anything on this colt. I roped a lot of calves on him, and he was a fine calf horse. The pony really liked that. He could run and he could sure stop. And he just wanted to do things."

By the time he was a 3-year-old, Skipper W had matured to around 15 hands and weighed a very evenly distributed 1,250 pounds. Mueller wanted to go on with the colt's roping training, but Wiescamp had decided to show him at halter.

Skipper W was shown only three times—all as a 4-year-old—and he stood grand at each show: the National Western Stock Show in Denver, the Colorado State Fair in Pueblo, and the New Mexico State Fair in Albuquerque. However, his AQHA record does not reflect these wins; this is not an unusual situation for horses shown in the 1940s when record-keeping was not as accurate as it became a few years later when the AQHA began keeping better records of show horses.

"I'm glad now that we didn't show him more," says Wiescamp, "because he would have been before the public so much that he probably would have been sold."

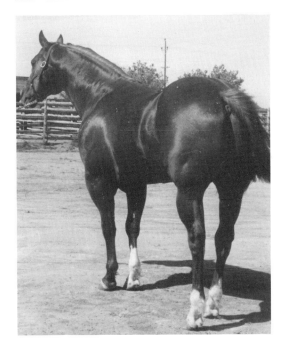

Here are two photographs of Skipper's King, whom many horsemen considered to be the greatest son of Skipper W. Foaled in 1954, Skipper's King was out of Santa Maria, by Plaudit. He became a tremendous broodmare sire, and at one time Hank had 70 of this horse's daughters in his broodmare band. Among his outstanding sons was Skip A Barb, an AQHA Champion stallion. In the show ring, Skipper's King earned 18 halter points and 4 performance points.

Photos by Darol Dickinson, Courtesy of Bill Gay

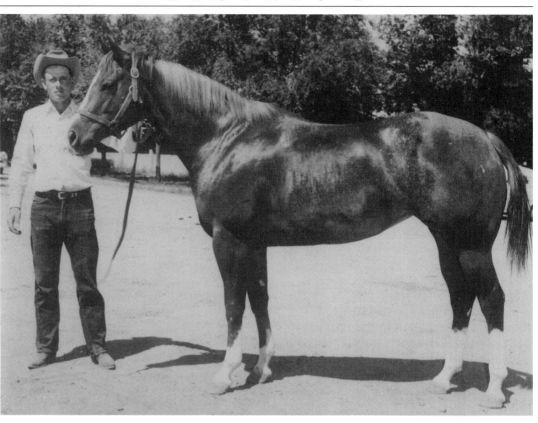

Skipperette, foaled in 1950, was one of Hank's all-time favorite mares, and was a full sister to Skipper's King. Although she never became an AQHA Champion, she earned 39 halter points and was named Grand Champion Mare at the 1955 National Western Stock Show and 1954 Colorado State Fair, where this photo was taken. The handler is Larry Walker.

Photo by Clarence Coil / Stewart's Photo

Skip's Princess, foaled in 1958, was by Skipper's King and out of H.J. Skippit, by Skipper W. An AQHA Champion, Skip's Princess also earned Superiors in halter, with 71 points, and reining. She had a total of 64 performance points. That's Leroy Webb holding her.

In early 1948, an accident had occurred on the Wiescamp ranch that effectively put a halt to any thoughts of a further show career for Skipper W. Nick Shoemaker, then barely 9 years old, was playing in his corral when he slipped on a patch of ice, hit his head on the fence, and broke his neck. In need of a replacement, Wiescamp gave the nod to Skipper W, and the die was cast for what was to become one of the most successful stud careers in the history of the breed.

Skipper W had been bred to a few mares in 1948, as a 3-year-old. Because of his plans to show him, Hank had instructed Mueller to hand-breed the youngster. Overly aggressive and under-experienced, Skipper would charge each snubbed-up mare that he was asked to breed, knock her over, and nearly scare her to death. As a result, he settled only a few mares that year.

After Skipper's short but successful show career, Mueller talked Wiescamp into pasture breeding Skipper. Again from Chamberlain's *QHJ* article, he tells of this incident:

"It was a terrible wreck. Those mares liked to have killed him that first night, kicking and biting and all. He looked like

Skip's Reward as a 2-year-old when he stood grand champion stallion at the 1960 Pikes Peak Quarter Horse show in Colorado Springs. He was shown by Leroy Webb, and earned 11 halter points in the show ring. Skip's Reward was by Skipper W and out of Show Lady, by Show Boat. This palomino sired a number of outstanding broodmares.

Photo by Clarence Coil / Stewart's Photo

a burro standing there the next morning with those ears lopped. I know it upset Hank, 'cause he didn't want to turn that colt loose to begin with. I thought he'd make me put the horse back in the barn and hand-breed him, but he didn't. So we left Skipper out a week, and then we caught him, put him back in the paddock, and let him rest a little bit—he was drawn up pretty bad. And the next time we turned him out, he was a different horse. He went way around those mares, and that was the last of it."

In his 18 years at stud, Skipper W never stood to outside mares. Wiescamp's philosophy regarding this was fairly simple and held true for not only Skipper W, but every other home-bred stallion that he used. "I set my sights on raising a particular type of horse years ago," he explains, "and I've never strayed from that type. By the time I put Skipper W at the head of my breeding program, I had a select band of Old Fred-bred mares to put under him—most of them Plaudit daughters or granddaughters. With this uniform set of mares, I felt that I could really work toward raising the type of horse that was my ideal.

"If I had to point to one single thing that was most responsible for Skipper W's success as a breeding horse, I would have to

Skip 3 Bar was out of Skipperette, and was sired by Bar Mount, a son of De Witt Bar, by Three Bars (TB). De Witt Bar was one of the first outcross stallions used by Hank. Foaled in 1960, Skip 3 Bar was an AQHA Champion, and earned a Superior in halter with 62 points. He had 12 performance points. **Photo by Darol Dickinson**

Skip's Barred, by Skip's Reward and out of Skipity Bar, by De Witt Bar. This sorrel mare, foaled in 1965, stood grand champion mare 33 consecutive times. She died at an early age.

Hank Wiescamp with Spanish Nick, an AQHA Champion foaled in 1948 by Nick Shoemaker and out of Mexicali Rose. A paternal half-brother to Skipper W, Spanish Nick sired several AQHA Champions. This photo was probably taken in the early 1950s.
Photo by Clarence Coil / Stewart's Photo

say that it was due to the family of mares that I bred him to. It was a family that he crossed well with, so I kept him there. That's the advantage of not standing a stud to the public—you can select his mares and then hold him to those mares. I've always said that a good mare is 60 to 70 percent responsible for what her foals are, and that a bad mare is 100 percent.''

Skipper W sired only 132 registered foals during his lifetime, averaging less than 8 foals a year. This light breeding use did not reflect any lack of confidence on Wiescamp's part in Skipper's siring ability; he was simply committed to a line-breeding program that put the emphasis on each succeeding generation.

Of the small number of registered foals that Skipper W did sire, 73 were shown and they accumulated 1,392 points at halter and 586.5 points in performance. These horses included seven who earned a Superior in halter; eighteen Register of Merit earners, one Superior performance horse, and thirteen AQHA Champions.

Among his more durable show performers were Skipper Jr., Skipity Skip, Silver Skip, General Skip, Skipper's Prince, Sailalong, Skipper's Smoke, Skip On, Skipette, Skip's Ink, Skip Sir Bar, Skip's Dilly, and Skip Beau. They were all AQHA Champions and, with the exception of Skip Sir Bar who was out of a Thoroughbred daughter of Three Bars (TB), all were out of Old Fred-bred mares.

Skipper's Image with 188 points, Skipette with 113 points, and Skipper's Smoke with 100 points were his top point-earning halter get. In addition, Skipper's Prince, Skip's Glory, Skip's Ink, and Skip Sir Bar were all Superior halter horses. Again, with the exception of Skip Sir Bar, all were out of Old Fred-bred mares.

Silver Skip, one of Skipper W's first sons to be named an AQHA Champion, was also one of his most versatile performers. Owned by Johnson and Kyle of Santa Rosa, N.M., and shown by Jack Kyle, Silver Skip earned his 41 performance points in roping, reining, cutting, working cow horse, and western riding.

Skip's Dilly, the last of the Skipper W daughters to earn an AQHA Championship, was the AQHA Honor Roll Western Pleasure Mare in 1966 and earned her Superior in that event.

Like their sire, the Skipper W's were

Skipadoo, another great daughter of Skipper W. Foaled in 1949, she was out of Miss Helen, by Plaudit, who also produced Skipper's Lad and Gold Mount. Skipadoo earned 44 halter points.

athletic and made good roping and reining horses. Skipette, the first of his daughters to earn her AQHA Championship, was the AQHA Honor Roll Calf-Roping Mare in 1964 and was just a few points shy of her Superior when she was retired and put in the Wiescamp broodmare band. Skip Sir Bar was the AQHA Honor Roll Steer-Roping Stallion in 1966 and ranked 5th among the high-point calf-roping horses that same year.

Skipper's Smoke with 47 points, Sailalong with 42 points, and Skip On with 31 points were three of Skipper W's top performers in reining, and all three could have easily garnered their Superiors in the event had they not been retired to stud.

The real value of the Skipper W horses, however, was not as show horses but as breeding horses.

In Hank's opinion, one of Skipper W's greatest merits as a breeding horse was that he was the sire of both sons and daughters who went on to become great sires and dams. "Usually a stud becomes better known as a sire of sires or a sire of broodmares," relates the venerable horseman. "Skipper W turned out to be a sire of both."

Skipper's King would have to head any list of top breeding sons of Skipper W. A 1954 sorrel out of the great producing Plaudit daughter, Santa Maria, this heavily-muscled stallion who, like his sire, stood grand at the Denver National Western, lived his entire life on the Wiescamp

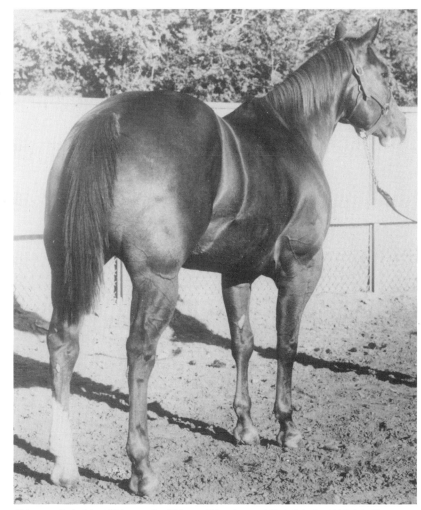

Skipette, foaled in 1959, was by Skipper W and out of Sis Nick, by Nick W. She was an AQHA Champion and earned a Superior in halter with 113 points. She also had 61 performance points, and was the 1964 AQHA High-Point Calf-Roping Mare.
Photo by Darol Dickinson

71

Skipper's Smoke, one of the best-looking sons of Skipper W. Foaled in 1956, he was out of Silver Leche, by Holey Smoke. This picture was taken at Denver's 1960 National Western Stock Show when he stood grand champion stallion. He was an AQHA Champion with 100 halter points and 64.5 performance points. Lawrence Wiescamp, Hank's brother, is at the halter.

This is Ted Waldhauser, of Clovis, N.M., on Saila-long, one of the breediest-looking sons of Skipper W. Foaled in 1956, he was out of Brushalong, by Brush Mount. Hank sold the horse to Ted, then later bought him back. Sailalong became an AQHA Champion, and is listed as the sire of Silent Sheila, one of Hank's best show mares.

Skip On, another great-looking son of Skipper W, died at an early age. Foaled in 1957, he was out of Scoot On, by Scooter W, and earned an AQHA Championship.

ranch. At one time, Wiescamp had over 70 daughters of Skipper's King in his brood-mare band.

Another Skipper W son who figured prominently in the Wiescamp program over the years was the beautifully-headed Skip's Reward, a 1958 palomino who was out of Show Lady; she was a double-bred Plaudit mare by Showboat, and was out of Santa Maria.

Other Skipper W sons who went on to become noted sires were Sailalong, Skip On, Skip Fare, Skipper's Lad, Spot Cash, Great Chance, Skipper Jr., Skipity Skip, Silver Skip, Beau Chance, Skipador, Stage-hand, Sir Skip, Sirlette, Skip Ahead, Skip On Bar, Skip School, and Skipper's Image.

Wiescamp kept a tight hold on the 68 daughters of Skipper W, and very few

Skippa String was a AAA stakes winner for Hank. Foaled in 1958, Skippa String was by Rukin String, by Piggin String (TB), and out of H.J. Skippa, by Skipper W. Shown in this 1962 photo, on the left, are Hank and his daughter, Charlotte, trainer J.J. Phillips, and jockey Bobby Harmon. Skippa String went on to establish an important male line within Hank's linebred family of horses. One of Skippa String's sons was the AQHA Champion String Of Gold, a gelding who earned 601 halter points.

of them ever left Alamosa while in their prime.

Skipperette, a full sister to Skipper's King, produced Skip 3 Bar, Skip Barette, Skip's Cadet, and Skip's Chant, four stallions who became noteworthy Wiescamp herd sires. H.J. Skippa, who was out of Question Mount by Gold Mount, was the dam of Skippa String, a AAA speedster who became the head of an exceptional male line within the family.

Other great producing daughters include H.J. Skippit, Skip Too, Skip Queen, Sea Skipper, Skipadoo, Skiparado, Skip's Glory, and Skipette.

Skipper W died in 1963, at the age of 18, of an apparent heart attack. At the time of his death, Hank had retained 7 of his sons and 57 of his daughters for use in his breeding program.

The Skipper W line of horses is still being raised today, not only by Wiescamp, but also by others breeders throughout the United States and in Europe.

Skipper W was never heavily shown or promoted, and he lived out his life in the relative seclusion of southern Colorado. He never stood to outside mares and was never put into mass production as a sire. Despite all of this, his name continues to be a household word within the Quarter Horse world.

A photograph of Silver Skip, an AQHA Champion, with Jack Kyle, taken about 1958 when Silver Skip stood grand champion stallion at Sonoita, Arizona. Foaled in 1954, Silver Skip was by Skipper W and out of H.J. Silver Finn, by Brush Mount. Hank sold this stallion as a 3-year-old to Jack Kyle, who was living in New Mexico at that time. Silver Skip sired five AQHA Champions: Jack Kyle, Leyba Skip, Mary Ann Murphy, Miss Blue Doll, and Ski Line Skip.

10 OKLAHOMA STAR

By Frank Holmes

He was the undisputed premier sire of rope horses.

FOR ALMOST as long as there have been organized rodeos, there have been Oklahoma Star-bred horses at, or near, the top in every event that required a contestant to be well-mounted.

In fact, someone once said that there were only two real sires of rope horses in Oklahoma, and that Oklahoma Star was both of them.

While this might have been overstating the case a bit, it does illustrate the high esteem of Oklahoma Star and his descendants held by rodeo contestants and ranch cowboys.

Oklahoma Star was foaled in 1915 near Slapout, Okla., on the farm of his breeder, Tommy Moore. Slapout lies in the "No Man's Land" of the Oklahoma panhandle, and Moore had moved there from Mulhall, Okla., a small community north of

Guthrie, in 1905 or 1907. After renting a place for a year, he homesteaded a farm of his own, where he raised the finest Percheron horses and the fastest race horses in the county.

One of Moore's most prized runners was a mare by the name of Cutthroat. She received her unusual name as the result of running into a barbed wire fence as a foal and severely injuring her trachea.

Cutthroat's breeding has always been, and will always be, a controversial subject. To begin with, not even her name remained constant throughout her life. In addition to Cutthroat, she was known at various times as May Mattison and as Bee Vee.

Early accounts give her sire as Bonnie Joe (TB), and her dam as Big Em, by Rocky Mountain Tom. She has also been listed as being sired by Glover and out of Miss Okla-

One of the very few pictures in existence of Oklahoma Star. He was obviously an aged horse when it was taken.

Photo Courtesy of the American Quarter Horse Heritage Center & Museum, Amarillo, Texas

This picture of Oklahoma Star was taken after he was purchased by Ronald Mason at the age of 17.

Photo Courtesy of the American Quarter Horse Heritage Center & Museum, Amarillo, Texas

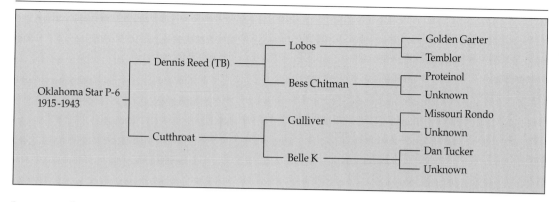

```
                                        ┌── Golden Garter
                           ┌── Lobos ───┤
                           │            └── Temblor
        ┌── Dennis Reed (TB) ──┤
        │                  │            ┌── Proteinol
        │                  └── Bess Chitman ──┤
Oklahoma Star P-6 ──┤                         └── Unknown
1915-1943           │
        │                               ┌── Missouri Rondo
        │                  ┌── Gulliver ──┤
        │                  │            └── Unknown
        └── Cutthroat ─────┤
                           │            ┌── Dan Tucker
                           └── Belle K ──┤
                                        └── Unknown
```

homa, and was once even represented as a daughter of Peter McCue.

The most current information available, however, which is recognized by the AQHA, identifies her sire as Gulliver, a son of Missouri Rondo, and her dam as Belle K, a daughter of Dan Tucker.

Franklin Reynolds, a noted Quarter Horse historian who wrote regular features for *The Quarter Horse Journal* during the 1950s, drove thousands of miles and interviewed scores of friends and neighbors of Tommy Moore (who, by that time, was deceased) in an attempt to pinpoint Cutthroat's true identity. By his own admission, he was no closer to the truth at the end of his search than he had been at the start.

As discovered by Reynolds, it was Tommy Moore, himself, who was at the heart of the confusion. It was he who, when queried, gave his race mare the various names and pedigrees by which she was known at various times during her life.

There is some evidence that Oklahoma Star was registered with The Jockey Club under a different name. If so, this would be in line with other Quarter Horses of that era who were registered as Thoroughbreds (with erroneous parentage) so as to have more racing opportunities.

Why the contradictory information? In an article on Oklahoma Star in the June 1957 issue of *The Quarter Horse Journal*, Reynolds probably comes as close to the truth as anyone possibly can.

"Horsemen in those days didn't so much boast of the races their horses had won, as they expressed a doubt their entry could outrun a certain other horse," he wrote. "But at the same time they would voice a willingness to try for a little money on the side. They weren't so likely to brag

Halter and Performance Record: None.

Progeny Record:

Foal Crops: 14	Race Money Earned: $185
Foals Registered: 119	Race Starters: 3
Leading Race Money-Earner: Sizzler ($185)	

of the royal blood of their horses, as they were to explain that: 'This colt's daddy was an Indian pony, and his mammy was a mare I got from a trader. I've been using this colt in the wagon, and my wife's been using him as a buggy horse. If there's any race blood in him, I don't know it, and I'm inclined to doubt it, but if you've got to have a race, we'll try him and see.'

"It wasn't always easy to match a horse known to have been high-born," continued Reynolds. "If a horse was well-bred, that fact, in the Oklahoma of the day, was more likely to remain a secret than to be revealed. It would even be heatedly denied at times.

"If he (Moore) concealed a pedigree truth, or misinformed on a pedigree fact, his intentions were not fundamentally dishonest," concluded Reynolds. "He was just simply being an Oklahoma horseman of the day and time."

Whatever her real name and pedigree was, one thing was certain—Cutthroat was a good-looking mare who had more than a little speed.

Arthur Ogden, an associate of Moore's during the years he lived in the Oklahoma

"Cutthroat never lost but one race."

panhandle, knew Cutthroat well and shared some of his recollections of her with Reynolds for Reynolds' *Journal* feature. Reynolds quoted Ogden as follows:

"If you have ever seen (Maddon's) Bright Eyes, she was near like Cutthroat. However, Bright Eyes was a bigger mare, and more leggy. Cutthroat was more muscled. Cutthroat never lost but one race. She was matched with a gray mare at Shattuck for a quarter. They scored a long time that afternoon and couldn't get off. Then we postponed it until the next morning, and that night a bunch of fellows who had bet on the gray mare went out and dug up about 20 feet of Cutthroat's path and filled it with sand. Tommy didn't ride down the track the next morning to see how it was, and when she hit that sand it almost threw her down, and certainly off stride, and we lost."

Because of her windpipe injury, Cutthroat was reported to be good for no more than an eighth of a mile. According to Ogden, however, this was simply not the case.

"Cutthroat could run the full quarter any time," he recalled. "Of course she would be breathing hard at the end, and you could hear her because of her injury, but she could run it. One time, three watches caught her in :22 when she was carrying 165 pounds."

Name and pedigree deceptions notwithstanding, the day arrived when Moore could no longer find any competition for Cutthroat.

He decided to breed her in 1914 when she was 6 or 7 years old and his choice of a stallion was a black Thoroughbred by the name of Dennis Reed, who was owned by Ned Snyder of Englewood, Kansas. Dennis Reed was a distance runner, but was credited with being able to run a quarter in :23 flat.

In the spring of 1915, Cutthroat foaled a dark bay colt with a small star on his forehead. Moore promptly named him Oklahoma Star.

Arthur Ogden, who had helped Moore break Cutthroat, also helped with Oklahoma Star.

Reynolds quotes Ogden as saying: "I can recall very clearly when he broke Oklahoma Star, then a 2-year-old. Tommy only rode him about half a mile before he called for a race between Oklahoma Star and Cutthroat. My brother was riding Cutthroat. Oklahoma Star outran her, but she had been nursing foals for 3 years and didn't have the strength to give him a tough race."

Moore felt that he had a runner, however, and set out to prove it.

In February 1918, he took Oklahoma Star to Covington, Okla., and matched him against a great runner named Slip Shoulder for an eighth of a mile. Star won with ease, but the locals were not convinced.

A second race was set up, this time against a fleet mare named Kate Bernard. The distance was the same and so was the result. In his report of the race which appeared years later in the March 1947 issue of *The Quarter Horse*, the official publication of the National Quarter Horse Breeders Association, author R.B. Potter related that, as a result of the second race, "all the cowmen of that section concluded immediately (that) Oklahoma Star was a better risk than big steers on cake and grass."

A year or so later, Moore moved back to Mulhall, taking seven or eight horses with him, including Cutthroat, Oklahoma Star, and three full brothers and sisters to Star.

Moore continued to match-race Oklahoma Star with considerable success. He met and defeated the fastest horses of his day, including Duck Hunter, Big Jaw, Henry Star, Ned S, Jimmy Hicks, Nellie S, and Bear Cat.

As quoted by Franklin Reynolds in the *QHJ* feature, Harvey Nealis, a well-known jockey at the time in the Guthrie area, recalled the race against Bear Cat.

"I rode Tommy's horses, because Tommy had gotten too heavy and was too old to do his own riding by that time. We didn't have any automobiles or trailers in that country then, and if we had to go any distance, we carried the horses in box cars. One day at Mulhall some fellows unloaded a horse they called Bear Cat, and they hunted Tommy up because they knew they could get a race out of him.

"I don't remember what horse we ran at them, but we got beat like Tommy expected. That was the way Tommy wanted

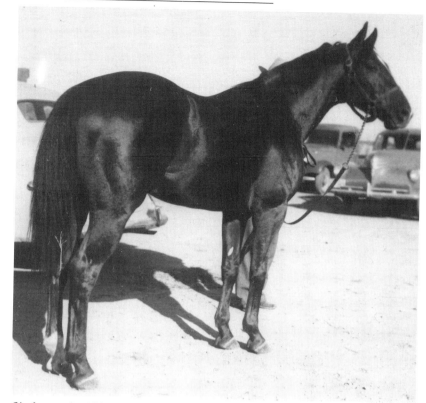

Sizzler was by Oklahoma Star and out of Lad's Run (TB). Foaled in 1937, Sizzler was a Register of Merit race horse and a successful sire. He stood for years at Brigham Young University in Provo, Utah. **Photo Courtesy of Phil Livingston**

Star Deck was one of Oklahoma Star's better-known sons. Foaled in 1940, he was out of Jane Hunt, a Coke Blake-bred mare. Star Deck sired six AQHA Champions, including NR Paul A (the NR was later dropped from his name). Raymond Guthrie, Prineville, Ore., owned Star Deck when this picture was taken.

Little Star, an own son of Oklahoma Star foaled in 1939, was owned by George Wingfield Jr. and Wilbur D. May, who stood him at the Spanish Springs Ranch, Reno, Nevada. This picture was taken in 1945; the gentleman on the left is not identified.

Photo by Tru Vencill

it. Then we matched Oklahoma Star at Bear Cat for a quarter up at Covington. We had found out what Bear Cat could do, and Tommy put up a pretty sizable bunch of money.

"Well sir, I was riding Oklahoma Star and we outran Bear Cat as far as from here to across that street out there. Tommy got well on that race and we weren't bothered with Bear Cat any more."

As was the case with his dam, Oklahoma Star soon ran out of horses to run against. Model T Fords were beginning to invade the countryside by that time, however, and Moore began racing his stallion against them. He would match Oklahoma Star for any distance between 20 yards and a quarter of a mile, doing his own riding, oftentimes in a stock saddle.

Then in 1925 or 1926, Moore suffered a severe injury while using a disc harrow that made it necessary for him to sell all of his horses, including Star.

Bill O'Meara, a local farmer, gave Moore $150 for Oklahoma Star and continued to stand him to outside mares for the same fee that Moore had charged—$10.

In 1932, Oklahoma Star changed hands once more and this time it was into the ownership of Ronald Mason, the man who would play a prominent part in Star's development as one of the foundation sires of the Quarter Horse breed.

Mason owned and operated the Cross J Ranch near Nowata, Oklahoma. At the time of Oklahoma Star's arrival, Mason had an outstanding set of mares to put him on. Included among them were daughters of Beggar Boy and Quarter Deck, both Thoroughbreds. Beggar Boy was a full brother to the famous Kentucky Derby winner, Black Gold, and Quarter Deck was an own son of the legendary Man o' War.

The remainder of the Mason broodmare band was made up of top Quarter-type mares of Coke Blake and John Dawson breeding. When put on mares of this quality, Oklahoma Star began to excel as a breeding horse.

Bob Denhardt, the dean of Quarter Horse

historians, paid a visit to Ronald Mason in the late 1930s to look over his stock. In an article on Oklahoma Star published in the December 1963 issue of *The Quarter Horse Journal*, Denhardt shared some of his impressions of the then aged stallion.

"It has been written that Oklahoma Star was 14.2 and weighed 1,200 pounds. I first saw him in the late '30s and he had a little age on him, but I doubt that he had been 14.2 since he was a long yearling. I would judge his normal weight to be under 1,100 pounds.

"Oklahoma Star was a beautiful mahogany bay with just two white areas on his body—a small star just above the eye line and a left hind foot white through the ankle," he wrote. "I thought he showed more Thoroughbred blood than his breeding warranted. This was especially noticeable in his ears, head, withers, and long bottom line.

"He showed his Quarter blood in his short pasterns and in the sloping rump and heavily muscled rear legs. His hind legs were as powerful as any I can remember on a horse. This no doubt explains why he was able to leave the starting chute so fast."

During the time Mason owned him, Oklahoma Star sired such famous sons as Congress Star, Starway, Osage Star, Nowata Star, Star Deck, Oklahoma Star Jr., Double Star, Hillside's Little Man, and Sizzler.

Congress Star, Starway, and Osage Star were all full brothers out of Quarter Lady, by Quarter Deck (TB). Congress Star and Starway were both multiple Register of Merit sires, and Osage Star was the sire of Snip Mac, an AQHA Champion. Osage Star was also the sire of Osage Lady Star, the dam of Palleo Pete, the 1954 Champion Quarter Running Stallion.

Nowata Star sired nine ROM race horses, sixteen ROM performance horses, and one AQHA Champion. He was also the sire of Star Duster who, in turn, sired four AQHA Champions and was a leading maternal sire of AQHA Champions. (Star Duster is featured in *Legends 1*.)

Star Deck sired six AQHA Champions, including Paul A., who, in turn, sired eleven AQHA Champions.

Oklahoma Star Jr. sired five AQHA Champions and became a leading mater-

Paul A, a grandson of Oklahoma Star, was out of Little Dixie Beach, by Tommy Clegg. Paul A was a leading sire of AQHA Champions, with 10 to his credit.
Photo by Stryker, Courtesy of Phil Livingston

nal sire of AQHA Champions. He also sired Pat Star Jr., who, in turn, sired 20 AQHA Champions and became a leading maternal sire of AQHA Champions.

Double Star and Hillside's Little Man were both multiple ROM sires.

Sizzler, a top son of Oklahoma Star, was an accident. In 1936, Mason took one of his favorite mares, an imported English Thoroughbred named Lad's Run, to the court of the Thoroughbred stallion Sheridan. The following year she produced a colt who was registered as a Thoroughbred. As a 2-year-old, he was put in race training,

Pony McCue, by Nowata Star, was a good performance horse in the Rocky Mountain region in the 1950s. He was owned and shown by Bill Sausser of Colorado Springs.

Photo by James Cathey

Nowata Star was an excellent son of Oklahoma Star. Foaled in 1940, he was out of Bay Lucy, by Chief P-5, and was bred by Ronald Mason of Nowata, Oklahoma. Nowata Star was a good broodmare sire, and his get included April Startip, an AQHA Champion, and Star Duster (featured in Legends 1*).*

with distance running as the goal.

Sizzler failed to live up to the potential that Mason thought his breeding warranted. Moreover, he did not look like a Thoroughbred; he looked like a Quarter Horse.

After a discussion with one of the men who had been working for him at the time Lad's Run was bred, Mason found out that Oklahoma Star had gotten in with Lad's Run upon her return from being bred to Sheridan, and had serviced her.

Now convinced that Sizzler was a son of Oklahoma Star, Mason cancelled the colt's Thoroughbred papers and registered him with the fledgling AQHA. He was, according to Mason, one of the best-looking horses he had ever raised.

While under Ronald Mason's care and guidance, Oklahoma Star proved to also be an outstanding sire of broodmares. Star's Lou, for example, produced Miss Meyers (sired by Leo), the 1953 Champion Quarter Running Horse.

Baldy Girl was the dam of Beggar Girl, one of Walter Merrick's first great race mares, and she, in turn, produced Leo Bingo, a AAA AQHA Champion.

V's Peaches produced Little Peach, a leading dam of ROM race horses with 11 to her credit. They included Tinky Poo, a AA AQHA Champion, who sired Hobby Horse, AAA and an AQHA Champion, who, in turn, sired Expensive Hobby, the great reining and working cow horse.

Star Bird C. produced War Bird, the dam of four AQHA Champions: War Leo, Ace Of Limestone, Limestone Bird, and Rondo Leo. Rondo Leo, in turn, sired Mr. Gun Smoke.

Other ROM-producing daughters of Oklahoma Star included Betty K, Diamond Jessie, Dona Hunt, Quarter Lady Star, G Fern Red Ribbon, Karen M, Star Babe, and Star Baby B.

And then there were the rope horses.

From the mid-1930s through the mid-1950s, Oklahoma Star was the undisputed premier sire of rope horses. During that time, such well-known rodeo performers as Bob Crosby, Buddy May, Ike Rude, Hugh Bennett, Ben Johnson, the Goodspeed brothers, Foreman Faulkner, John Scott, Jim Snively, Everett Bowman, Chalk Dyer, the Burk brothers, Andy Juaregui, and Floyd Gale all roped off Oklahoma Star get or grand-get.

By the time the AQHA was formed in 1940, Oklahoma Star was one of the most influential Quarter sires in existence. He was recognized as such by the organization and, at the age of 27, was assigned the registry number, P-6, distinguishing him as one of the breed's foundation sires.

Oklahoma Star died on Mason's ranch on February 14, 1943, at the age of 28, and was buried on a hill overlooking the Cross J Ranch.

Although a part of Oklahoma Star's heritage will probably forever be unknown, his role in the development of the Quarter Horse breed is secure. He was one of its brightest stars.

Starway was a full brother to Osage Star, and was foaled in 1939. He sired a number of good colts, including six ROM race horses, and five ROM performance horses.

Osage Star, by Oklahoma Star and out of Quarter Lady, by Quarter Deck (TB), by Man o' War, was foaled in 1938, and was well known as a broodmare sire. He was the maternal grandsire of the great race horse, Palleo Pete AAA.

11 OKLAHOMA STAR JR.

By Frank Holmes

He was a worthy namesake of his famous sire by virtue of the family of horses that he, himself, founded.

OKLAHOMA STAR JR. was not one of the best looking or most athletic horses sired by Oklahoma Star P-6. By the time it was all said and done, however, he did prove that he was a worthy namesake of his famous sire by virtue of the family of horses that he, himself, founded.

Oklahoma Star Jr. was bred by pioneer Quarter Horse breeder John Dawson of Talala, Okla., located in the northeastern corner of the state. At the time of Star Jr.'s foaling in 1934, Dawson had been breeding good working horses for almost 50 years. He began with the purchase of "a pretty good 2-year-old mare" in

1887 when he was 16 years old.

By the time the AQHA was formed in 1940, John Dawson was considered one of the premier Quarter Horse breeders in the land. His accomplishments were recognized by the AQHA when a horse bred by him, Old Red Buck, was given the registration number of 9 as one of the breed's foundation sires.

Oklahoma Star Jr. was out of one of Dawson's most famed producers, Babe Dawson, who was a linebred Little Earl, being by Little Earl Jr. and out of Queen, by Little Earl. Little Earl was a Missouri Mike stallion from the Cold Deck family of horses that had been popularized by S. Coke Blake of Pryor, Oklahoma.

In addition to Oklahoma Star Jr., Babe Dawson was also the dam of Baldy, one of the greatest calf-roping horses of all time. Baldy, who was known for his tremendous stop, carried Clyde Burk to the R.C.A. calf-roping championship in 1944 and did the same for Troy Fort in 1947 and 1949.

At one time or another, Baldy was ridden by many of the top-notch calf ropers of that era, including Ike Rude, Irby Mundy, Everett Shaw, Jess Goodspeed, Dick Truitt, Jiggs Burk, Dee Burk, Jack Skipworth, Cotton Lee, Roy Lewis, and Earl Moore.

Getting back to Oklahoma Star Jr., John Dawson liked the chestnut colt well enough to leave him as a stallion and to use him as his principal breeding stallion for 6 years. While Star Jr. was broke to ride at some point during his early life, he was never extensively trained due to a hock injury he had received as a youngster.

By 1942 or 1943, Dawson had a pasture full of Oklahoma Star Jr. mares and a new

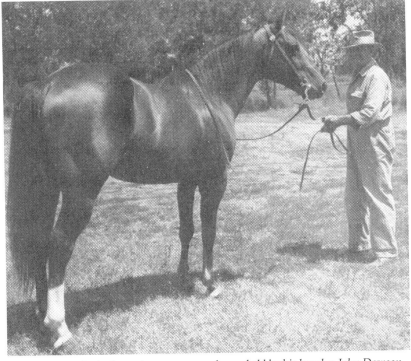

Oklahoma Star Jr. is shown here as a young horse, held by his breeder, John Dawson. Star Jr.'s smooth lines and good flat bone are evident in this photo.

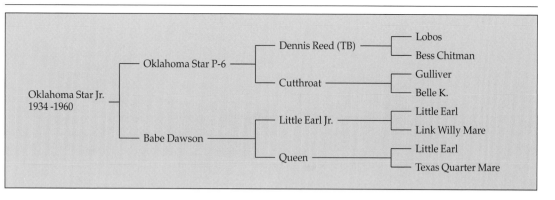

Oklahoma Star Jr.
1934 -1960

- Oklahoma Star P-6
  - Dennis Reed (TB)
    - Lobos
    - Bess Chitman
  - Cutthroat
    - Gulliver
    - Belle K.
- Babe Dawson
  - Little Earl Jr.
    - Little Earl
    - Link Willy Mare
  - Queen
    - Little Earl
    - Texas Quarter Mare

stallion, Wimpy II, to breed them to. As a result, Star Jr. was sold to Ronald Mason of Nowata, Okla., the last owner of Oklahoma Star.

Mason, in turn, sold Star Jr. to R.W. Viersen of Okmulgee, Oklahoma. Like Dawson and Mason, Viersen was one of the outstanding breeders of Quarter Horses in that part of the country. One person who was familiar with both Viersen and Oklahoma Star Jr. during that time period is Nick McNair of Adair, Oklahoma.

McNair rated Oklahoma Star Jr. as the best breeding horse he ever knew, although he never considered him a very impressive looking individual. According to McNair, Star Jr. was a small horse, not weighing more than 950 pounds, but a breedy looking animal none-the-less.

Larry Kilgore of Broken Arrow, Okla., was also an admirer of Oklahoma Star Jr.

Kilgore spent a year working for Ralph Viersen during the time he had Star Jr. and remembered that Viersen also had the stallions Little Jodie, Star McCue, Grey Question, and Hysition (TB), and that he bred most of his good Bert daughters to them. Star Jr., with his super disposition, was used primarily as a teaser.

Star Jr. was bred to a few mares, however, and Jack Henson, who, at the time, ran things for Viersen, was quick to notice that his offspring were the kind of horses a man liked to own. Slowly, but surely, Jack started breeding more and more mares to him. Kilgore also rode Oklahoma Star Jr. several times to bring in the milk cows. He has been quoted as saying the stallion was an exceptionally good-natured stud who had a healthy dose of "cow" in him.

Like McNair, Kilgore did not consider Star Jr. to be a really nice-looking horse. In

Halter and Performance Record: None.

Progeny Record:

AQHA Champions: 5	Performance Points Earned: 202
Foal Crops: 22	Performance Registers of Merit: 11
Foals Registered: 131	Race Money Earned: $10,250
Halter Point-Earners: 24	Race Registers of Merit: 1
Halter Points Earned: 374	Race Starters: 2
Performance Point-Earners: 19	Superior Halter Awards: 2
Leading Race Money-Earner: War Star ($10,250)	

fact, he remembered that when people started asking Henson about breeding to the stallion, the foreman would tell them to just send their mares . . . not to come look at him first.

Kilgore also recalled that everyone who had a Star Jr. horse out of a Bert mare always wanted another one. They were known as natural cow horses who were easy to break and who wanted to do whatever was asked of them. According to Kilgore, they were good, solid, using horses with enough speed to get the job done.

In 1955, R.W. Viersen had a complete dispersal sale. Oklahoma Star Jr., then 21 years old, was a feature of the sale and was purchased by Paul Lomax of Skiatook, Oklahoma. He remained in Lomax's ownership for 5 years, until his death in 1960.

While by most accounts Oklahoma Star Jr.'s looks left something to be desired, his record as a sire definitely did not.

Only two of his offspring were race

V's Sandy, a good-looking gelding by Oklahoma Star Jr., out of Adonna, by Bert. Foaled in 1948, V's Sandy is shown here with his owner, Jane Mayo, of Okemah, Okla. after being named grand champion gelding at an AQHA show held in Plainview, Tex., in June 1958. V's Sandy went on to earn his AQHA Championship and a superior in halter with 108 points. He also carried Mayo to two world championships in barrel racing.

Oklahoma Star Jr. not only proved that he was worthy of his name, he added to its luster.

starters, but one of these, War Star, achieved a speed index of 95 and had $10,250 in earnings.

As a sire of show horses, Oklahoma Star Jr. proved versatile indeed.

V's Sandy, a 1948 gelding out of Adonna, by Bert, became an AQHA Champion in 1956 with 108 halter and 31 performance points. Ridden by Jane Mayo of Okemah, Okla., V's Sandy also became one of the first truly great barrel-racing horses. To-

gether, the pair won the Girls Barrel Racing Association world title in 1959 and 1960.

V's Jose, a 1951 stallion out of V's Lucy, by Little Jodie, earned his AQHA Championship in 1956 with 35 halter and 23 performance points.

V's Lady Star, a 1951 mare out of Lady Panita, by Bert, became an AQHA Champion and Superior Halter Horse in 1957 with 64 halter and 29 performance points.

Star Jr.'s Joie, a 1956 mare out of V's Beggar Jo, by Little Jodie, was the 1959 AQHA high-point calf-roping mare.

Mr. Star Jr., a stallion foaled in 1958 out of Ingersoll's Miss Snip, by Tamo, earned his AQHA Championship in 1963 and was also the AQHA high-point barrel-racing stallion that same year.

Baby Doll Combs, one of Oklahoma Star Jr.'s most famous offspring, does not even appear on his official AQHA get-of-sire performance record. She is a legend, none-theless, in the world of pro rodeo. Known simply as Baby Doll, she was one of the greatest bulldogging horses of all times.

Baby Doll was foaled in 1947 and was out of Miss Boctick, by Bert. From 1953 through 1960, she carried a multitude of R.C.A. cowboys to bulldogging wins of over $400,000. She was so well known throughout the country that *LIFE* maga-zine ran two feature articles on her.

As good a sire as he was, Oklahoma Star Jr. was an even better broodmare sire.

When crossed by John Dawson on Wimpy II, the Star Jr. mares excelled as producers. For example:

Kate Dawson produced Dawson No-wata, the 1961 AQHA Honor Roll Pole-Bending Horse. Nellie Dawson produced Dawson Jack, an AQHA Champion and Superior Halter Horse, and Nellie Don Dawson produced Dawson's Surprise, an AQHA Champion.

And the Star Jr. mares crossed just as well with other stallions.

When bred to Gold King Bailey, Socks Dawson produced Pat Dawson, an AQHA Champion and the 1961 and 1962 AQHA Honor Roll Barrel-Racing Horse.

Crossed on Chico Dawson, Dawson's Fan produced Slats Dawson (registered by the AQHA as Dawson's Slats), the 1958 NCHA World Champion Cutting Horse and an eventual inductee into the NCHA Hall of Fame.

When bred to King Sunday, Susette Clap-per produced Sundalene Dee, an AQHA Champion and Superior Cutting Horse; when bred to M&M's Major's Mangum, she produced Raysette, an AQHA Cham-pion and Superior Halter Horse; and when bred to Joe Norfleet, she produced Kiowa Dusty, a Superior Cutting Horse.

Star Jr.'s Sue produced three AQHA Champions: Tabano Star Jr., by Tabano King; Benear Jr's Sue, by Sandy Benear; and Two Eyed Star Jr., by Two Eyed Jack.

When bred to King Command, the Oklahoma Star Jr. daughter Hat Band produced Frosty Star, the 1971 AQHA high-point cutting stallion. Likewise, when bred to Docs Diablo, Star Jr's Cat

Old Red Buck P-9, foaled in 1924. This foundation Quarter Horse sire was also bred by John Dawson and was by Red Man, by Tubal Cain, and out of Pet Dawson, by Jeff. Dawson crossed Oklahoma Star Jr. on daughters of Old Red Buck with consider-able success. Later, Old Red Buck was owned by the well-known Rocky Mountain horseman King Merritt of Federal, Wyoming. This photo appeared in AQHA's Stud-book No. 2, published in 1943, and is reproduced courtesy of AQHA.

Here is a classic photo of the famous roping gelding, Baldy, with Clyde Burk in the saddle. Baldy was a half-brother of Oklahoma Star Jr., being sired by Old Red Buck P-9 and out of Babe Dawson. Apparent in this photo are Baldy's neck, shoulder, and leg scars, the result of a trailer fire. **Photo by Stryker**

Slats Dawson is shown here at a December 1960 cutting held at the B.F. Phillips Ranch, Frisco, Texas. He is receiving the award for being named champion cutting horse of the North Texas Cutting Horse Association. Slats, who was owned at the time by George Pardi of Uvalde, Tex., was another outstanding maternal grandson of Oklahoma Star Jr. He was foaled in 1947 and was by Chico Dawson and out of Dawson's Fan. Also pictured are (left to right): NCHA President Byron Matthews; trainer Minor Johnson; Pam Phillips; and B.F. Phillips. Slats Dawson was the 1958 World Champion Cutting Horse and is a member of the NCHA Hall of Fame.

Photo by James Cathey

John Dawson chose Wimpy II, by Wimpy P-1, to cross on his Oklahoma Star Jr. mares. This is a photo of Dawson Jack, one of the results of that cross. Dawson Jack, a gelding foaled in 1948 out of Nellie Dawson, was an AQHA Champion and also earned a Superior in halter with 94 points. He is shown here with his owner, Dr. H.P. Kemmerly of Tulsa in the saddle, after standing grand champion gelding at Wetumka, Okla., in May 1957.

Photo by James Cathey

produced Doc Diablo Star Jr, the 1987 AQHA high-point cutting stallion.

Crossed on Coy's Bonanza, June Twilight produced the Superior western pleasure horse Bonanza's Bay Lady. When bred to Julio's Bar, Sandra Star produced Red Star Bar, who earned an AQHA Championship and Superiors in both halter and western pleasure.

In all, the daughters of Oklahoma Star Jr. produced 15 race Register of Merit earners, 42 performance ROM earners, 11 AQHA Champions, and 12 Superior event earners.

Oklahoma Star Jr. was also the sire of Pat Star Jr., a 1953 stallion who was out of V's Patsy Ann, by Bert.

Although he died at the relatively young age of 14, Pat Star Jr. did live long enough to help make Howard Pitzer, of Ericson, Neb., a leading breeder of halter and performance horses.

Pat Star Jr. sired 20 AQHA Champions and 10 Superior halter horses. Among his noteworthy get were Dot Pat Star, Babe Pat Star, Johnny Pat Star, and Dina Pat Star. Each of these horses were AQHA Champions and each of them earned over 100 halter points.

Pat Star Jr. was also the maternal grand-

The famous bulldogging mare Baby Doll was by Oklahoma Star Jr. and out of Miss Boctick, by Bert. Foaled in 1947, she was bred by H.M. Boctick of Oktaha, Oklahoma. She is shown here in action at a 1958 rodeo in Burwell, Nebraska. Her owner, Willard Combs, is the bulldogger, and the hazer is believed to be Willard's brother, Benny. Both men won PRCA bulldogging championships off Baby Doll.

Photo by Devere, Courtesy of Professional Rodeo Cowboys Association

sire of 23 AQHA Champions and the earners of 42 Superior event awards.

Another noted producer within the Oklahoma Star Jr. family was War Bird, by War Star. War Bird was the dam of the following horses: War Leo, an AQHA Champion with a Superior in halter and an NCHA Bronze Award winner and the 1963 AQHA high-point cutting stallion; Rondo Leo, an AQHA Champion with 362 performance points; Ace of Limestone AA, AQHA Champion; War O'Lee, Superior cutting horse with 180 points and an NCHA Bronze Award winner; and Limestone Bird, AQHA Champion.

War Leo, in turn, went on to become a leading cutting horse sire, and Rondo Leo sired Mr. Gun Smoke, a Superior cutting horse who became a leading sire of reining and cutting horses.

Pat's Dusty Star, by Barry Pat Star, by Pat Star Jr., was the dam of Skipa Star, the 1975 AQHA World Champion 2-Year-Old Stallion at halter, and a leading sire of halter and performance horses.

Naming a horse after his sire is a risky proposition, particularly if that sire happens to be famous. But it was no problem with Oklahoma Star Jr. He not only proved that he was worthy of his name, he added to its luster.

Star Jr.'s Sue, a daughter of Oklahoma Star Jr., shown here after winning the 2-year-old mare class at an AQHA show held in Wetumka, Okla., in May 1957. Star Jr.'s Sue was out of San Sue Darks, by San Siemon, who also produced the well-known sire Leo San. At the time this picture was taken, Star Jr.'s Sue was owned by Turner Meadows of Wetumka.

Photo by James Cathey

12 DRIFTWOOD

By Phil Livingston

A great match-race horse, Driftwood is best remembered as a sire of outstanding performance horses.

KNOWN AS Speedy during his rodeoing days, Driftwood left an indelible mark on the using horse world of the Southwest and West Coast. Foaled in 1932 near Silverton, Tex., the bay stallion was bred by a Mr. Childress (known locally as "Old Man" Childress).

At the time Driftwood was foaled, there was no American Quarter Horse Association, and breeding records were often loosely kept. Many breeders, especially if they were racing their horses, preferred that the breeding of their horses not be known. It was easier to match a horse that way, especially if a horse was by a known sire of speed.

AQHA records list Driftwood as being sired by Miller Boy, and out of The Comer Mare. The dam of The Comer Mare was a Thoroughbred mare, who supposedly came from Kentucky, and was owned by Old Man Childress. The top side of The Comer Mare's pedigree shows her sire as Barlow. Some horsemen have maintained that Barlow was by Texas Chief, but the record states that he was a son of Lock's Rondo. Lock's Rondo had quite a reputation as a match-race horse.

Driftwood's sire was Miller Boy, by the Hobart Horse. Little is known about the Hobart Horse other than he was thought to have been brought to the JA Ranch, outside of Clarendon, Tex., around 1920 by T.D. Hobart, who was then general manager of

Driftwood in a 1944 photograph with Jim Carr, one of the most respected California trainers at that time.

Photo Courtesy of Katy Peake

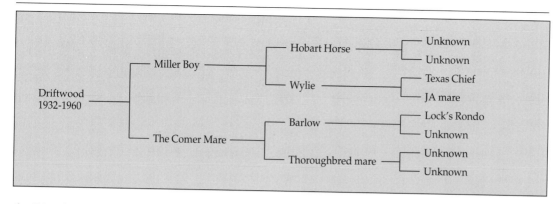

the JA. The Hobart Horse was remembered as an outstanding individual. Some horsemen of the time said that he was a son of John Wilkins, who was by Peter McCue, but that has never been verified.

Miller Boy's dam was by the celebrated Texas Chief, by Traveler, who stood at the Shely Ranch outside of Alice, down in the Texas brush country.

There's an interesting variation on Driftwood's breeding that appeared in the 1944 edition of *Racing Quarter Horses*, prepared by Melville Haskell for the Arizona Quarter Racing Association. It concerns a 1935 son of Driftwood called Cowboy Schell. In the pedigree for Cowboy Schell, Haskell lists Driftwood's sire as Line Up (TB), by Upset and out of Perling. And Haskell lists Driftwood's dam as a daughter of Peter McCue. This same breeding also appears in the 1945 and 1946 editions of the same yearbook. Was it a mistake, or wishful thinking? Or, was it possibly true, thus explaining Driftwood's Thoroughbred looks and speed?

Regardless of the lack of solid information on his pedigree, Driftwood's bloodlines were good, and they produced a horse with outstanding physical ability and speed. For a number of years, he was a hard-knockin' match race horse all over the Texas Panhandle, winning at distances from 220 yards to ⅜ of a mile.

During those early match-racing years, there were no starting gates. Instead, horses were flagged off the starting line in what were called lap-and-tap starts. "Lap" meant that the horses had to lap each other when they came up to the starting line. In other words, if the horses were in a straight line, the starter, who was standing either to the right or left of them, could only see the entire body of the horse

Halter and Performance Record: None.

Progeny Record:

Foal Crops: 25	Performance Points Earned: 242.5
Foals Registered: 153	Performance Registers of Merit: 19
Halter Point-Earners: 5	Race Money Earned: $60
Halter Points Earned: 34	Race Registers of Merit: 1
Performance Point-Earners: 26	Race Starters: 2
Leading Race Money-Earner: Calzona Katy ($60)	

The late Driftwood

Driftwood as an aged horse. His bone, balance, and alertness were still evident and gave an indication of how the horse must have looked during his rodeoing days.

Photo Courtesy of Phil Livingston

As a young horse, Driftwood certainly looked agile and athletic. Note the length of his hip. A dark bay with no white markings, he weighed approximately 1,075 pounds.

Photo by Katy Peake

Driftwood and Asbury Schell in 1943.

Photo Courtesy of Katy Peake

closest to him. When the horses were "lapped" like this, the starter "tapped" them off. If they weren't lapped, he yelled to pull up and try again.

The term "tap" came from colonial days when the starter either tapped a stick against a board, or had a drummer tap the horses off.

For practice, and for conditioning purposes, trainers would "score" their racers. This meant they would practice coming up to the starting line, let them break, then pull them up. Sometimes the trainers would do this for hours on end, to see which one would blow up first.

In his book titled *13 Flat*, Willard Porter discussed Driftwood's ability to remain quiet in lap-and-tap starts. Porter quoted an old-timer as saying, "Driftwood never blew. One time, Driftwood was matched against one of the best lap-and-tap horses in the Sweetwater country for 220 yards. They scored for an hour and a quarter, until both horses were drenched with sweat from the start of so many un-lapped starts. The other horse was high, and fretting, and obviously tiring. But Drifty was

Seven-year-old Catherine Anne Peake on Driftwood in 1945 or '46. The daughter of Channing and Katy, Catherine Anne was the little girl who separated Driftwood and Booger H when they were fighting.

Photo Courtesy of Katy Peake

still calm. When they finally broke, Drifty never made a mistake. He broke straight and on top, and he won by 2 lengths."

Early in his career, Driftwood was sold to Roy McMurtry, who, in turn, sold him to Ross Brinson, who eventually took him to Arizona. There, he ended up in the hands of Ab Nichols, the legendary race horse man and breeder who lived in Gilbert. There, Driftwood added to his reputation as a tough match horse.

It was during his tenure at the Nichols ranch that Driftwood, so the story goes, outran Clabber, the 1940-41 Champion Quarter Running Horse also owned by Nichols at the time. It took a real race horse to do that.

In an article about Driftwood in *Hoofs and Horns*, Willard Porter quoted Ab Nichols' son, Buck, as saying: "Driftwood was 6 or 7 years old when we bought him. He was a race horse, but I broke him to be a rope horse and rodeoed on him. As far as I know, he'd never experienced anything like that before we got him.

"He was a blood bay; not real big, and definitely showed his Thoroughbred breed-

Poker Chip Peake, by Driftwood and out of Sage Hen, was foaled in 1950. The good-looking gray is still considered by many calf ropers to have been the greatest calf-roping horse of all time. He was owned by Dale Smith, shown here, and roped on by Dale and other top hands.

Photo Courtesy of Phil Livingston

Speedy Peake, by Driftwood and out of Shu Cat, by King P-234, was a winner in calf roping, team roping, steer stopping, cutting, and working cow horse.

Photo by Katy Peake

Wooden Nugget, a 1957 bay stallion by Driftwood and out of Nugget Hug, by Bear Hug. He was a good-looking rascal that Walt Mason rodeoed on.

Photo by Katy Peake

ing," continued Nichols. "And he could run! He was also an extremely smooth riding horse with an easy disposition.

"We didn't keep him more than a couple of years, but we thought a great deal of him. As a matter of fact, we bred a lot of our Clabber mares to him."

Since that happened before the AQHA was organized, there is no record of those sons and daughters. It can easily be assumed, however, that the combination of Driftwood and Clabber bloodlines produced some outstanding match-race, ranch, and rodeo mounts for Arizona cowboys.

Porter's article continued to quote Buck Nichols: "George Cline, of Roosevelt, Ariz., came to us about buying the horse. We sold him for $600. The Depression of the 1930s wasn't over yet and that was an unheard-of price for a horse. The Clines liked to rope, and Driftwood got to look at lots of cattle."

In 1941, when he was 9 years old, Driftwood was sold to Asbury Schell of Tempe, Arizona. Asbury was a tough calf and team roper, and a former world champion in the second event. As you might expect, he augmented his ranching income with rodeo winnings. The horse fit in well with that program, and before long he was a fixture at the big rodeos across the country. From the Mexican border to Calgary, from California to Madison Square Garden, Driftwood was ridden by some of the top timed-event hands in the business. Schell began calling the horse Speedie (later, the Peakes spelled it Speedy) based on the speed with which he caught cattle, and the name caught on with the cowboys.

In those days, most outdoor rodeos were held in large arenas and over a long score. Because of his match-race experience, Speedy broke from the roping box extremely fast and learned to hunt, or track, cattle in the quickest way possible. Ropers of the time still talk about the way that he ate up ducking, dodging calves and steers.

At a rodeo at Payson, Ariz., probably in 1941, the spectacular bay stallion was ridden in every timed event—calf roping, team tying, single steer roping, and bulldogging. And he carried his riders into the money in every one of them. Then, he won the stock saddle cow horse race down the length of the arena. The story passed into rodeo legend and was recounted for many years by the ropers who were there to see it.

Driftwood was a tough horse. He stood

up under the pressure of rodeoing with the long hauls, numerous riders, and changes of climate and feed. Even with all the hard use, however, he never lost his good disposition.

Then, early in 1943, his life took a different trail when he was purchased by Channing and Catherine "Katy" Peake, who owned Rancho Jabali in Lompoc, California. Several years earlier, the Peakes had purchased five mares of One-Eyed Waggoner breeding from Duwain E. Hughes of San Angelo, Texas. These mares were of strictly Quarter Horse type. The Peakes already had five RO mares from the Greene Cattle Company of Cananea, Sonora, Mexico.

According to Willard Porter, the couple had decided to develop a breeding program to produce the best rodeo and ranch horses possible. Although they had the mare power to do it with, they didn't have a stallion. So they began to search for a suitable one. For a year or so it was a difficult hunt. The Peakes weren't in the market for just any stallion. As Porter has written, they wanted one with proven, outstanding roping ability. While they were interested in a horse with the conformation that would enable him to stay sound under hard use, their primary objective was a horse with performance ability, heart, and the speed to catch cattle in winning time. And they wanted a prepotent horse who could pass these traits on to his get.

One day, Gordon Davis, a rancher and roper from nearby Templeton, stopped by the Peakes' ranch. Willard Porter quoted him as saying, "Katy, I've got the horse for you. They call him Speedy, and he's owned by Asbury Schell of Tempe, Arizona. He's a rope horse all the way!"

In the spring of 1942 the Peakes, along with Davis, went to the Hayward, Calif., rodeo where Schell was competing. They would not only see what the horse looked like, but could judge his performance as a contest mount in both the calf roping and team roping.

The well-balanced, good-looking bay stallion lived up to his advance billing. He was alert, had a kind eye and a quiet disposition, and was the kind of rope horse the Peakes had visualized. Seeing Speedy ended the Peakes' search for a stallion.

There was just one problem. Schell

The renowned Jimmy Williams on Henny Penny Peake, a Driftwood daughter who was an outstanding stock horse. Foaled in 1949 and out of Sage Hen, Henny Penny Peake was a full sister to Poker Chip Peake.
Photo by John Williamson, Courtesy of Susan Hutchison

A 1957 picture of Katy Peake with Driftwood.

Photo Courtesy of Katy Peake

Jimmy Williams on another Driftwood who went by two names: Wood Wind and Hot Toddy. In 1961, Wood Wind was the ASHA Stock Horse of the Year and PCHJSHA Stock Horse Champion (A Division).
Photo by George Axt, Courtesy of Susan Hutchison

Mescal Brownie, a top rope horse by Driftwood, with Chuck Sheppard. Brownie carried Chuck to lots of money in both calf roping and heeling. This picture was taken at Tucson (date unknown) where Brownie won the registered heeling at an AQHA show.

didn't want to sell the horse. He was winning money off him in the rodeo arena and, like most ropers, when he had a horse that fit him, he didn't want to give him up. However, Channing and Katy did talk the Arizona cowboy into coming to their ranch for a short visit and breeding Speedy to several of their mares.

When Schell headed back to Tempe, the Peakes asked if they could have the first chance to buy the horse if Schell ever decided to sell him.

After he returned home, Asbury did decide to sell Speedy, and so informed the Peakes. But later, he changed his mind, and hectic correspondence flew back and forth between Arizona and California. Asbury didn't know what to do. He was winning off the horse, but World War II had started and gas rationing was imminent. Rodeos would certainly be limited, and it would be hard to travel, anyway. He finally agreed to part with Driftwood.

On March 9, 1943, Channing Peake paid Asbury Schell $1,500 for the stallion that he and his wife wanted to head their breeding program. Channing drove to Phoenix and picked the horse up right after the big Phoenix rodeo, where Schell had wanted to rope on him one last time. At the time, Speedy was 11 years old, and the Peakes got their first foals by him that spring, since they had bred mares to him in 1942.

In writing about Driftwood, Willard Porter had said that even though Speedy had won more money at Phoenix than his purchase price, Schell had decided that the best place for Speedy was at Rancho Jabali. There, he would have a good home as well as the opportunity to sire more top rope horses.

The stallion, even after being retired to stud duty, was always a gentle, tractable individual. An incident one year at the Peakes' ranch proved that. One night, as reported by Porter, another stallion, Booger H, got loose, kicked the lock off of Speedy's stall, and went in after him.

The two stallions fought, first in the stall and then outside. Channing and Katy Peake weren't home but their young daughter, Catherine, was. She went out and drove Booger H off. Then, she called to Speedy. The stallion came to her, she slipped a halter on him and led him to a safe stall.

During the years at Rancho Jabali, the Peakes made a practice of never breeding Speedy to nervous, high-strung, or un-

Jay Wood, a 1950 gelding by Driftwood and out of Black Maria D., was the grand champion working horse at the 1962 Bay Counties Quarter Horse Show in California. He was owned by Kathryn Donovan of Santa Maria.

Ropers knew that buying a Driftwood weanling was almost a sure-fire guarantee of being well-mounted in the years to come.

proven mares, either their own or others, wrote Porter. Undoubtedly that, along with his own quiet manner, was a big reason why most of Driftwood's get had good dispositions.

"The conformation of Speedy's get is variable," said Katy Peake in another Willard Porter article in *The Quarter Horse Journal* of December 1955. "We have been careful of the mares we have bred to him, and by and large they carry more Quarter Horse characteristics than he does himself. He passes on his intelligence, kindness, speed, and way of moving with great fidelity."

For 2 decades, ropers from California, Arizona, Oregon, and Nevada purchased weanlings by Driftwood. They knew that owning one of his weanlings was almost a sure-fire guarantee of being well-mounted in the years to come. Katy adds that most

of the ropers would buy the foals sight unseen; they made their selections according to the mares. "For example, Oscar Walls wanted the foals out of Smoky McCue, one of the One-Eyed Waggoner mares."

For years, the major rodeos and team ropings in California and Arizona were a showcase of Driftwood offspring—usually geldings—since so many of his get would be in action.

One of the first of the Driftwoods to carry on his sire's winning tradition was owned, appropriately enough, by Asbury Schell. The Arizona roper knew what he had had in Driftwood, and was sure that Cowboy Schell, who was mentioned earlier, would put him ahorseback again. By Driftwood and out of a Will Stead mare, Cow-

Red Button, who was called Roany, was by Driftwood and out of Sage Hen. Foaled in 1945, he was a full brother to Henny Penny Peake and Poker Chip Peake. Roany was owned by Pat Smith and later by Joe Bergevin, and was one of the top horses going down the road for many years. This picture was taken at the Ellensburg, Wash., rodeo; the date is unknown.

Photo Courtesy of Phil Livingston

boy was foaled in 1935 and was owned by a member of the McLoud family near Silverton, Texas. Wayne McLoud took Cowboy to Arizona and for several years, the bay gelding tore up the short tracks while under the ownership of several people.

Incidentally, Cowboy Schell was best known as just Cowboy. Evidently when Asbury Schell later bought him and registered him with the AQHA, Schell was added to Cowboy's name to distinguish him from Cowboy P-12.

Writing about Cowboy Schell in the 1944 edition of *Racing Quarter Horses,* published by the Southern Arizona Horse Breeders' Association, Melville H. Haskell commented, "A nicely made little gelding—perhaps a bit light in the bone to quite live up to the top Quarter Horse

standards—with a whole lot of speed. In 1943 he crowded Clabber to track record time for 350 yards and finished ahead of Red Man and Painted Joe. Arizona Girl topped him in the Speed Stakes, but he won a handicap from her when she had to give him 5 pounds."

Cowboy was 11 years old when Asbury Schell purchased him from Abe Graham. Until 2 years before, the horse had been principally a race horse, and won 14 out of 17 match races. However, it has been said that he spent some time on the Boquillas Ranch as a ranch mount until his speed was discovered. During his years on the track, Cowboy ran against the best and frequently beat them. When Cowboy was 9, Graham decided that it was time the horse began a second career. So Graham began training him as a rope horse.

That same year, after Cowboy had been introduced to the arena, Buckshot Sorrells and Homer Pettigrew took him to the Madison Square Garden rodeo to rope and bulldog on. Cowboy was still pretty high from the track, but did well over the short score there. Schell paid out $3,500 in 1946 dollars to own the blaze-faced bay. The war was over, gas rationing had been lifted, and rodeo hands were on the road again. In Schell's first two rodeos (Lehi, Utah, and Reno, Nev.) with his new mount, he won more than he had paid for his new horse. Before long, Arizona ropers were telling each other that Schell was once again one of the best mounted hands in the country.

Another of Driftwood's good sons was Mac McCue W., better known as Old Blue. An outstanding race horse, and later a top calf and team roping mount, he was foaled in 1943, had been bred by the Peakes, and was out of Smoky McCue. He was first purchased by Oscar Walls, who reportedly match raced the horse 57 times and won 50 of them.

Old Blue was later purchased by Buck and Gilbert Nichols, who had also owned Driftwood. A top calf and team roping mount, Blue was an outstanding race horse during his younger years.

A Driftwood horse known both as Hot Toddy and Wood Wind was Stock Horse of the Year in both the Pacific Coast Hunter Jumper Stock Horse Association and the American Horse Shows Association. He was trained and shown by the renowned Jimmy Williams. Hot Toddy also twice carried Stu Gildred to the AHSA Stock Seat Medal finals. One of Driftwood's best show-ring performers was the talented Henny Penny Peake. She was out of Sage Hen, by One-Eyed Waggoner. A terrific stock horse, she was trained and shown by Jimmy Williams. This was in the 1950s, before Jimmy gave up showing stock horses (forerunners of today's reining and working cow horses) to concentrate on hunters and jumpers. Katy Peake says that they gave Henny Penny to Jimmy because they felt she had tremendous potential, and they knew Jimmy could develop it better than anybody else. And he did.

Henny Penny Peake was Stock Horse of the Year (high point) in both the PCHJSHA and the AHSA, and was the Pacific Coast

DRIFTWOOD IKE P-47645
By Driftwood P-2833 — Hancock Belle P-5593

Driftwood Ike, a dun foaled in 1954, was by Driftwood and out of Hancock Belle, a maternal granddaughter of Joe Hancock. Owned by Roy Wales of Queen Creek, Ariz., Ike was a top rope horse who was ridden by some of the best in the business.
Photo Courtesy of Phil Livingston

Hackamore Champion in 1953 and 1954. Those are just a few of her many impressive wins, some of which were earned with Luann Beech in the saddle, according to Katy Peake. The mare also became a movie star, and played the role of The Bay Lady in the Walt Disney movie, *The Horse of the West.* Jimmy later sold the mare.

Red Button, also by Driftwood and out of Sage Hen, was a top calf and heel horse owned by Pat Smith and later by Joe Bergevin. Red Button was better known as Roany.

Wood Wasp, one of the better cutting horses on the Pacific Coast, was by Drift-

Here's a 1959 picture of 4 fillies from Driftwood's last crop. They were given by the Peakes to Cal Poly at San Luis Obispo where they were broke and trained by students. From left: Tweedle Dum, ridden by Mervyn Becker; Annie Wood with Glenn Gimple; Quick A. Lick with Norbert Oliviera; and Tweedle Dee with Jim Flanagan.

wood and owned by W.P. Roduner.

Driftwood Ike, by Driftwood and out of Hancock Belle, was owned by Roy Wales of Queen Creek, Ariz., and ridden by some of the best professional calf ropers in the business before he was retired to stud. Among the roping toughs who went to the pay window on his stout back were Donnie Nichols, Sonny Davis, Bill Barbers, Bill Rush, B.J. Pierce, Bill Lowe, and Walt Nichols.

Two more Driftwoods were Wooden Nugget, shown by Walt Mason, and Mescal Brownie, who carried Chuck Sheppard to lots of heels in both the show ring and rodeo arena.

Asbury Schell also roped on another Driftwood, Cherokee Jake. Dusky Peake, owned and ridden by John Bacon of Los Olivos, Calif., was a winning team roping mount and became a popular sire, as well.

There is no doubt, however, that Driftwood's best-known son was Poker Chip Peake, the gray calf roping mount owned by Dale Smith of Chandler, Ariz., during the 1950s and early 1960s. Dale served nine times as president of the Rodeo

Cowboys Association (R.C.A. and PRCA). Poker, as the ropers still refer to him, has gone down in rodeo history as one of the greatest calf roping horses of all time.

Foaled at Rancho Jabali, Poker was also out of Sage Hen, one of the original One-Eyed Waggoner-bred mares obtained by the Peakes. Poker was purchased as a weanling by Oscar Walls of Welton, Arizona. The gray was owned and roped off by Duane Ellsworth and then J.K. Harris before Dale Smith traded for him. With Dale and other top calf ropers in the saddle, Poker made money in the arena for nearly a decade before an injury sustained in a trailer wreck finally sidelined him.

Not only was the horse a solid campaigner, but he was also spectacular to watch. His sparkling gray color, outstanding conformation, and smooth way of working made him really stand out, both to spectators and other ropers who wished that they could get a "seat" on the gray. He was especially attention-getting on television, which, during the early 1960s, was beginning to cover rodeo as a sport.

When Dale returned one year from the Cow Palace rodeo in San Francisco, which had been nationally televised, Roy Wales greeted him with: "You should have seen him, Dale. You should have seen ol' Poker. He looked great on TV . . . made Roy Rogers' Trigger look like an old dawg." Wales was a rancher and roper from Queen Creek, Arizona.

Poker Chip Peake is buried on the Trail of Great Cowponies at the Cowboy Hall of Fame in Oklahoma City.

Dale also roped on another Driftwood son, Speedywood.

Speedy Peake, owned by Katy Peake, was another top son of Driftwood, and was out of Shu Cat, by King P-234. The sale catalog for the Rancho Jabali dispersal in 1966 described Speedy Peake as "versatile, capable, and tough, like his sire." He earned ROMs in reining, cutting, and calf roping. According to the sale catalog, "In 1965 Speedy won the $1,000 Championship Working Horse Stake at Santa Barbara. He placed first in three of the five stake events—cutting, calf roping, and steer stopping—and was second in the working cow horse section."

Jimmy Williams, who passed away in 1993, was one of the great stock horse and hunter-jumper trainers of all time. In Willard Porter's *Hoofs and Horns* article about Driftwood, Williams was quoted as follows in describing Speedy's foals: "They are the best. You ask 'em to do anything and they'll do it. They want to learn, and they have the ability to do something when you've finished with them. I think Speedy is as good a sire as there is any place."

A number of Driftwood's sons and daughters, however, were not registered with the AQHA, or were not shown in AQHA events. Otherwise, his AQHA progeny record would be far more impressive.

The ability to perform under saddle didn't stop with the sons and daughters of Driftwood. Notable grandget included Shady (by Cherokee Jake), who carried Dale Smith to two PRCA world champion team roping titles, Redwood Jake, Whizwood, Six Pac, War Drift, and Doc's Drift. These are just a few of the grandget who kept Driftwood's reputation alive in arenas and on ranches across the country.

In addition to the Peakes' own band of select mares, Driftwood was bred to a number of outside mares. Many of them came from Arizona, where the horse's reputation as a sire of rope horses was so strong. In addition to the foals out of the Hughes mares owned by the Peakes, his most popular crosses came from daughters of Red Man, by Joe Hancock, and Lucky Blanton. Both were outstanding race and rope horses in their day.

Although Driftwood had been a hard-knocking race horse, few of his get went to the track. The rodeo arena was their destination, although more than one was match raced when the opportunity arose. And usually the Driftwood crossed the finish line first. Driftwood's biggest money-winner on recognized tracks was Calzona Katy, out of Smarty Pants, by Sergeant Hogan (TB).

While the Driftwood line is now getting thin, there are a few breeders scattered around the country attempting to carry it on. And, when possible, the ropers still like to own the Driftwoods. Even today, a cowboy will occasionally comment that his top horse goes back to old Speedy. This usually means that he is well-mounted.

Driftwood died at Rancho Jabali on October 20, 1960. During his career as a sire he proved, conclusively, that the Peakes' dream of raising top horses who excelled in roping and other performance events was possible.

13 JESSIE JAMES

By Phil Livingston

HE MAY have been named after one of the most notorious outlaws of the American West, but the Quarter Horse Jessie James built his reputation as one of the "good guys" of the early-day cutting horse scene. In fact, he was considered by many of the cutting horse trainers in the 1950s and 1960s to be one of the greatest cutting horses to ever look through a bridle.

According to Jim Reno, the noted cutting horse trainer and western sculptor who owned him for several years, "Jessie James was a tremendous athlete who could run, stop hard, and turn around quickly.

"He was a master at using his head and neck to control a calf. He worked with his ears back, and looked like a striking snake as he reached for the calf. He kept his ears pinned flat to the back of his head all the time that he was working a cow, almost like he didn't have any ears. He probably worked a cow more with his head than any other horse I've ever seen.

"I saw the horse do things that were equal to anything we see our good horses do today, and more," continued Reno. "There was no limit to his ability. If we'd worked horses in those days like we do now, and if we'd known how to train horses then like we do now, there's no telling how great that horse could have been."

Reno also noted that Jessie James' conformation was probably the key to his ability to stop, turn, and block a yearling. "He was a little bit short in the croup as well as being flat-crouped, he said. "He was also an extremely straight-legged horse behind, almost post-legged."

Reno, an outstanding sculptor and student of equine anatomy, has found the latter conformation feature to be true with some other outstanding equine athletes. Two other examples of top cutting horses who were very straight behind were Gandy's Time and Lena's Super Cool.

Jessie James, with Snooks Burton in the saddle, after winning the open cutting at the 1950 Southwestern Exposition & Fat Stock Show in Fort Worth.
Photo by Skeet Richardson

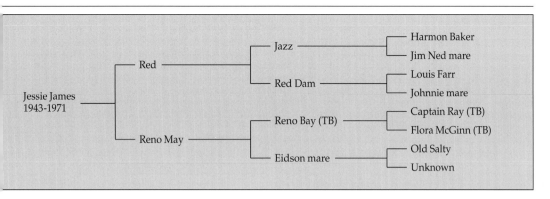

Jessie James 1943-1971
- Red
  - Jazz
    - Harmon Baker
    - Jim Ned mare
  - Red Dam
    - Louis Farr
    - Johnnie mare
- Reno May
  - Reno Bay (TB)
    - Captain Ray (TB)
    - Flora McGinn (TB)
  - Eidson mare
    - Old Salty
    - Unknown

Jim Reno summed up Jessie James' place in cutting horse history by comparing him to another sports legend. "I've always felt that he was to the early-day cutting horse world what Babe Ruth was to early-day baseball. Babe Ruth was the greatest baseball player of his era and I thought that Jessie James was the greatest cutting horse of his time. He certainly was a fantastic individual."

Jessie James was foaled in 1943 on the Odessa, Tex., ranch of Tom Elrod, a long-time breeder of good Quarter Horses and an early supporter of the AQHA.

Jessie James was sired by Red, a double-bred descendant of Harmon Baker. Harmon Baker, of course, was by Peter McCue. Red was a top conformation horse, winning the champion Quarter Horse stallion title at the Sand Hills show at Odessa in both 1942 and 1944.

Red's sire, Jazz, was bred by William Anson of Christoval, Tex., one of the greatest of the pioneer Quarter Horse breeders. Anson, an English nobleman who came to Texas in the early 1890s, got his start in the horse business by purchasing horses and mules for the British Army for use in the Boer War.

Jessie James' dam was Reno May, who was sired by the Remount Service Thoroughbred stallion Reno Bay. During the 1920s, 1930s, and 1940s, the government stallions provided by the U.S. Remount Service were popular with ranchers and put some of the finest Thoroughbred blood in the world into the remudas and brood-mare bands of western breeders.

As a 2-year-old, Jessie James was purchased by E. Paul Waggoner of Vernon and Arlington, Texas. The Waggoners always had an eye for a good horse, and E. Paul was no exception. During his 3 decades in the business, he either bred or owned many of the top Quarter Horses in the nation.

Jessie James began his career as a working horse at Waggoner's Three D Stock Farm outside of Arlington. Bob Burton, a Waggoner ranch hand, was the first person to ride both Jessie James and his stablemate, Poco Bueno. In comparing these two great horses in Mary Ellen Harris' *Western Horseman* story "Jessie James" (December 1975), Burton remarked, "I don't think there was a whole lot of difference between the two horses. Jessie wasn't near as stout a horse as Poco Bueno; they were just two different types of horses. I don't think there ever was a horse like Jessie James."

Matlock Rose was the next in the chain of riders to ride Jessie James. "Bob started the horse and was roping calves on him," recalled Rose. "Then, they bulldogged a little on him. I started riding Jessie James after I went to work for Mr. Waggoner. I roped calves on him for a while and then I started cutting on him.

"He was a nice kind of horse, but would hump up and buck a little. Bob took most of the rough out of him, but he'd still try to

He was considered to be one of the greatest cutting horses to ever look through a bridle.

A classic photograph of Jessie James in action, showing his snake-like method of working cattle, with his head and neck extended, and ears flat back. Matlock Rose is in the saddle in this 1951 photo, riding with one hand free of the saddle horn, as was the style in those days.

Photo by James Cathey, Courtesy of Phil Livingston

An advertisement, probably from the late 1940s, for Elrod Quarter Horses, Odessa, Tex., featuring Red, the sire of Jessie James.

Photo Courtesy of Phil Livingston

Elrod Quarter Horses

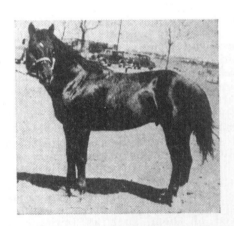

RED No. 204

Red was the champion Quarter Horse stallion at the Sand Hills Show at Odessa in 1942 and again won this same class in 1944.

We now have for sale a nice selection of his colts and a few one and two-year-old stud colts and fillies. Would sell a few brood mares with or without colts.

ELROD RANCH

Box 2248
ODESSA, TEXAS

Box 33
RANKIN, TEXAS

buck you off if anything out of the ordinary happened."

Jessie James took to cutting like a duck takes to water, demonstrating his own, unique style immediately.

"He was one of the best handling horses I ever rode in my life," continued Rose. "He had a lot of handle to him and could spin faster than any horse I've ever ridden.

"Jessie was an easy horse to ride. He'd stop and stay stopped all the time. All you had to do was say *whoa* and that was the end of it right there. I rode him with just a little old rope noseband and that's what I showed him in."

Rose left Waggoner's ranch in May of 1949, before he was able to show Jessie James as a cutting horse. The horse was turned over to Elmo Favor who showed him at a Fourth of July cutting a couple of months later. The pair won first place. This was the beginning of many trips to the pay window by the talented dun.

In 1950, Ben Fussell of Eagle Lake, Tex., bought Jessie James from Waggoner, and showed the horse in NCHA open cuttings. The following year, Fussell reunited Matlock Rose and the dun stallion for the entire show season.

Hitting the road hard, the team earned $7,352 and the title of 1951 NCHA Reserve World Champion, finishing behind the great cutting horse gelding Skeeter, owned and ridden by Phil Williams of Tokio, Texas.

Jessie James returned to the NCHA Top Ten in 1953 with a seventh-place finish, one notch behind his daughter, Fannie James. He earned $4,397, and was campaigned this time by George Tyler.

His career at AQHA shows was also impressive, although he was shown primarily in Texas. During 1951 through 1955 there were few major shows within an easy haul from Eagle Lake that Jessie James did not win or place in the cutting at one time or another.

In addition to those men already mentioned, such top cutting horse trainers as Cotton Merriott, Billy Bush, Bubba Cascio, James Boucher, Nolan Powell, and Amye Gamblin rode Jessie James in competition.

Jessie James collected his last major win at the age of 18 at the 1961 Houston Livestock Show with Nolan Powell in the saddle. He was the reserve champion of the NCHA contest.

Fussell sold Jessie James to Jim Reno in 1962. The horse was officially retired from arena competition with lifetime NCHA earnings of $18,961 and the NCHA Bronze Award (signifying that he had earned $10,000 or more in NCHA-sanctioned cuttings). He earned 121 AQHA cutting points, a Superior in cutting, 3 reining points, and 1 halter point.

In 1965 Jessie James changed hands again, going to T.O. Collins of Searcy, Ark., who had been a long-time admirer of the horse. His last recorded owner was HCM Enterprises, Gurnee, Illinois.

Although his reputation as one of the great cutting horses is secure, Jessie James' record as a sire is limited. This is perhaps because he wasn't bred to that many good mares as a young horse, being overshadowed by Poco Bueno when he was owned by Waggoner's Three D Stock Farm.

Jim Reno agrees: "He just wasn't bred to that many good mares as a young horse. It's important for a horse to have the best opportunity while he's young, and Jessie James didn't have that opportunity."

He sired only 143 registered AQHA foals, 36 of whom were AQHA performers. Sixteen of his get earned their Registers of Merit and one attained his AQHA Championship. Although the list of his offspring is short, Jessie James stamped his get with his athletic ability, cow sense, and, in many cases, his handsome dun color. He also sired more fillies than he did colts.

Cindy James, a 1947 mare, was the first

Jesse James Has a New Home

We recently purchased Jesse James 2257 pictured right from the Three D Stock farm, Arlington, Texas, and he is now on our ranch located near Eagle Lake, Texas, where he will be used in our breeding program. Our brood mare prospects, we feel, will make one of the best bands of mares ever assembled and the breeding of Jesse should combine to produce outstanding Quarter Horses. Jesse James is a grand champion at halter, reining and cutting, having won these awards in the top shows of the Southwest.

★

Our band of brood mares represents top blood lines such as Joe Reed, Little Joe, Harmon Baker and Hickory Bill. They are all top individuals from the Southwest's leading breeders.

★

We Are Breeding
Quarter Horses that feature working performance and showing ability.

B. D. FUSSELL COLUMBUS, TEXAS

Ranch Located 3 Miles N. W. of Eagle Lake, Texas, Hy. U. S. 90 A.

ALWAYS A FEW FOR SALE...GOOD ONES!

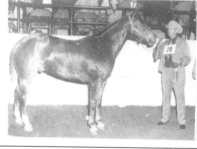

George T No. 1535, Grand Champion Gelding, San Antonio, 1950.

A group of our future brood mares.

This B.D. Fussell ad in the September 1950 issue of The Cattleman *announced Fussell's recent purchase of Jessie James from E. Paul Waggoner. The ad features one of the few conformation shots taken of Jessie James. Note that "Jessie" is misspelled.*
Photo Courtesy of Phil Livingston

of Jessie James' get to earn an ROM, which she did in 1957.

Next came RL Banjo Eyes, a 1947 daughter who was out of the famous producer Pretty Rosalie (the dam of Poco Stampede and Poco Pine).

RL Banjo Eyes earned her ROM in 1947. After she was retired to the broodmare band, she produced Poco Jessie, an AQHA Champion and Superior cutting horse.

Jessie James sired one other daughter out of Pretty Rosalie. Her name was Jessie Rose and, although unshown, she was the

Here is another shot of Jessie James with Snooks Burton aboard. The pair is shown here after winning the senior cutting at the Santa Rosa Roundup, Vernon, Tex., in May 1955. Jessie James' good head and intelligent expression are apparent in this photo.
Photo by James Cathey

dam of Poco Imprint, an AQHA Champion and Superior cutting horse.

Poco Imprint, in turn, sired Imprint's Hope, an AQHA Superior cutting horse; and Imps Double Jessie (out of Mae Wood, by Jessie James), earner of 34 performance points.

Fannie James, a daughter of Jessie James foaled in 1948, was one of his most accomplished competitors. She earned her ROM in 1957 with a total of 26 performance points. In NCHA competition, she finished ninth in the 1952 NCHA Top Ten with earnings of $2,857, and she was sixth in 1953 with earnings of $4,823. She also won an NCHA Bronze Award.

Fannie James is the second dam of Fannin Sugar, who was the 1988 NCHA Super Stakes Classic Champion, and the winner of over $90,000 in NCHA aged events.

Martin's Jessie, a 1961 dun stallion, was the only get of Jessie James to achieve an AQHA Championship. He accomplished this feat in 1965 and added a Superior in cutting the following year.

Competing in the NCHA, Martin's Jessie placed seventh in the Top Ten in 1972, with $6,260 in earnings. He also went on to earn an NCHA Bronze Award.

Jessie's Pride, a 1958 mare, was Jessie James' top halter point-earning get, with 44 points.

Other top performers by Jessie James included Jaime Jess, with 56 performance points; Red Miller James, with 36 performance points; Mae Wood, with 34 performance points; and Mae James, with 34 performance points.

While in the ownership of T.O. Collins, Jessie James sired several top horses, including Collins James, Collins Jessie, Daisy James, and Collins Daisy.

Collins James was trained for cutting by Matlock Rose and competed in the 1972 NCHA Futurity under Sam Rose, Matlock's son. He also sired Dot's Jessie, the 1980 AQHA World Champion Senior Reining Horse, and 1983 AQHA World Champion Senior Working Cowhorse.

Both Daisy James and Collins Daisy were ROM performance horses, and Collins Daisy held an NCHA Certificate of Ability for earning $1,500 or more in officially sanctioned contests.

Although Collins Jessie was not shown, he did distinguish himself as a sire. Among

Jessie James and Willis Bennett after winning the cutting at Fort Worth in 1950.

Photo by James Cathey

the top horses he sired are Jess Ta Lady, the 1979 AQHA high-point cutting mare; and Jess An Impression, an AQHA Champion with over 131 open and youth points.

Although Jessie James sired more daughters than sons, they must have been valued more as saddle horses than as producers, for only 27 of them have any produce listed with the AQHA.

Mae Jessie, a 1954 daughter, produced 10 foals by Poco Red Ant, by Poco Bueno. Six of those were AQHA performance point-earners: Red Ant's Lil, AQHA Champion; Red Ant's Annie, AQHA Champion; Red Ant's Jessie, 17 performance points; Red Ant's Emmy, 10 performance points; Copoco, 4 performance points; and Red Ant's Shane, 3 youth performance points.

Suzyque James, by Jessie James, produced four AQHA performance point-earners, including Jessie James Leo, the 1970 AQHA Honor Roll Cutting Horse.

Esoba James was the dam of Traildust Toby, a youth Superior western horsemanship horse and a youth Superior trail horse. This smooth-working grandson of Jessie James earned 315 youth working points and 57 open working points.

Jessie James died in 1971. He was owned by HCM Enterprises of Gurnee, Ill., at the time of his death.

He is remembered as a great cutting horse personality, with a distinctive style of working that, once seen, was not easily forgotten. And, as one cutting horse trainer and exhibitor of the period remarked, "He made the reputation of more good trainers than any other horse."

Although he did not sire the number of foals that other well-known working horses did, Jessie James was still a sire of considerable influence.

14 KING'S PISTOL

By Phil Livingston

He founded one of the first great families of cutting horses.

KING'S PISTOL was the 1957 NCHA World Champion Cutting Horse, and he founded one of the first great families of cutting horses. However, the start of the road that led to these accomplishments was a bit rocky.

Jim Calhoun of Cresson, Tex., is the man most associated with King's Pistol—as owner, trainer, and rider. Looking back on his acquisition of the famous stallion, he recalls that the purchase was not without a certain amount of risk.

"I was going to college at Oklahoma A&M (now Oklahoma State University) in 1952, saving my money, and planning on getting married during the Christmas break. That fall, I drove over to Bud Warren's place at Perry to look at Leo and all those good mares. We looked at all the horses at the ranch and then went to town to see some colts that Bud's trainers were just starting.

There was a short-legged, pot-bellied, coming 2-year-old bay stud colt tied up

King's Pistol, as portrayed by Orren Mixer in 1958.

Photo Courtesy of Orren Mixer and Jim Calhoun

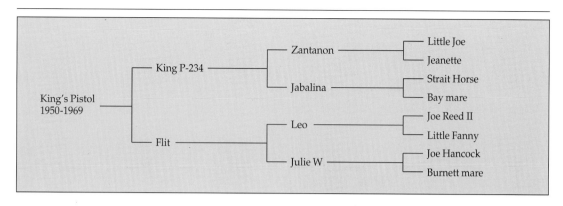

			Little Joe
		Zantanon	Jeanette
	King P-234		Strait Horse
		Jabalina	Bay mare
King's Pistol 1950-1969			Joe Reed II
		Leo	Little Fanny
	Flit		Joe Hancock
		Julie W	Burnett mare

that they were just starting to break. Well, I liked him so well I went back to the house and bought him. The problem was, I spent all my money that I'd saved. Skeet and I did get married, but it was later than we'd planned. We didn't have any money, but we did have a horse."

King's Pistol was sired by Jess Hankins' famous King P-234, who had established himself as one of the premier sires of performance horses in the breed. His dam, Flit, was by Leo, out of Julie W, by Joe Hancock. Flit was one of the first great daughters of Leo. She was AA race-rated, when that was the highest rating available, and set a track record at Enid, Okla., while carrying King's Pistol. In addition to King's Pistol, Flit also produced Sugar Leo, AAA, AQHA Champion; and Leo Bar, AAA.

When asked why Bud Warren would take a speedy mare like Flit to King, rather than breed her to one of his running stallions, Calhoun said, "Bud and Jess used to trade breedings each year, and this was one of them. Besides, King had a pretty good background of speed in his own pedigree, since he was sired by Zantanon, who was once known as the Mexican Man o' War."

Although King's Pistol was never aimed toward the racetrack, he did have one moment of glory there.

"Two men from *The New York Times* came down and wanted to compare Quarter Horses and Thoroughbreds," recalled Jane Calhoun, who goes by her nickname, "Skeet." "Pistol was 3 or 4 at the time and had never run. Jim took him over to Sid Richardson's Thoroughbred training track anyway.

Well, Pistol came out of the gate in front of the Thoroughbreds, and the men got their pictures. Jim put Pistol back in the trailer, saying, 'Let's go home. The

Halter and Performance Record: 1957 NCHA World Champion Cutting Horse; AQHA Champion; AQHA Superior Cutting Horse (65 Points); Halter Points, 30; Reining Points, 2.

Progeny Record:

AQHA Champions: 5	Performance Registers of Merit: 35
Foal Crops: 16	Race Money Earned: $1,356
Foals Registered: 238	Race Registers of Merit: 1
Halter Point-Earners: 27	Race Starters: 3
Halter Points Earned: 198	Superior Halter Awards: 1
Performance Point-Earners: 47	Superior Performance Awards: 4
Performance Points Earned: 1,448.5	
Leading Race Money-Earner: Pistol Mike ($1,356)	

only track you're going to see from now on is the track of a cow.' That was the end of Pistol's racing career."

Calhoun's initial plan for King's Pistol was to make a good ranch gelding out of him. He took his new purchase back to the Calhoun Ranch near Cresson, which lies just west of Fort Worth. The idea was to let the colt grow over the winter and spring and then start him under saddle. Jim's father, H. Calhoun, one of the founders of the NCHA and a knowledgeable horseman in his own right, commented that he felt that his son should leave his new horse a stallion until they saw how he worked out under saddle. He was just too well bred and well built not to give him a chance. After some thought, the younger Calhoun decided to take his father's advice.

Like most of the Kings, it took Pistol awhile to grow out. He was long-bodied, short-legged, and didn't look too promising. When some of the local horsemen first saw the young stallion, there was a lot of

King's Pistol and Jim Calhoun in action. This photo was used by the NCHA for many years as its logo.

Photo Courtesy of Jim Calhoun

Although King's Pistol had a good disposition, and was an easy horse to train, he did have an independent streak.

kidding about "Calhoun's Shetland." That came to a halt when they saw how the bay grew out and took to working cattle. Although King's Pistol had a good disposition, and was an easy horse to train, he did have an independent streak. He was his own horse, so to speak, and throughout his entire life, he never let his owner forget it.

"The first time I saddled him," remembers Calhoun, "he just stood there like it had been happening every day. I turned him around a time or two and stepped up. Without making any fuss about it, he flat bucked me off and then looked at me like he was telling me who the boss really was. I got up and back on and we never had any more trouble.

"He was a smart horse. After I got to cutting on him, I'd get out in the pasture, cut a cow out of a herd, and practice holding her. If she got away, Pistol would have to really run to put her back against the fence. Well, the next cutting we went to, I drove a yearling out of the bunch and the old horse just held her up against the arena fence and

wouldn't let her go anywhere. I couldn't keep him off the fence without taking hold of him. He'd jump out there and head the cow before she ever got started.

"It was a long way across the arena and he didn't want to run. He was beating the cow to the punch just enough to head her, then he'd pop back and wait on her. I got to thinking about it later, and that long trip across the pasture was what had caused him to do that. If a horse is smart, he'll figure out how to get the job done with the least amount of effort."

At that time, the rolling prairie southwest of Fort Worth was all steer country. Ranchers like George Glascock, Ray Smyth, Loyd and T.C. Jinkens, Volney Hildreth, H. Calhoun, T.B. Saunders, and the Slochum brothers all ran large bunches of yearling steers on pasture, backgrounding them for the feedlots. These ranchers were constantly gathering, working, and shipping cattle; and it was an ideal place for a young horse to learn his lessons. There were lots of wet saddle blankets pulled off Pistol's back that first year and he quickly learned the easy way to handle a cow with "quit" on her mind. In fact, he developed so rapidly that Jim began to think seriously about making an arena cutting horse out of the talented colt.

The fact that Jim was constantly exposed to such horsemen as George Glascock, Ray Smyth, T.B. Saunders (Jim Calhoun's father-in-law), the Jinkens brothers, and his father, all founders of the NCHA, had a great deal to do with his decision. These men were top hands and knew what it took to "make a horse," and they all thought that Pistol had the makings of a top cutter.

When Jim Calhoun purchased King's Pistol, he wasn't a beginner at riding cutting horses. He had been doing it all of his life. He was a member of the NCHA at 14 and, at 18, in 1951 at Amarillo, rode A.R. Eppenauer's Caesar's Pistol in a 10-head matched cutting against E.P. Waggoner's Snipper W, with Pine Johnson in the saddle. It was a tight cutting, but Snipper W came out on top.

Calhoun and Caesar's Pistol came back to win the rich cutting at San Antonio shortly afterwards against the pair. A win picture of that event shows Calhoun on Caesar's Pistol, Andy Hensley on Poco Bueno, Milt Bennett on Poco Tivo, Phil Williams on Skeeter, and Matlock Rose on Jessie James, all toughs of the period who have gone down in the record book.

When King's Pistol was 4, he was a top cow horse, used to long circles, working cattle on the range or in the alleys, and dragging calves to the branding fires. He had also been introduced to the cutting pen and begun his show career, winning AQHA points at halter, reining, and cutting. Calhoun hauled the young stallion to seven jackpot cuttings close to home that summer, winning three of them.

In 1955 Calhoun and Pistol competed at one AQHA show and four cutting contests, all scheduled around ranch work. In 1956 they went to 15 cuttings, including 9 AQHA events, and won 9, in addition to acquiring points in halter and reining. All of this competition was close to home and didn't make too large a dent in the work schedule on the Calhoun Ranch. In fact, Calhoun and Pistol sometimes worked cattle all day and then went to a cutting on a Friday night.

"There was one morning that I saddled up Pistol and loped over to George Glascock's ranch at Cresson, about 6 or 7

This picture of King's Pistol and Jim was probably taken in the mid-1950s. Pistol's head reflects the intelligence for which he was noted.

Photo by James Cathey, Courtesy of Jim Calhoun

miles from our place," remembers Calhoun. "We worked cattle, and I roped and dragged a bunch of yearlings across the highway that day, until about 5 p.m. with only a short lunch break. Skeet came by with a trailer and we hauled over to George's where I cleaned up before we went to the cutting. Pistol really worked good that night, and we won part of it. We were back over at George's bright and early the next morning.

"I didn't start Pistol in cutting with the championship in mind, but, after he got so far along, there was no doubt in my mind

King's Pistol, nose to nose with a critter at a jackpot cutting at Godley, Tex., just a few miles from the Calhoun Ranch at Cresson.

Photo Courtesy of Jim Calhoun

King's Pistol and Jim cutting in the mud at the 1956 Santa Rosa Round-up in Vernon, Texas. Pistol would work anywhere, under any circumstances.

Photo Courtesy of Jim Calhoun

King's Michelle, by King's Pistol, winning the 1962 Southern Arizona Livestock International at Tucson with Glen McWhorter in the saddle. Owned by Dr. and Mrs. E.F. Meredith, Olney, Tex., King's Michelle had an outstanding career in the cutting arena.

that he was good enough," continued Calhoun. "I'd been showing him more than usual in 1957 and he was winning more than his share. I was judging a show one weekend and asked myself, 'What am I doing here, judging, when I have a good horse at home?' Stanley Bush, on Snipper W, was already leading for the year with about a $2,600 lead, but I decided that I'd give Pistol a try."

Well, by the end of the point year, King's Pistol was the 1957 NCHA World Champion Cutting Horse, with earnings of $16,217. Says Calhoun, "We were gone every weekend that year, and were home only once for 10 days straight. That's when the nearby Weatherford rodeo and cutting was going on. We beat Snipper W by better than $4,000. That was a lot of money back then. Stanley and I traveled together that year, and we just kept winning at most of the places we went."

In January 1958, Calhoun took Pistol to the big Odessa, Tex., livestock show, which had an AQHA show as well as an NCHA cutting. "Pistol won everything we entered," Calhoun remembers. Pistol stood grand champion at halter, and won the registered cutting and the NCHA open cutting.

"After Odessa, we showed one more time," Calhoun continues, "at the Fort Worth Fat Stock Show, a few weeks later,

Pistol Toter, a 1957 son of King's Pistol, was out of Duchess Bonnie, by Jiggs H. Pistol Toter was an AQHA Champion with 12 halter and 18.5 performance points. He also sired the ROM performance horse Toter's Angel.

Photo Courtesy of Phil Livingston

111

[handwritten annotations:]
...tennial Race Track
...lenn Bracken, Owner
...A. Blasingame, Trainer
"Tonto's Angel", 2nd

Pistol Mike

Oct. 19, 1963.
Donald Allison, up
400 yards : 20 4/10
"M. Walt." 3rd

Pistol Mike, by King's Pistol, shown here after winning a 400-yard race at Centennial in Denver on October 19, 1963. Although primarily of working-horse bloodlines, Pistol Mike was a AAA race horse.

Photo Courtesy of Phil Livingston

King's Pistola was another AQHA Champion by King's Pistol. This good-looking dun mare, who was out of Ken Ada Jane, by Waggoner's Rainy Day P-13, was a Superior halter horse with 62 points. **Photo Courtesy of Phil Livingston**

and won the NCHA open cutting. Then I called it quits on going down the road. But I will say that Pistol was a tougher cutting horse when we quit than when we started hauling. With the will that he had, there's no doubt in my mind that we could have done it again."

One example of Pistol's will to win, and the determination that it took to be a champion, happened at Tucson in 1957. Pistol had won the first go-round and was doing a good job in the second when he lost a calf. Because he never lost cattle, Calhoun couldn't figure out the why. After they were through working, however, he looked closely at his horse and saw that one eye was swollen shut. A hay stem had blown into the eye and the horse was temporarily blinded on that side. King's Pistol worked well until he turned his blind side to the calf. Although he couldn't see it any longer, he kept on trying.

King's Pistol was the first stallion to win an NCHA World Championship. Until then, people didn't haul stallions during the breeding season because they caused too much fuss. "But, I didn't have any trouble with him," remembers Calhoun "He was a good horse to haul, would eat and drink

Pistol Lady 2 Be, a gray daughter of King's Pistol, in action with Jim Calhoun aboard. Pistol Lady 2 Be was the last horse that Calhoun competed on before he quit showing. She was the dam of House Mouse and Miss Silver Pistol, two great cutting mares who, between them, won over $1,200,000 in NCHA competition.

Photo by Dalco, Courtesy of Jim Calhoun

anywhere, and a good horse to be around. He stood up well under riding in the trailer all the time that we were on the road, something that a lot of horses can't do.

"Pistol was also smart enough not to fret and fuss as so many stallions do when they are around a bunch of horses. Perhaps that was the result of years of ranch work when he learned that it might be a long, hard day before he was unsaddled. There was no sense in wasting energy when it might be needed before the day was over."

After the horse's retirement at the Fort Worth Fat Stock Show in 1958, Calhoun cut on King's Pistol only one more time. "It was a couple of years afterwards and we were having a little get-together at our place outside of Cresson. Well, Pistol was hanging his head over the stall door like he wanted to work. I went and got him, warmed him up, and then cut a couple of yearlings. He hadn't forgotten a thing and really had a good time out there."

It's evident in any conversation with the Calhouns that King's Pistol was a major part of the family, and unlike some outstanding horses, was not for sale. One instance, in particular, illustrates that point.

Cresson is a small town, and the telephone lines in the area at that time all went through a single operator who knew all the subscribers in the exchange. Late one night Calhoun received a phone call from a fan of King's Pistol, who offered a

lot of money for the stallion. Calhoun turned the man down, as well as mailing back the blank, signed check that he later received from the same individual. The next morning he walked into the single cafe, where the locals all gathered to drink coffee, and sat down at a table. He hadn't been sitting there long when the telephone operator passed by, stopped, and told him that he was a damn fool for turning down that much money for a horse. The man had been listening in on the conversation, as country operators frequently did.

As a sire, King's Pistol had an enviable record. Like their sire, his foals had the serviceable conformation, the athletic ability, the cow sense, and the trainability to make performance horses. His get have excelled in the show ring, the cutting pen, the rodeo arena, and out on the ranch.

King's Michelle was probably King's Pistol's best known performer. This 1954 mare, who was out of Brown Shorty, was eighth in the NCHA top ten in 1960 and third in 1961. In 1962 she was the NCHA Reserve World Champion Cutting Horse and the World Champion Cutting Mare. She was also an NCHA Silver Award winner, for having earned $20,000 or more in NCHA-approved contests.

In AQHA cutting competition, King's

As a sire, King's Pistol had an enviable record.

113

Miss Silver Pistol, a 1982 maternal granddaughter of King's Pistol. Sired by Doc's Hickory, she is shown here winning the non-pro division of the 1985 NCHA Futurity at Fort Worth, with Wes Shahan in the saddle. Miss Silver Pistol had lifetime NCHA earnings of over $500,000.

Photo Courtesy of NCHA

Michelle was a Superior cutting horse with 352 points.

King's Pistola, a 1956 mare out of Ken Ada Jane, by Waggoner's Rainy Day P-13, was the first of King's Pistol's get to earn an AQHA Championship, which she did in 1962. She also earned a Superior in halter with 62 points.

Janie Cal, a 1954 mare out of Ceaser's Bonnie, by Brown Ceaser, was also an AQHA Champion and earned a Superior in cutting with a total of 114 points.

In addition to King's Pistola and Janie Cal, King's Pistol sired three other AQHA Champions: Pistol Toter, Kamay, and Pistol's Lotsip.

Rock Pistol, a 1956 son out of Zantanon Babe, by Zantanon Sorrel, was a Superior cutting horse. Pistol's Machete, a 1960 stallion out of Jazz Band, by Little Jazz, was the AQHA high-point reining stallion in both 1968 and 1971. Pistol's Machete also earned a Superior in reining and had a total of 133 performance points.

Surprisingly, King's Pistol sired one AAA race horse. Pistol Mike, a 1959 stallion out of Lady Mike Bracke, by Cowboy Mike, earned a AAA rating in 1963.

Other noted performance horses by King's Pistol included Tina Pistol, with

67 points; Question Pistol, 126 open and youth points; Pistol's Ace, 46 points; Jimbo Pistol, 42 points; and King Rocky, 42 points.

Pistol's Man, a 1956 stallion out of Jazz Band, by Little Jazz, earned his ROM in performance and went on to become a good sire of performance horses in his own right. Among the notable performers he sired were Pistol's Bit, who earned 540 halter points; and Pistol's Hornet, an AQHA Champion and the 1966, 1967, and 1968 AQHA Honor Roll Calf Roping Horse.

Although many of the daughters of King's Pistol performed creditably under saddle, it is as producers that they were most appreciated.

One such mare was Bonnie Pistol, who foaled the bay stallion Smokin Pistol, by Mr Gun Smoke. Ridden for the most part by Jim Calhoun Jr., Smokey, as he was called, earned a Superior in cutting with 110 points. In NCHA competition, Smokin Pistol earned $13,771, a Certificate of Ability, and a Bronze Award before his death in the spring of 1994.

Competing in the relatively new American Cutting Horse Association, Smokin Pistol was reserve champion open cutting horse in 1985 and champion open cutting horse in 1988. With Jim Jr.'s wife, Beverly, in the saddle, he was also the champion amateur cutting horse in 1988.

According to Dave Brian, Jim Jr.'s brother-in-law and an owner-rider of

Smokin Pistol, by Mr. Gun Smoke and out of Bonnie Pistol, by King's Pistol. Smokin Pistol was an AQHA Superior cutting horse, and a winner in AQHA, NCHA, and American Cutting Horse Association contests before being retired to stud. He died in the spring of 1994.

Photo Courtesy of Dave Brian

the stallion, Smokey was a good ranch horse as well, and sure fun to drag calves on. The ability to work outside the arena was, and still is, the basis for developing a good cutting horse as far as the Calhouns are concerned.

Pistol Lady 2 Be is another King's Pistol daughter who has proven to be an outstanding producer. The gray mare is the last cutting horse that Calhoun competed on before he hung it up. She is the dam of the sensational House Mouse, by Tanquery Gin. House Mouse was the earner of over $700,000 in NCHA competition.

Miss Silver Pistol, by Doc's Hickory, was another daughter of Pistol Lady 2 Be. She was the 1985 NCHA Futurity Non-Pro Champion.

With Tom Lyons aboard, she was the 1986 NCHA Co-Reserve Open Super Stakes Champion. Miss Silver Pistol's earnings in NCHA events totaled over $500,000.

It's easy to determine Pistol's get who were successful in the show ring and cutting arena; but there is no way to total the number of geldings who earned their oats as ranch or rope horses. They were popular with the ropers because of their cow sense, quick speed out of the box, and ability to gather and stop. The rugged conformation was also another plus.

For 17 years King's Pistol was the pride of the Calhoun Ranch. In fact, as the years went on, he became more like a member of the family than just a horse. Jim Calhoun Jr. remembered that Pistol would back clear across the corral to have a person scratch under his butt, something that disturbed first-time visitors since they thought that the stallion might kick. "If a person was seated, Pistol never missed the chance to drop his head in their lap so that he could have his jaw scratched," he added.

Finally, in 1969, with arthritis crippling the stallion so bad that he could hardly get around, Calhoun made the decision to put his old partner to sleep.

"My wife suggested that I have a vet do it, but he was my horse and I felt it was my job," said Calhoun. "I finally got primed to do the chore and drove on out to the ranch one morning. Well, Pistol had passed away during the night. He always could figure out how to stay ahead of a feller."

Author's note: *I interviewed Jim Calhoun for this story early in 1994. He later died of a heart attack, at the age of 63, on July 19, 1994.*

15 MY TEXAS DANDY

By Jim Goodhue

His legend lives on to his present descendants.

HOW CAN a stallion with a decidedly mediocre racing career found a dynasty of runners with such brilliant speed that it is carried on generation after generation? Well, in the case of My Texas Dandy, there are three possible explanations for his indifferent race record.

The first is offered by Will Hysaw, a jockey who helped break My Texas Dandy and who rode him in many of his races. He explained that the stallion broke and ran with such tremendous early speed that he could not make the turns on the small bull-ring tracks available to him. Hysaw said that he usually had to pull My Texas Dandy up to keep him from running through the outside fence after his usual fast breaks and increasing momentum.

Clyde Smith, one of My Texas Dandy's owners during his racing days, pointed to a bad scar on one of the horse's legs as another possible explanation for his mediocre racing career. Although the injury apparently healed, Smith felt that it may have caused strain or pain when My Texas Dandy reached top speed. This may

My Texas Dandy, circa 1945, is shown here at the Uvalde, Tex., ranch of his last owner, George Herndon. Herndon's son, Russell, who had just returned from duty in World War II, is at My Texas Dandy's halter.

Photo Courtesy of Carrie Herndon

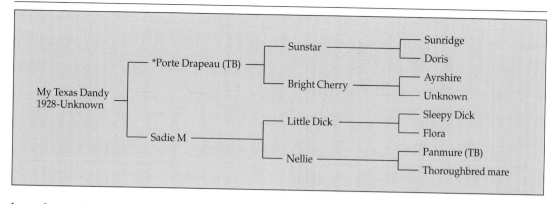

My Texas Dandy
1928-Unknown

- *Porte Drapeau (TB)
  - Sunstar
    - Sunridge
    - Doris
  - Bright Cherry
    - Ayrshire
    - Unknown
- Sadie M
  - Little Dick
    - Sleepy Dick
    - Flora
  - Nellie
    - Panmure (TB)
    - Thoroughbred mare

have been the reason for his races which were so fast at the front end and so slow nearing the finish line. Perhaps the injury also increased the difficulty in his making sharp turns on the small tracks.

Finally, as it appeared from the sidelines, My Texas Dandy simply lost interest in the race after he had gone to the front in the early stages of the race and felt he had shown that he was the best. This quirk might account for the one race credited to him as a win. It has been reported that in that race at Cuero, Tex., the jockey finished the race by throwing the reins away and concentrating on whipping the horse across the finish line.

Note that all three theories are based on the fact that My Texas Dandy broke so fast that it appeared that the other horses had gotten bad starts, and then he kept that speed up at least until he was well in the lead. Certainly My Texas Dandy had the breeding to be a fine race horse.

Back in the 1920s, C.F. Meyers at Ellinger, Tex., was breeding and racing both Thoroughbreds and Quarter Horses. Among other horses, he had an exceptional race mare named Sadie M (sometimes called Sadie Mae). Although she was a part of his Quarter Horse band, she could hold her own at distances up to 5 furlongs.

At this same time, there was a promising young Thoroughbred stallion named *Porte Drapeau, owned by Dr. A.I. Clark, standing at stud in nearby Schulenburg. Though imported from France, *Porte Drapeau was sired by the noted English

sire Sunstar. In addition to *Porte Drapeau, Sunstar made his mark on Quarter Horse racing through his sons *Hand Grenade and *North Star II.

When Smith bred Sadie M to *Porte Drapeau, the result was a powerfully built sorrel colt who was so special looking that he immediately was named Boy Howdy.

About then, one of *Porte Drapeau's Thoroughbred sons, named My Dandy, won several important races in the East and brought considerable prominence to himself and his sire. As a result, *Porte Drapeau was shipped out of Schulenburg and Boy Howdy's name was changed to My Texas Dandy.

It should be noted here that the year in which My Texas Dandy was foaled is somewhat in question. In a feature article on him

117

The QUARTER HORSE

Vol. 3 - No. 7   Entire contents copyrighted 1948   OCTOBER · 1948

Subscription price: $2 per year   *Official Publication of*   Single copies 25c

THE NATIONAL QUARTER HORSE BREEDERS ASSOCIATION

R. J. (Rusty) Bradley, Jr., *President*   DALE GRAHAM and DAVE WOODLOCK, *Editorial Staff*   J. M. Huffington, *Sec'y-Treas.*

His Is the Story of A Bloodline

MY TEXAS DANDY — Twenty-two Years Old Now, This Famous Stallion Has Truly Earned His Title of SIRE OF SPEED — Read His Story on Page Eight

Entered as Second Class matter at the postoffice at Knox City, Texas, July 1, 1946, under Act of March 3, 1879. EDITORIAL, ADVERTISING and CIRCULATION OFFICES: 6204 COLLEGE, HOUSTON 5, TEXAS, Phone Madison 2-1982. DAVE WOODLOCK, Advertising Manager. STAFF: Photographers, TIL THOMPSON (Photochart), 6623 Melrose Ave., Phone York 2759, Hollywood 38, California, specialist in livestock photography and photo-finish; WILCOX PRECISION RACE CAMERAS, Inc., Box 333, Olympia, Wash., photo-finish. Editorial contributors, DANA STONER, Houston; NELSON C. NYE, Tucson; MRS. LUTHER BULLOCK, Springer, New Mexico. While exercising reasonable care the publishers will not be responsible for the safe return of unsolicited manuscripts or photographs sent in for publication.

Picture Credits In This Issue—Page 2, Victoria race strip, Tel-A-Win Photos, Cuero, Texas; Amarillo race, Photochart; Raton race, Til Thompson and staff; Pages 10-11, Billings Show, Western Livestock Reporter, Billings, Montana; Page 25, Kerrville race strips, Til Thompson and staff.

Another shot of My Texas Dandy that was also taken while he was owned by George Herndon, and which appeared on the cover of the October 1948 issue of The Quarter Horse. *Although of dubious quality, this photograph shows that My Texas Dandy was still a good-looking individual at age 22.*

that appeared in the October 1948 issue of *The Quarter Horse*, My Texas Dandy is said to have been foaled in 1926. However, AQHA Stud Book No. 5 lists his foaling date as 1928. At this point, neither date can be proved or disproved.

Most of the Meyer-bred Thoroughbreds were sent to Louisiana to be campaigned because of higher purses and the popularity there of longer races. The newly re-christened My Texas Dandy, with his infusion of Quarter Horse blood, was not eligible for such racing, however, and remained in Texas with its bull-ring tracks.

As a 2-year-old, My Texas Dandy was acquired by Dr. Henry Mayer of Hondo, Tex., and was put in race training with Charley Brenham. It was Brenham who broke and first tried to race the good-looking youngster at the Texas tracks.

After several unprofitable races, My Texas Dandy was bought for $250 by J.C. Smith, who made the purchase on behalf of his father, Clyde Smith, at Big Foot, Texas. The senior Smith was a well-known breeder and it is reported that, after viewing the newcomer, he gave his son some rather pointed parental advice pertaining to buying losers.

When Clyde Smith saw My Texas Dandy running, however, he changed his tune and kept the blaze-faced sorrel in training. The results, however, were no better. But Smith still was impressed with My Texas Dandy's early speed and decided to use him for breeding purposes.

Before My Texas Dandy's foals became well-known, though, Smith sold him to a Mr. Winn of Uvalde, Tex., for $400. Winn, in turn, sold the stallion for $400 in 1939 to Carroll Thompson of Devine, Texas. Thompson wanted the horse because he was so impressed with a My Texas Dandy filly he owned named Ginger Rogers.

Unfortunately, no one else discerned the

possibilities in the My Texas Dandy foals and Thompson had trouble selling them. One sold for as little as $60 and Thompson, disheartened, sold My Texas Dandy in 1941 to George R. Herndon of North Uvalde, Texas. Herndon kept My Texas Dandy until the castoff stallion died many years later—no one seems to remember exactly when.

Slowly but surely, however, the value of the sons and daughters of My Texas Dandy became apparent. They began to acquire the reputation for being speedy, athletic horses who could pass on their speed and athleticism.

Three of his sons, in particular, figure in giving My Texas Dandy the reputation of being a "sire of sires." They were Colonel Clyde, Clabber, and Texas Dandy.

The earliest of these, Colonel Clyde, was foaled in 1932 or 1933, depending on whose memory was called upon to supply the foaling date. M.S. (Morris) Ridgeway, who is usually credited with breeding Colonel Clyde (though not by the AQHA Stud Book at the time he was registered), remembered it as 1933.

On his ranch at Devine, Tex., Ridgeway had a mare he called Old Red. She traced to Traveler (through his sons Captain Joe and Possum) and once through a daughter who was the second dam of Old Red. After developing a fistula as a filly, Old Red never was given the chance to run. As a broodmare, however, she showed her mettle. She first produced a noted polo pony named Trixie and then came up with a filly called Whirlwind (by Uncle Jimmie Gray). Whirlwind beat some excellent horses during her racing career and later became a highly successful roping horse in professional rodeos.

My Texas Dandy was very easy to handle, according to Ridgeway, and so Clyde Smith hauled him around in a pickup truck to mate with mares in that region. Since the Ridgeway ranch and the Smith ranch adjoined, however, Ridgeway simply took Old Red next door to be bred to My Texas Dandy.

A light sorrel colt was the product of

Colonel Clyde, a great son of My Texas Dandy, hazing at a Reno, Nev., rodeo with John Bowman in the saddle. Colonel Clyde was a well-known race horse, ranch horse, and rodeo mount in the Southwest during the late 1930s and early 1940s. He also sired several Register of Merit race and performance horses including Catch Rope, Duke, Just Luck, Major Clyde, Prissy, and Decoration.

The ill-fated Prissy, by Colonel Clyde. The 1947 yearbook of the American Quarter Racing Association, from which this photograph was taken, listed Prissy as one of the top stakes horses of that year. On April 17, 1947, however, both Prissy and her jockey, Carl Ewing, were killed in a tragic racing accident that occured at Eagle Pass, Texas.

My Texas Dandy Jr, a top son of My Texas Dandy. Foaled in 1944, the sorrel stallion was out of Dandy Beth Herndon, by Tom Mix, by Uncle Jimmie Gray (TB). My Texas Dandy Jr was bred by the Herndons and was raced for the most part in AQRA-sanctioned events, under the name of Texas Jr. He does hold an official AAA rating with the AQHA, however, and once held the world record for 250 yards. My Texas Dandy Jr sired a number of ROM race and performance horses and was the maternal grandsire of Miss Louton, the 1958 Champion Quarter Running 2-Year-Old Filly. In this picture, the two handlers are not identified, but the jockey is Santos Lopez.

Photo by Tommy Thompson, Courtesy of Carrie Herndon

Here's another picture of My Texas Dandy Jr. Russell Herndon is holding him. In those early racing days, young boys were often used as jockeys and this jock looks like he learned to ride before he learned to walk. He is not identified.

Photo Courtesy of Carrie Herndon

this union and Ridgeway was going to name him Clyde in honor of the sire's owner. When the Smith family named one of their My Texas Dandy colts Captain White Socks, though, Ridgeway decided to practice a bit of one-upsmanship. He started calling the youngster Colonel Clyde, instead of just Clyde.

Colonel Clyde was allowed to run in the pasture until he was about 20 months old. He was easy to handle and Ridgeway did the breaking and training honors himself.

As a test of the two young horses, Ridgeway and Smith matched Colonel Clyde and Captain White Socks in a 350-yard race. The Colonel outranked the Captain in this race, too, as Colonel Clyde won by a length.

Then Ridgeway put Colonel Clyde in a 3-furlong race on the small circle track at Seguin, Texas. He broke like a veteran and was 5 lengths ahead of nine other 2-year-olds when he came to the first turn. At that point, however, he repeated his sire's history and failed to make the turn. Drifting to the outside rail, he slammed on his brakes in time to avoid going through the rail. The jockey apparently was not aware of this

This is V Dandy, a good-looking ROM son of My Texas Dandy, out of Dandy Miss Eight. This picture was taken after V Dandy won a 220-yard race, probably at Eagle Pass, Tex., on October 21, 1949. Shown are George Herndon at V Dandy's head and George's brothers Elmer (left) and Pal (right).

Photo Courtesy of Carrie Herndon

family trait, though, and he became air-borne, landing on the other side of the rail.

The last race Colonel Clyde ran under Ridgeway's ownership was another 3-furlong event at Seguin, even though Ridgeway knew by that time that 3 furlongs was beyond Colonel Clyde's true inclinations. However, Colonel Clyde had learned how to get a big lead at the start and still manage to make the turn. At the head of the stretch, he was 10 lengths in front of the field. Gamely, Colonel Clyde held on to win by a margin of less than a head.

Later, Colonel Clyde became a part of the stable of A.A. "Ab" Nichols, the famous Arizona race horse man. Nichols campaigned Colonel Clyde successfully until the horse got the attention of noted all-around rodeo contestant John Bowman of Oakdale, California. After seeing Colonel Clyde beat one of the leading Arizona sprinters in a matched race, Bowman decided he could use this son of My Texas Dandy. Colonel Clyde had matured to just under 15 hands, and weighed about 1,100 pounds.

By 1938, Nichols had on his Gilbert ranch another outstanding My Texas Dandy race prospect named Clabber. Although both Nichols and Bowman have

Texas Dandy, a 1942 son of My Texas Dandy was out of Streak, by Lone Star. He was owned by the Finley Ranches of Gilbert and Dragoon, Arizona. The sire of numerous ROM race horses, he is listed as a leading maternal grandsire of ROM race horses. He also sired three AQHA Champions, and seven ROM performance horses, and Dandy Doll, the dam of Doc Bar. This picture appeared in AQHA Stud Book No. 5, and is reproduced here courtesy of AQHA.

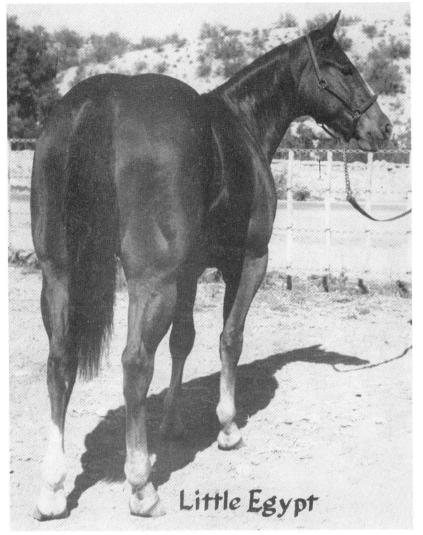

Little Egypt

Little Egypt was by Texas Dandy and out of Jezebel, by Pigeon, by Red Joe of Arizona. She was one of the first eight AQHA Champions ever named, receiving that honor in the fall of 1952. She was also the breed's first AAA AQHA Champion and the 1952 Honor Roll Race Horse. Bred and owned by Finley Ranches, she was the dam of Bank Night AAA, Bar Flirt AAAT, Casbar AAA, and Garter Gal AAA.

Photo by L.F. Henderson

reported that Colonel Clyde could beat Clabber at one-eighth of a mile, and Nichols had Colonel Clyde open to the world at that distance, Nichols was persuaded to part with Colonel Clyde.

Bowman changed directions with his new mount and started using him for all kinds of ranch work, including cutting and branding. Colonel Clyde proved to be a level-headed and alert cutting horse. He was gentle enough to become a favorite mount for Bowman's young children. He also won the only two races in which Bowman matched him.

After becoming a real using horse, Colonel Clyde almost immediately moved on to professional rodeos where he got on-the-job training in actual rodeo events. Colonel Clyde carried Bowman and his brother, Everett, to roping wins at most of the major rodeos of the era. He was also the mount of champion Homer Pettigrew in steer wrestling events. Carl Dorsey and Buckshot Sorrells both roped and wrestled steers from this versatile performer.

As a sire, Colonel Clyde also proved to be superior. During the 1940s, one of the leading sprinters was his ill-fated daughter, Prissy. She set a world record for 350 yards and beat such classy runners as Miss Bank, Blondie, and Queenie. After several successful years as a runner throughout the Southwest, Prissy was killed when she went through the inside rail during a race at Eagle Pass, Tex., although there was no interference from other horses in the race. Since her jockey, Carl Ewing, was killed at the same time (April 17, 1947), there was never an explanation for the accident.

Decoration, a good-looking son of Colonel Clyde, was another versatile performer. He carried his breeder, John Bowman, to wins in both calf roping and steer roping at major rodeos. Bowman won the all-around cowboy title at the

1945 Pendleton Round-up on Decoration. Upholding his sire's tradition, Decoration also was an adept cutting horse.

The second of My Texas Dandy's greatest sons was Clabber, who was foaled in 1936, out of Blondie S, by Lone Star. Clabber's colorful life is detailed in another chapter in this book.

The third My Texas Dandy son to ensure that his sire's name would go down in history had the somewhat confusing name of Texas Dandy. A foal of 1942, Texas Dandy was out of Streak, a daughter of Lone Star, by Gold Enamel (TB). His breeder was R.C. Tatum of Junction, Texas.

In Arizona, about three-fourths of a mile from the Nichols Ranch at Gilbert, was one of the Finley ranches. There, two young men named Jack and Tom Finley worked with their father in the ranching enterprise.

The Finleys were acquainted with Colonel Clyde and had seen Clabber contested both on the racetrack and in rodeo roping events. Tom Finley recalls that the Nichols family also successfully used a daughter of My Texas Dandy, called Blue Bonnet, in roping events. Tom says that Blue Bonnet was one of the most beautiful mares, in an athletic way, he ever saw.

So, when the younger Finleys decided in 1946 that they wanted to move up in the Quarter Horse world, they began to look for a stallion from the My Texas Dandy line. Tom says, "We were looking for a horse with speed and cow sense." They heard that Texas Dandy had been put in an auction by W.A. Northington of Egypt, Tex., so Tom and Jack journeyed to Texas to have a look.

They liked what they saw—a speedy-looking horse with the conformation to indicate all-around athletic ability. By this time, Texas Dandy had run a couple of races at Eagle Pass and was a winner. They also liked the looks of two of Texas Dandy's foals who preceded him in the sale ring.

When Texas Dandy came into the auction, the Finleys sat patiently while the auctioneer seemed to have some difficulty in knowing when he had actual bids. So when the bidding was started over, the Finleys got into the fray. They bought the

Dandy Time was a AAA-rated son of Texas Dandy, and was out of Fleet F, by Chicaro Bill. Foaled in 1951, Dandy Time is shown here immediately after tying the gelding world record for 330 yards at Rillito in March 1953. Owner Tom Finley is at Dandy Time's head and John Hazelwood, an early-day AQHA inspector, is standing next to Finley.
Photo Courtesy of Jim Goodhue

123

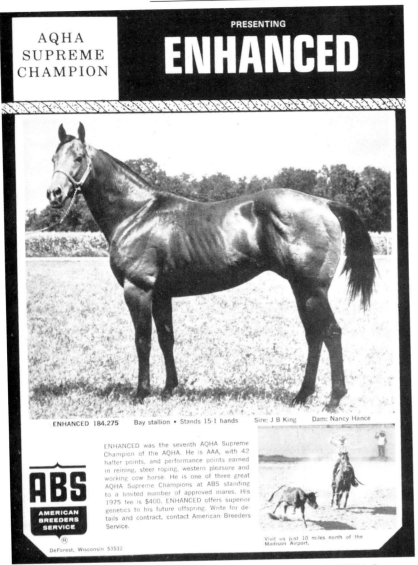

ENHANCED 184,275   Bay stallion • Stands 15-1 hands   Sire: J B King   Dam: Nancy Hance

*Enhanced, a maternal grandson of My Texas Dandy, was the seventh AQHA Supreme
Champion. Foaled in 1961, Enhanced was by J.B. King and out of Nancy Hance. In
addition to a AAA race rating, this bay stallion had 42 halter points and 19.5 performance points in reining, steer roping, western pleasure, and working cow horse.*

admitted the price tag. When their father
asked where the other horses were that
they got for their $5,250, they owned up
to the fact that there was just one horse
involved. Gradually, the elder Finley came
to agree that the price was reasonable.

The Finleys raced Texas Dandy a few
times—winning a race at Sportsman Park
in Phoenix and another at Rillito Race
Track over such horses as Hill Country and
Annetta—before they began using him full
time as a ranch using horse and as a sire.

Early on, Texas Dandy sired the Register
of Merit runners Chicaro Dandy and
Dandy Duke, the latter being one of the
top 2-year-olds of 1949, according to the
American Quarter Racing Association Year
Book. He later sired Dandy Time who, as a
2-year-old, was the co-holder of the 330-
yard world record for geldings of all
ages. As a matter of fact, Texas Dandy
sired a string of winners on the racetrack,
the performance arena, and the halter ring.

Texas Dandy's 239 registered foals include 137 performers in official AQHA
events. Among them are three AQHA
Champions, one Youth AQHA Champion,
three Superior race horses, and two Superior halter horses. He sired eight Register of
Merit qualifiers in performance events and
forty-nine in racing (including one TAAA,
thirteen AAA, and twenty-two AA).

When asked about the most outstanding foal by Texas Dandy, Tom Finley does
not hesitate to name Little Egypt. Not only
was this filly an AAA AQHA Champion,
she was the very first horse to earn both of
those honors.

Tom recalls the time he took Little Egypt
to show in halter at Tucson the day before
she was to run an important race at Rillito.
He says, "John Hazelwood sure was mad
at me about that." Hazelwood, trainer of
the Finley race horses and who later became a very respected inspector for the
AQHA, felt better when Little Egypt not
only won the race, but also set a record for
2-year-old fillies at 330 yards. Too, she had
been the grand champion mare in the
show the day before.

The Finleys also bred another noteworthy
daughter of Texas Dandy. She was a good
AA runner named Dandy Doll, who won

young stallion for $5,250, a big price in
those days and about twice what they had
come prepared to pay.

Then they returned to Arizona to show
the new purchase to their father. With the
price in mind, Tom says, "The closer we got
to Arizona, the slower we drove." Carefully
not telling the senior Finley what they paid,
they made sure he got a good look at the
handsome Texas Dandy before they

at distances from 220 yards to 440 yards. She will live in the annals of Quarter Horse history, however, as the dam of Doc Bar. A son of Lightning Bar, Doc Bar was a flop as a runner, but was a good halter winner and then proved to be brilliant as the sire of cutting horses. (Doc Bar is featured in *Legends 1*.) Texas Dandy died on the Finley ranch at Gilbert and was buried in a paddock near his stall.

Other acknowledged speedsters that My Texas Dandy sired included Texas Jr (registered as My Texas Dandy Jr), Ginger Rogers, Battle Creek, Texas Star, Nancy Hance, Captain White Socks, Free Silver, Oscar, Tiny Texas, Chew, Peter Pan Dandy, and Golden Slippers. He also sired the speedy calf roping stallion Dynamite.

My Texas Dandy also excelled as a broodmare sire. His daughters produced a total of 157 starters, 54 of whom qualified for their Registers of Merit. Racing mostly in the 1950s and 1960s, they won 243 races and $152,364.

Chain Lay, a 1941 daughter of My Texas Dandy, and out of Manosa, by Uncle Jimmie Gray (TB), produced five ROM runners including Boom Chain AAA; Chain Truckle AAA; and Gill Chain AAA.

Nancy Hance, a 1942 daughter out of Herndon's Dolly, by Uncle Jimmie Gray (TB), produced eight ROM horses including Enhanced, AQHA Supreme Champion; Nancy Twist AAA; Half Twist AAA; Nancy Parsons AAA; and Big Nance AAA.

Among the other ROM-producing daughters of My Texas Dandy were Buttermilk Thompson, Dandy One, Fanny, Kneeka, Indian Girl Canales, Texas Pride W, Cameo Girl, Carole Dandy, Golden Slippers W, Miss Texas Gal, Texas Star Miers, Ida Redsailes, Lows Elsie, Yeager's Miss Texas, Dianna Dandy, Dandy Midget, Skeet Doll, May Dandy, Shrimp Boat,

Mayflower W, a good-looking daughter of Flying Bob, out of Texas Pride W, by My Texas Dandy. Foaled in 1945, Mayflower W was a hard-knocking competitor in both AQRA- and AQHA-sanctioned races and earned an official AAA rating from the AQHA. At one time, the speedy filly held track records for 300, 330, and 440 yards.

and Hovito Dandy.

The legend of My Texas Dandy lives on through his sons and daughters, his grandget, and to his present descendants. Each generation has added even more acclaim to the family history and has proven additional justification for the faith C. R. Herndon had in his undervalued horse. It's a remarkable record for a stallion whose various owners despaired of ever winning races with him.

16 CLABBER

By Phil Livingston

He was nicknamed the Iron Horse because he stayed sound in spite of years of hard use.

HE WAS big, rawboned, plain-headed, tough as a piece of sun-dried rawhide, and he had an independent disposition that kept a rider alert. But, Clabber could win a race, work cattle all day, and carry a roper to a set of horns or to a calf to win a roping. Frequently, he did all three in the same day. He also stayed sound and usable in spite of all the hard use. This trait helped to earn him the nickname of the Iron Horse.

More importantly, he sired horses who were capable of doing the same things and who had the same physical characteristics. All of those traits endeared him to southwestern horsemen during the 1940s and 1950s, and riding a Clabber meant that a man was mounted.

Twenty-seven of his get, as well as numerous grandsons and granddaughters, had a Register of Merit in racing. Since many of his early foals were not regis-

Clabber as a mature horse during the years he was owned by Frank Vessels. This photo shows the overall conformation and dense bone that allowed him to stand up under the years of racing, roping, and ranch work. His head, however, left something to be desired.

Photo Courtesy of Phil Livingston

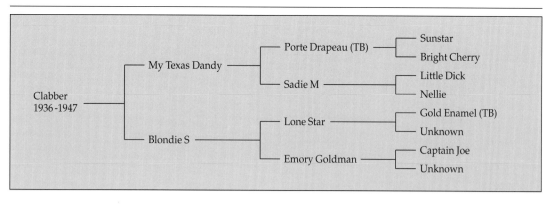

```
                                          ┌─── Sunstar
                        ┌─ Porte Drapeau (TB) ─┤
            ┌─ My Texas Dandy ─┤              └─── Bright Cherry
            │           │                     ┌─── Little Dick
            │           └─ Sadie M ───────────┤
Clabber ────┤                                 └─── Nellie
1936-1947   │                                 ┌─── Gold Enamel (TB)
            │           ┌─ Lone Star ─────────┤
            └─ Blondie S ─┤                    └─── Unknown
                         │                    ┌─── Captain Joe
                         └─ Emory Goldman ────┤
                                              └─── Unknown
```

tered, there is no record of those used as ranch or rodeo mounts over a 20-year period, but it had to be considerable. The list of Arizona and California ropers who went to the pay window on Clabber-bred geldings would be impressive. This would include Ike Rude, who tripped steers on the reliable Buster.

As broodmares, the Clabber daughters were in demand and carried on the chestnut stallion's legacy of speed. A horseman could easily tell a Clabber, since the prepotent stallion stamped his get with his image, speed, and athletic ability.

In describing Clabber's get, one Arizona rancher and roper in the 1950s stated, "They can all run, you can't kill 'em off, they savvy a cow, and if you rub 'em the wrong way, they can sure buck you off."

Considered to be the greatest son of My Texas Dandy, the hard-knocking Clabber established an enviable reputation as a race horse and sire of speed in the short decade that he lived. Even now, many years after his death in 1947, his name in a pedigree still denotes physical toughness and the ability to streak down the track.

While there is no doubt about the identity of Clabber's sire, there exists some confusion about just who his dam was. Volume I of the AQHA studbook lists Clabber as being out of Golden Wheel, by the U.S. Government Remount stallion Uncle Jimmy Grey (TB), by Bonnie Joe. Bob Denhardt, first secretary of the AQHA, later commented that he felt the pedigree was incorrect; he blamed it on his poor handwriting, with someone misinterpreting *Girl* as *Wheel*. Then he failed to catch the mistake during the proofreading process before the book went to print.

Melville Haskell of the American Quarter Racing Association was working independently on pedigrees at that same time and listed Clabber as being out of Golden Girl, a granddaughter of Possum (who was

Halter and Performance Record: Register of Merit Racing; 1940-41 World Champion Quarter Running Stallion; 1940-41 World Champion Quarter Running Horse.

Progeny Record:

Foal Crops: 10	Performance Points Earned: 2
Foals Registered: 116	Race Money Earned: $46,114
Halter Point-Earners: 1	Race Registers of Merit: 27
Halter Points Earned: 1	Race Starters: 52
Performance Point-Earners: 1	World Champions: 1
Leading Race Money-Earner: Clabbertown G ($16,132)	

Clabber as a younger horse, in good working condition.
Photo Courtesy of the American Quarter Horse Heritage Center & Museum, Amarillo, Texas

first known as King). This is also the way that Clabber's pedigree is listed in the first edition of *Racing Quarter Horses*, edited by Melville Haskell for the Southern Arizona Horse Breeders' Association in 1943. It was also substantiated by Jo Flieger and

Clabber as a ranch horse.

Photo Courtesy of Phil Livingston

This photograph of Clabber was taken after he won the Tucson Derby in August 1941.
Photo Courtesy of Buck Nichols

other Arizonans who knew the horse well, both during his racing and rodeo days and after he was retired to stud duty.

Later issues of the AQHA studbooks show Clabber's dam as being Blondie S, by Lone Star, by Gold Enamel (TB). Blondie's dam is given as a Captain Joe

mare, Emory Goldman. The October 1948 issue of *The Quarter Horse* (published by the National Quarter Horse Breeders Association), in an article about Clabber's sire, My Texas Dandy, also lists Clabber as a son of Blondie S, one of the great Lone Star mares. In either case, the bottom side of Clabber's pedigree was loaded with speed to match that of his sire's.

Bred by Frank Smith, Clabber was foaled in 1936, on Smith's south Texas ranch near Big Foot. The stout, chestnut colt already had a host of well-known half-brothers and sisters. To name three: Colonel Clyde, Captain White Sox, and Ginger Rogers, all of whom had made reputations on the short tracks of the Southwest.

Another half-brother, foaled a few years later in 1942, was Texas Dandy, who became an outstanding sire. Among his get was Dandy Doll, who became the dam of Doc Bar.

A.A. "Ab" Nichols, of Gilbert, Ariz., had owned and liked several horses sired by My Texas Dandy, including Colonel Clyde and Captain White Socks, and he wanted another. He went to Big Foot in the spring of 1938 and purchased Clabber. He picked the colt for two reasons. He liked his looks, and his dam was a top mare from a line known for speed.

At that time, the chestnut was without a name. His older brother, Captain White Socks, had demonstrated a fondness for soured milk while owned by Ab, so the amused Nichols boys named the second My Texas Dandy colt "Clabber" when they got him home.

This ad for Clabber appeared in the September-October 1941 issue of Western Horseman *magazine.*

It didn't take long for Nichols to put his new horse to work on the ranch. Ab was a cowman of the old school and he expected every man and horse on the place to earn his keep. Clabber learned his lessons rapidly and became an all-around cow horse. He probably headed more cattle in one spring for Nichols than most cow horses ever do in a lifetime.

The Nichols boys didn't waste any time in showing Clabber what a calf looked like either. The big chestnut took to roping like a duck takes to water. In fact, the calves looked as if they were running in deep sand since Clabber caught them so rapidly. And he had a hard stop. He was also used for heading and heeling which, in Arizona in those years, was team tying. In this event, it took a tough, stout, nervy horse to stand up under the strain.

Nichols quickly realized how much speed the colt had, and Clabber was soon matched at local ropings, rodeos, and Sunday afternoon race meets.

Clabber matured into a powerfully made individual, with dense, heavy bone, a functional frame, and solid muscling. In fact, if it hadn't been for his big, coarse head, he would have been a good-looking horse. But, as the cowboys said, that head was just to hang the bridle on; looks didn't have anything to do with what was in it or the desire to win. His coat was a bright chestnut, with a sock on his left rear foot and a wandering streak down his face.

It was during those early years of match racing that the title of the Iron Horse was pinned on Clabber. Nichols didn't go in for special training of his race horses. There was just ranch work . . . and lots of it. As far

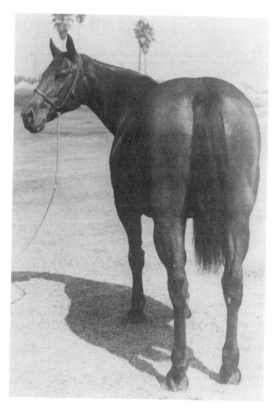

Clabber's Flossie V., an unraced daughter of Clabber, out of Flossie, by Duggan. Foaled in 1946, she was a tremendous producer, with six AAA foals and seven who earned their ROM in racing. Among them was Clabber's Win, by Direct Win (TB), who was the 1957 Champion Quarter Running 3-Year-Old Stallion.

Clabber matured into a powerfully made individual, with dense, heavy bone, a functional frame, and solid muscling.

as bandages, blankets, liniment, a deeply bedded clean stall, and lots of brushing, Nichols just didn't see any sense in it. In a 1964 *Quarter Horse Journal* article, Bob Denhardt quoted Nichols as saying, "He (Clabber) could outrun those pampered horses that smelled like a drug store any day of the week and twice on Sundays."

And Clabber could. While he was owned by the Gilbert rancher, he ran at all of the scheduled meets at Tucson's Moltaqua Racetrack. Many times Clabber

ture event of the day, he defeated the top Texas horses of the year, including the King Ranch's Nobody's Friend, Balmy L., and Little Joe Jr., to become the talk of the meet.

Racetrack legend had it that no small amount of money changed hands that day, most of it leaving Texas for Arizona. The story is also told that, according to one man who was there, Clabber also was bred to a mare between the last two races. "I know, because I owned the mare," he said.

Richard Kleberg, of the King Ranch, had a story about that final race. He was there to see it, and was involved in the aftermath. Bob Denhardt told the story in his book, *The King Ranch Quarter Horses*. George Clegg was running Nobody's Friend for the King Ranch and, the morning after the race, several of Clegg's friends rubbed in the defeat.

"George's room was next to mine at the hotel in Eagle Pass," commented Kleberg. "About 5 a.m., I heard a knocking on the door. I thought it was at mine and got up to answer it. There at the next door, which was George's, were a couple of his friends bringing him a big bowl of clabber."

The American Quarter Racing Association awarded Clabber the titles of World Champion Quarter Running Horse and World Champion Quarter Running Stallion for 1940-41.

During one of his races at Tucson's Moltacqua Racetrack, Clabber acted up in the starting gate, and it took two men to hold him in with a rope run through his bit. When the gates opened, Clabber lunged and jerked the rope away from his handlers. This caused Clabber to fall to his knees, and he was virtually left at the post with his jockey desperately trying to get off his neck and back into the saddle. That would have been enough to eliminate most horses, but the Iron Horse got up, turned on the gas, and won the race with the rope still dangling from his bit.

The time for the 440 yards was :22.4. The start, from an open gate set back from the line, was timed from a flag and cannot be compared with modern times.

Writing in *The Running Quarter Horse*, Melville Haskell commented: "Clabber is a horse of great power—he seems to thrive on rough treatment. During his racing career he has served about 100 mares a year, been used as a cow horse and rope horse, been turned out to pasture and then taken up, been hauled several hundred

Tonto Bars Hank, a paternal great grandson of Clabber. He was rated TAAA, won the 1960 All-American Futurity, and was the 1960 Champion Quarter Running 2-Year-Old Colt and Champion Quarter Running Stallion.

Photo by Wayne Hunt, Courtesy of Phil Livingston

worked cattle all morning, was trucked to a brush track to sprint 440 yards, and then was trucked home to finish the chores in the cutting or branding pen. On at least one occasion, he spent the morning moving cattle, the afternoon at a rodeo where he was ridden by several contestants in both roping events, and then won a quarter-mile dash after that.

There was no doubt in anyone's mind that he had to be made of iron to stand up under it all.

More than once, he ran two races on a Sunday, after chasing cows all week on the ranch and maybe going to a roping on Saturday. At one time, Nichols issued an offer to match any horse for any amount for a quarter-mile. After Clabber daylighted two challengers in one afternoon, other running horse owners quit coming around.

More than a few of Clabber's races were run under an impost of 135 pounds, and he was competition for any horse regardless of the weight. In 1941, at Eagle Pass, Tex., he ran three quarter-mile sprints in one afternoon and won each of them in 23 seconds. The last two sprints were only an hour and a half apart. In the final one, the fea-

It was as a sire that Clabber really made his mark. His best get seemed to come from daughters of Possum (King), who could run a little themselves.

miles in a trailer to race, without training, and hauled home the same day. In spite of all these handicaps, he is one of the most consistent performers we know of."

Clabber's racing career peaked in 1941. The rough treatment, ranch and rodeo use, plus heavy stud duty, apparently began to take its toll, for in 1942 the big-hearted chestnut lost both the AQRA World Championship to Elmer Hepler's Shue Fly by a neck and the stallion championship to the King Ranch's Nobody's Friend (TB). He did give a good account of himself, however, being individually timed in :22.4.

Nichols sent him back to the track in 1943 and he was again narrowly beaten for both championships, again by the great Shue Fly for the world champion title, and by Joe Reed II for the stallion title. There was a lot of run left in the old horse, however, and he lowered the track record at Tucson to :18.4 for 350 yards.

The hard-knocking chestnut was still held in high regard by horsemen, and Haskell wrote: "During the 1943 Quarter Horse Speed Trials, the track at Moltacqua was slow and the wind blew a gale straight up the track, but we had a good measuring stick in Clabber, the honest, big, chestnut son of My Texas Dandy who runs his race every time for all there is in him, and he isn't often beaten by anything but a champion.

"In the world's championship, Shue Fly showed her class by beating him a scant neck. In the stallion championship, Joe Reed II caught him at the eighth pole, but he hung on gamely to the wire in one of the most exciting finishes ever seen at Moltacqua and was called second by a nose," continued Haskell.

Like all racers, Clabber was not invincible. In addition to Joe Reed II and Shue Fly, he was beaten by such celebrated speedsters as Red Man, Cyclone, Driftwood, and Arizona Girl. He could be outrun, but it took a real race horse to do it, and he never gave up.

By 1944, the Iron Horse was really showing the wear and tear of the lack of training, heavy stud service, and the miles of cowboying. But he did beat the colorful Painted Joe in two matches. The best, however, that he could do in the stallion race at the Speed Trials at Moltacqua was a dead heat with Bartender in :24.2. Although Clabber's racing star had set by 1944, two of his sons were building his reputation as a sire of

Tonta Gal, Clabber's best-producing daughter, was an exceptional race mare. From 28 official starts, she had 13 wins, 3 seconds, and 6 thirds. As a broodmare, she produced six ROM runners, including the well-known Tonto Bars Gill AAA.

Photo Courtesy of Phil Livingston

Tonto Bars Gill AAA, the 1952 Champion Quarter Running 3-Year-Old Colt, was a maternal grandson of Clabber. As a breeding horse, he sired Tonto Bars Hank TAAA, and Miss Louton TAAA and the Champion Quarter Running Filly at ages 2 and 3.

Wagon N, a chestnut horse foaled in 1945, was by Clabber and out of Lady Luck, by Lucky. He was generally considered as the best son of Clabber. In addition to being a good race horse, rated AA, he looked good in a halter class, could cut a cow, was a top rodeo horse, and sired more just like him. **Photo Courtesy of Phil Livingston**

speed. The publication, *Racing Quarter Horses*, carried this interesting piece by Melville Haskell: "It is beginning to look as though the name Clabber will live on through his get. His 2-year-old son, Jeep, distinguished himself at Rillito and has set remarkable records for the 220 (12 flat) and the 330 (:17.4 to defeat the good mare Prissy), at Corona, California.

"Chester C proved to be a fast colt as well, a credit to his sire. Another 3-year-old son, Buster (300 yards in :16.1), made a name in Arizona last season in match races, and Flicka (220 yards in :12.1 and 350 in :11.2) showed her class."

As with any individual with an outstanding reputation, stories abound about Clabber. One is told about his first appearance at the Eagle Pass, Tex., race meet, about 1940.

Seeking to match his still unknown speedster against the Texas horses, Ab Nichols took advantage of the fact that the Army was in the area for maneuvers. He led his rough-coated, big-headed horse over to the field artillery picket lines (light cannons were still pulled by four-horse teams at the time) and tied him up. No one has ever told the details, but it is probable that Ab had made some arrangements with the soldiers.

After a suitable buildup, Nichols offered to run one of the Army horses against a challenger. The laughing Texans took him up on the deal, sensing some easy money. Clabber may not have been known before the race, but he definitely was afterwards, and the bankroll of his backers was substantially enlarged.

When his racing days were over, Clabber went back to ranch work, rodeoing, and breeding all the mares who came his way. It was said that "a person could breed him to a packing crate and get a pretty fair colt." The stallion passed on a considerable amount of his speed, rugged conformation, and toughness to his get.

After World War II, Frank Vessels purchased Clabber from Nichols and moved him to his Los Alamitos, Calif., stables. Vessels built the Los Alamitos racetrack and was a well-known breeder of speed horses. After Clabber spent years on the Arizona ranch, on racetracks, and in roping arenas, his new life must have been a peaceful one. At Los Alamitos, Clabber was bred to a variety of mares, the majority of them proven producers of speed, and he had the opportunity to sire some really top individuals. Yet, he also sired exceptional horses who were out of average mares.

Vessels was once quoted by the well-known Quarter Horse writer Nelson Nye as follows: "Clabber produced some very good horses from some very ordinary mares, and although most of the offspring had many of his conformational defects, they also had much of his ability, desire to run, and general intelligence."

It was as a sire that Clabber really made his mark. His best get seemed to come from daughters of Possum (King), who could run a little themselves. (Note: Possum was first known as King, but he is not the same horse as King P-234.) The Clabber-Possum cross produced such speedsters as Buster, Jeep, Chester C., Flicka, and Tonta Gal, all of whom earned ROMs.

Tonta Gal, out of Peggy Cooper, by Doc, was rated AAA and set records at two tracks. She was bred by Chester Cooper, and her race record shows 13 wins, 3 seconds, and 6 thirds in 28 official starts. As a broodmare, she was Clabber's best-producing daughter. Among her offspring was Tonto Bars Gill, by Three Bars (TB). Foaled in 1949, he was sensational on the track, earning a AAA rating and the title of 1952 Champion Quarter Running Stallion.

When retired to stud, Tonto Bars Gill became a leading sire of ROM race colts and a leading maternal grandsire of ROM race colts. Among his sons was the celebrated Tonto Bars Hank AAAT, winner of the first All-American Futurity in 1960.

Bombardier was considered as the best-looking son of Clabber, and he accumulated points at halter and reining.

Wagon N would probably get the nod as the best son of Clabber. Bred by Buck Nichols and foaled in 1945, he was out of Lady Luck, by Lucky, by My Texas Dandy, and earned his ROM in racing. Like his sire, he was extra tough and raced for seven long seasons, taking on and defeating many quality horses—such as Silhouette, Black Easter, Ariel Lady, Tess S., and Little Sister W.

Wagon N's daily schedule often included being used as a pony horse in the morning, breeding a mare right after lunch, and then being loaded into the gate for an afternoon stakes race. He also won at halter and cutting, and was used as a heeling mount. He sired a number of racing, using, and show mounts, including Clabber Juan AAAT, and the 1954 Champion Quarter Running 3-Year-Old Stallion.

Although Clabber had many more outstanding sons and daughters, and although space prevents listing all of them, here are a few:

Clabber II, foaled in 1946, out of the mare Do Good, by St. Louis; was AAA and a leading maternal grandsire of ROM race colts.

Clabbertown G, foaled in 1946, out of Caroline, by Ben Hur; was AAA and the 1951 Champion Quarter Running Stallion.

Peggy N, foaled in 1941, out of Peggy Cooper, by Doc; a leading dam of ROM race colts.

Clabber's Flossie V, foaled in 1946, out of Flossie, by Duggan. This mare was never raced, but produced seven ROM race foals, including six who were AAA. Among them was Clabber's Win AAAT, by Direct Win (TB), the 1957 Champion Quarter Running 3-Year-Old Stallion.

Clabber Girl, foaled in 1942, out of a mare by Mark. Bred by Ab Nichols, she was owned by Tom Finley, was a champion halter mare, and produced four ROM race foals.

Clabber earned his position on the AQHA List of Leading Sires and Grandsires, along with his sons Clabber Bar

CLABBER II AQHA #P-14,556
Sire: CLABBER, AQHA #P-507　　Dam: Do Good, AQHA #P-4864

This ad for Clabber II appeared in the 1948 edition of The Quarter Running Horse, *published by the American Quarter Racing Association.*

and Clabber II; grandson Tonto Bars Gill; and great-grandsons Tonto Bars Hank, Tiny Charger, and Tiny Watch. Clabber is also on the list of all-time leading maternal grandsires.

It was Clabber's ability to sire stallions and broodmares who could pass on his speed and durability that made him so valued by Quarter Horse breeders. Clabber died on January 1, 1947, at Frank Vessels' Los Alamitos ranch. He left behind the reputation as being one of the toughest Quarter Horses who ever looked through a bridle.

133

17 ROCKET BAR (TB)

By Diane Simmons

Not only was he a "wonder horse" on the tracks, but he also became a "wonder sire."

ROCKET BAR (TB) was known throughout his racing career as a horse who ran with a lot of heart, putting everything he had into each race. Retired to stud, he gained additional fame as one of the greatest siring sons of Three Bars (TB).

Rocket Bar's breeder is listed as Charles H. Reed of Midlothian, Virginia. But the horse was apparently bred in Arizona, where Three Bars was standing, and was foaled in 1951 at the Talmadge Ranch near Tucson.

Rocket Bar's dam, Golden Rocket, was reported to be an outstanding mare and was the winner of the Washington Futurity.

Her dam, Morshion, had 16 wins, including the Rosedale, Consolation, and Montauk Claiming Stakes.

As a weanling, Rocket Bar was sold for $5,000 to Dr. Harold Donovan, a Tucson physician who had relocated to Raton, N.M., to open a hospital near La Mesa Park.

Rocket Bar (TB), a leading sire and leading maternal grandsire of AQHA Register of Merit race horses. He stood 16.2 hands and weighed 1,250 pounds.

Photo by Darol Dickinson, Courtesy of S.F. Henderson

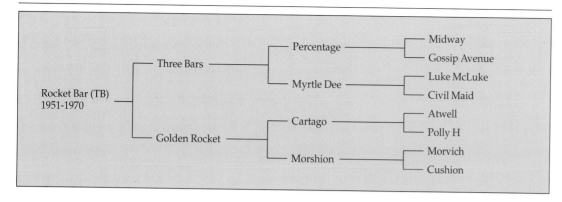

Rocket Bar (TB)
1951-1970
├─ Three Bars
│ ├─ Percentage
│ │ ├─ Midway
│ │ └─ Gossip Avenue
│ └─ Myrtle Dee
│   ├─ Luke McLuke
│   └─ Civil Maid
└─ Golden Rocket
   ├─ Cartago
   │ ├─ Atwell
   │ └─ Polly H
   └─ Morshion
      ├─ Morvich
      └─ Cushion

Rocket Bar won his maiden race for Donovan in October of 1953 by an incredible 45 lengths while covering 4 furlongs at Raton, New Mexico. Two weeks later, in his second race, he fell to his knees at the break. He struggled up, regrouped, and headed for the finish line. In an amazing come-from-behind performance, he wound up as the only horse in the finish photo! From that moment on, he was known as the "Wonder Horse."

As a result of his starting gate accident, Rocket Bar suffered an injury to his left knee that would trouble him for the remainder of his racing career. Dr. Donovan spent hours applying ultrasound treatments to Rocket Bar's knee. These, combined with 2 to 3 weeks of rest between races, served to relieve the pain and reduce the heat when he wasn't running.

As a 5-year-old in 1956, Rocket Bar set a track record at Turf Paradise in Phoenix when he covered the 5 furlongs of the Phoenix Gold Cup in :57.8. Later in that same season, he lowered his own record when he clocked :57.6. The world record for that distance was :57 flat. He returned in 1957 to win the same race by 3 full lengths.

In 1958, Donovan decided it was time to retire Rocket Bar. Over the course of a 5-year racing career, the chestnut stallion competed in a total of 35 races, winning 16, placing second 6 times, and third 4 times. His total race earnings amounted to $22,904. He also made one start in 1953 in an AQHA-recognized race. He placed third in a 440-yard event at Albuquerque and earned a race Register of Merit.

Donovan wasn't interested in standing a stallion, and he knew Rocket Bar could present problems in terms of finding a home in the breeding world. The Thoroughbred racing industry wasn't interested in him as a sire. He was too much of a sprinter for them. And the Quarter Horse breeders

Halter and Performance Record: Won 16 Thoroughbred Races; AQHA Racing Register of Merit (placed third in his only AQHA race).

Progeny Record:

AQHA Champions: 7
Foal Crops: 15
Foals Registered: 454
Halter Point-Earners: 18
Halter Points Earned: 285
Performance Point-Earners: 33
Performance Points Earned: 897
Performance Registers of Merit: 17
Leading Race Money-Earner: Osage Rocket ($266,645)

Race Money Earned: $4,214,921
Race Registers of Merit: 287
Race Starters: 368
Superior Halter Awards: 1
Superior Performance Awards: 3
Superior Race Awards: 46
Supreme Champions: 3
World Champions (Racing): 5

An unknown photographer took this shot of Rocket Bar, when he was a long yearling or 2-year old.
Photo Courtesy of S.F. Henderson

135

Rocket Bar after winning a 5-furlong race, sometime during the middle or late 1950s. His owner, Dr. H.E. Donovan, is at Rocket Bar's head in this photograph, and trainer John Cheeney is on the far left. Rocket Bar's jockey in this race is identified only as S. Miller.

**Photo Courtesy of
S.F. Henderson**

Note: *Over the years, Dr. Donovan's name has also been spelled as Donavon and Donavan, but we believe Donovan is correct.*

Another conformation shot of Rocket Bar, circa 1961, that is reminiscent of the early photographs taken of his famous sire, Three Bars (TB).

weren't exactly banging at the door to take their mares to a Thoroughbred stallion. There was, however, one horseman who had kept his eye on Rocket Bar.

George Kaufman, one of the leading Quarter Horse race trainers of that era, had been racing in California, mostly at Los Alamitos. Kaufman and his wife, Josephine, were interested in Rocket Bar.

It took awhile for everybody's paths to cross. Donovan stood Rocket Bar in Arizona, advertising a $200 breeding fee and free breedings to AAA mares. The Kaufmans had been standing the great sire, Tinky Poo, who had become sterile in the late 1950s. They had a bunch of Tinky Poo, Barred, Joe Reed II, and Red Joe of Arizona daughters, but no stallion.

George Kaufman explained his thoughts about Rocket Bar to this writer for an article in the November 1982 *Speedhorse* magazine. "I knew Thoroughbred stallions weren't all that popular in the Quarter Horse world;

but I also knew that a new futurity (the All American) had started in New Mexico with a gross purse of more than $100,000. Maybe, I thought, we might be ready for some sprinting Thoroughbred blood.

"Anyway, I decided to breed three mares to Rocket Bar—one free AAA mare and two others. When I delivered them, I asked Donovan how much he would ask if he decided to sell Rocket Bar. He said $36,000. That did it. There was no way I could come up with $36,000. Heck, I didn't even have $1,000."

Kaufman returned to Arizona a few months later to pick up his mares. When he arrived, Donovan had drawn up a sale contract for Rocket Bar to Kaufman in the amount of $36,000. Donovan would keep six breedings, reducing the figure to $30,000. Kaufman still couldn't cover the price, so he and Donovan did some serious negotiating.

Eventually, with the free breedings taken into consideration, and a few other concessions made, a deal was struck and Kaufman made arrangements to take Rocket Bar to his ranch in Modesto, Calif., a ranch that was later named Rocket Bar Ranch.

Josephine Kaufman's maiden name had been Starlin. Her father was O.M. Starlin, who used to match Thoroughbreds down the main streets of Kansas towns. In 1959, Starlin moved to California and partnered with his daughter and son-in-law on Rocket Bar. Mares such as Sue Wood and Suleo were his most significant contribution to the partnership.

The first year, Kaufman stood Rocket Bar for $300. He bred 30 outside mares and 28 of his own. He consigned the first Rocket Bar colt to the second All American Sale in 1962 at Ruidoso Downs. His name was Mr. Tinky Bar and he brought $3,500. The following year, Mr. Tinky Bar won the Kansas Futurity and placed second in the All American. He earned $98,371 and was named the 1963 Champion Quarter Running 2-Year-Old Colt.

The next Rocket Bar offspring to be sold

Here is a shot of Rocket Bar getting some exercise in his paddock on the George Kaufman ranch, Modesto, California

Photo by Darol Dickinson, Courtesy of S.F. Henderson

Kaufman's strategy for promoting Rocket Bar was simple. He bred the best mares he and Starlin had to the chestnut stallion.

at the All American went for $16,000. The prices then went to $20,000 and more.

Kaufman's strategy for promoting Rocket Bar was simple. He bred the best mares he and Starlin had to the chestnut stallion. He then trained the offspring and took them to the track. And he would do whatever was necessary to get high-quality outside mares. There were instances when he drove from

Rocket Wrangler, by Rocket Bar and out of Go Galla Go, by Go Man Go. This 1968 stallion earned $252,167 in 23 starts and won the 1970 All American Futurity. He sired the earners of over $7,000,000, and is the sire of the great Dash For Cash.

Three Jets AAAT was another good-looking son of Rocket Bar. Foaled in 1962, Three Jets was out of the famous race matron, Miss Night Bar, who also produced Jet Deck.

**Photo by
Darol Dickinson**

California to Oklahoma with a trailer, picked up a customer's mares, took them to California, bred them to Rocket Bar, and drove them back to Oklahoma.

It didn't take long to find out that the "wonder horse" of the tracks was also going to be a "wonder sire." For example, almost every one of Kaufman's Tinky Poo mares, when crossed on Rocket Bar, produced runners.

On April 3, 1965, the Pacific Coast Quarter Horse Racing Association Spring Futurity was run at the Sacramento fairgrounds. Five of the ten finalists were by Rocket Bar, and they finished in the top five spots. They were Suleo's Rocket, Cape Canaveral, Rocket Vandy, Rocket's Glare, and Clabber's Rocket. The following year, 15 Rocket Bar get ran in AQHA-recognized races, and 14 earned their Registers of Merit.

In 1965, Kaufman bred 50 outside mares at a $2,500 stud fee. Then, in 1966, he sold the stallion to Billy and Harriet Peckham, and Sonny and Sarah Henderson for $360,000. Within a short time, Rocket Bar's consortium of owners consisted of the Peckhams, the Hendersons, Z. Wayne Griffin, Leo Winters, Jacob Bunn, Mr. and Mrs. Tom Carter, Dan Urschel, and Mr. and Mrs. Bert Hall. It was one of the first multiple ownerships in the Quarter Horse racing industry.

Having sold Rocket Bar, the Kaufmans held a complete dispersal sale on April 7, 1967. A letter included in the sale catalog read, in part, "As you know, when the heart is removed, it's hard to keep the rest of the body alive, and when Rocket Bar left, it removed the heart. Those Rocket Bar foals have been the very heart of the whole picture for us, and when we realized that we wouldn't have any more of them, we just couldn't seem to picture us in the business without them. So the only thing was to find a way out."

Reflecting on Kaufman's contribution to the Rocket Bar success story, Harriett Peckham noted, "Really, none of this would have worked without George Kaufman. He was a great trainer and a great horseman. More importantly, he had the vision to know that Rocket Bar would work in the Quarter Horse world."

In 1967 Rocket Bar sons and daughters won 10 futurities and derbies. The following year brought more of the same, with Rocket Bar's sixth crop adding 17 new stakes winners to the list. In 1969, a sports journalist wrote, "No one knows what the future will bring for the 'Wonder Sire.' But, if Rocket Bar continues to work his magic through his offspring, he may well reach the heights of being the greatest sire of running Quarter Horses the world has known."

Because of an imposing tax that California levied on breeding stallions, Rocket Bar was moved from the West Coast to Texas in the late 1960s.

By that time, Rocket Bar's popularity as a sire had risen to unforeseen heights, as reflected in a letter written on November 25, 1969, by part-owner Sonny Henderson to George Kaufman.

"The big horse has gotten greater and become the super stallion we knew he would be," wrote Henderson. "This should make you feel enlightened and proud that you made the horse what he is today. He is standing at Buena Suerte (then located at Richmond, Tex., and later moved to Roswell, N.M.), and Gerald Wells is handling him. (Wells also showed and stood the great Scooper Chick.)

"Please come down to see us and the big horse. He is in excellent health and always wanting attention. . . . and we have expectations of another great year, with commitments of 70 mares such as Chicado V, Noorella, Straw Flight, Fly Straw, Cute Trick, Top Ladybug, Leocita, Miss Top Flame, and many others."

Unfortunately, the 1970 breeding season that Henderson referred to with so much optimism turned out to be Rocket Bar's last.

On October 23, 1970, at the height of his popularity, Rocket Bar died after colic surgery. He was 19 years old.

Rocket Bar sired a total of 287 horses

50 VOO DOO ROCKET 287,196 Stallion

Chestnut – Age 6 – Foaled April 14, 1961

Sire: ROCKET BAR (TB) — Three Bars {Percentage, Myrtle Dee}; Golden Rocket {Cartago, Marshion}

Dam: TET'S BABY 128,284 — My Tet Rambler (TB) {Tetros, ----}; Little Nettie {Eddie, ----}

Voo Doo Rocket AAAT, a 1961 son of Rocket Bar, out of Tet's Baby, by My Tet Rambler (TB). Voo Doo Rocket sold for $29,000 in the Kaufman ranch complete dispersal on April 17, 1967. He went on to sire numerous ROM race horses including the good Northwest sire, Terrible Scotch, who was AAA and an AQHA Champion. This photo and pedigree were reproduced from the sale catalog. Note the spelling of Marshion; according to the AQHA, the correct spelling is Morshion.

He Rocket, an AQHA Supreme Champion. Foaled in 1969, he was by Rocket Bar and out of Lady Me, by Joe Reed II. In addition to his racing points, He Rocket had 36 halter, 12 western pleasure, and 8 team roping points.

Photo by Alfred Janssen III

who earned their racing ROMs. Included among these were 46 Superior Race Award winners; 138 horses with speed indexes of 90 or higher; and 32 horses with speed indexes of 100 or higher.

In addition to Mr. Tinky Bar, Rocket Bar's champion get included, Nug Rock, 1964 Champion Quarter Running 2-Year-Old Gelding; Top Rockette, 1968 Champion Quarter Running 3-Year-Old Filly, 1968 and 1970 Champion Quarter Running Mare; Rocket Wrangler, 1970 Champion Quarter Running 2-Year-Old Colt and winner of the 1970 All American Futurity; and Osage Rocket, 1971 Champion Quarter Running 2-Year-Old Filly.

Among his other top runners were

Rocket Elaine, Quincy Rocket, Marble Man, and Flying Rockette, each of whom earned over $100,000 during their racing careers.

Rocket Bar also sired seven AQHA Champions: Rocket Hug, Heza Rocket, Rocket's Chick, Rocket Little, Fire Rocket, Sugar Rocket, and He Rocket.

Fire Rocket, He Rocket, and Sugar Rocket went on to attain their AQHA Supreme Championships, making Rocket Bar the second leading sire of Supreme Champions. Only Three Bars, with four to his credit, sired more.

As proof that speed is speed, no matter what the surface, Rocket Bar also sired Rocket Bar Boy and Rocket Bracket, both of whom earned their Superiors in cutter and chariot racing. Both of them also had speed indexes of 90+.

And Rocket Bar's daughters became some of the industry's best producers.

La Ree Bar, out of Tinky Ann, by Tinky Poo, produced the great Charger Bar. In 5 years of campaigning, Charger Bar won 21 stakes events and earned $495,437. She also earned nine champion titles.

Gay's Delight, out of Miss Ginger Gay by Palleo Pete, produced Tiny's Gay, the winner of $444,721 and earner of three champion titles.

Apachette's Bar, out of Apachette, by Super Charge, produced Laderago, who earned $206,800; Mid Rocket, out of Mickey Bar, by Mid Bar, produced Wanta Go, winner of $175,568. And the list goes on and on.

In all, the daughters of Rocket Bar produced 632 race ROM horses who earned $8,060,907. They also produced 67 halter and performance point-earners who earned a total of 1,341.5 open show points. SR Hometown Girl, a 1988 mare sired by Doc's Hickory, and out of Rocket Jo Dee, by Rocket Bar, was the 1993 AQHA high-point senior reining horse with 36.5 points. She had a total of 113 open performance points.

Among the many sons of Rocket Bar who contributed to this bloodline's heritage as sires is Rocket Wrangler, who was out of Go Galla Go, by Go Man Go.

Rocket Wrangler sired Dash For Cash, holder of five champion titles, earner of $507,687, and a leading sire of money earners, stakes winners, and running champions.

In addition to Dash For Cash, Rocket Wrangler sired such other notable stakes winners as War Star Wrangler, American Speed, Double Dutch Bus, Rambling Sallye, The Heat Is On, Wrangler Sam, Tisa Golden Dream, Rockay, Rockets Magic, and Quick Wrangler.

Through each successive generation, the speed and determination of the Rocket Bar line has been carried on.

It seems only fitting, then, to end his story with one last observation regarding heart. An autopsy on Rocket Bar revealed that he had an exceptionally large windpipe and lung capacity, and that his heart was 2½ times larger than normal. Rocket Bar did, literally, have a lot of heart.

Top Rockette had a speed index of 101. A 1962 mare by Rocket Bar, she was out of Kay Deck, by Top Deck (TB). She is shown here in 1967, with Bobby Yanez in the irons. Top Rockette was a three-time champion, who earned $217,900, and won seventeen stakes races.

LIGHTNING BAR

By Diane Simmons

Although Lightning Bar died at an early age, his legacy lives on through his descendants.

THE STORY of Lightning Bar began in 1945 when Art Pollard travelled from the Dallas area to Arizona to visit his sister, who was suffering from tuberculosis. He fell immediately in love with the desert landscape—so much so that he and his recent bride, Phyllis (Phee), decided to buy 115 acres of raw land east of Tucson and develop it into a horse breeding operation. He named it the Lightning A Ranch.

Not long thereafter, Pollard met the well-known race horse man, W.D. "Dink" Parker of Patagonia, Arizona. From Parker, he purchased his first Quarter Horse, Hula Girl P., a daughter of Ed Echols. She became his first champion show horse and, as the direct result of some friendly chiding from some race-horse friends about what he was going to do with his "pretty little mare," his first champion race horse. As a 3-year-old, she won the Arizona Derby and, in another race, equalled the 3-year-old record for 350 yards.

Hula Girl P., who went on to earn her AQHA Championship, also became the

An April 1955 photograph of Lightning Bar, with Art Pollard at the halter, when he was grand champion stallion at the Tucson show.

Photo by Matt Culley

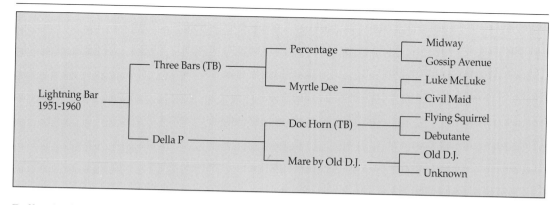

Lightning Bar 1951-1960
- Three Bars (TB)
  - Percentage
    - Midway
    - Gossip Avenue
  - Myrtle Dee
    - Luke McLuke
    - Civil Maid
- Della P
  - Doc Horn (TB)
    - Flying Squirrel
    - Debutante
  - Mare by Old D.J.
    - Old D.J.
    - Unknown

Pollards' first top-notch producing mare. She was the dam of War Chant AAA; Arizonan, AAA and Champion Quarter Running Gelding of 1955; Hula Baby AAA; and Sonoitan AAA, AQHA Champion.

Over the course of the next several years, Pollard continued to avail himself of Dink Parker's vast store of equine knowledge and experience. He also purchased several more mares from him, including Della P.

"Dink had bought Della P from Claude Morein of Ville Platte, La.," says Pollard, who now lives in Washington state. "I liked her and wanted to buy her. Dink had paid more for her than for any of his other horses—including Ed Echols.

"I kept after Dink and finally, after Della P had some age on her, he agreed to sell her to me for $1,750, provided I promised to breed her to Three Bars (TB). I said okay."

In 1949, Pollard took Della P to Melville Haskell's Rincon Stock Farm at Tucson where Three Bars was standing for $250. "Charlie Hall was handling him," Art recalls. "We bred Della P and, in 1950, Bardella was foaled." In an article on him that appeared in the December 1954 issue of *The Quarter Horse Journal*, written by George C. McLeod, Pollard shared some thoughts on what producing Bardella meant to his fledgling breeding program.

". . . Hula Girl gave us our start," he remarked. "But Bardella finished the job. She did more to establish the Lightning A Ranch than anyone can imagine. In her first racing season at Rillito track, she won $5,100." Pollard also tried to match race his chestnut 3-year-old, without much success. "At Bay Meadows we accepted a challenge from the trainer of Little Request, a Thoroughbred who supposedly was unbeatable at a quarter of a mile. But when we went to the Coast with Bardella, Little Request

Halter and Performance Record: AQHA Champion Racing Register of Merit.

Progeny Record:

AQHA Champions: 5
Foal Crops: 8
Foals Registered: 148
Halter Point-Earners: 21
Halter Points Earned: 421
Performance Point-Earners: 8
Performance Points Earned: 209.5
Leading Race Money-Earner: Lightning Belle ($60,134)

Performance Registers of Merit: 4
Race Money Earned: $477,436
Race Registers of Merit: 77
Race Starters: 108
Superior Halter Awards: 4
Supreme Champions: 1 (Lightning Rey)

Lightning Bar at the age of 23 months.   **Photo Courtesy of Art Pollard**

Art Pollard says this is his favorite picture of Lightning Bar; it was taken when the sorrel was 4 years old. The youngster schooling ol' Lightnin' on the how-to of working a rope is Roman Figueroa, who became a top jockey.

Hula Girl P. was Art Pollard's first show horse and first race horse. She was AA on the track (when AA was the highest speed rating) and an AQHA Champion. When bred to Lightning Bar, she produced Hula Baby AAA.

and his owners took to the brush."

Bardella was the Co-Champion Quarter Running 2-Year-Old Filly in 1952 (with Chicado V.) and the Champion Quarter Running 3-Year-Old Filly in 1953.

Having been pleased with Bardella from the moment she hit the ground, Pollard bred Della P back to Three Bars in 1950 and got Lightning Bar in 1951.

"I always had the greatest respect for Three Bars, and I still do," says Pollard. "But I'll tell you something . . . Della P was such an astounding producer that you could breed her to a jack and get a stakes-winning mule. She was like Hula Girl in that respect. Everything Hula Girl had was a bullet on the racetrack—and they could do things other than run.

"Why, when Arizonan was at his toughest on the tracks, those Figueroa boys who were working for me at the time would take him to roping contests on the weekends when he didn't race and rope off him. There wasn't a cowboy in southern Arizona who wouldn't have jumped at the opportunity to rope off Arizonan."

Pollard still had a lot to learn as a horse breeder when Lightning Bar was foaled—so much so that he took a long look at the colt and thought he should probably put him down. In September 1973, he told the story of his near-fatal mistake to *Quarter Racing World* (now *Speedhorse* magazine),

Lightning Rey, shown here with Dwight Stewart aboard, was an AQHA Supreme Champion son of Lightning Bar, and a Superior halter horse. He earned 50 halter points, 93.5 points in performance, and was AAA on the track.

in an article written by Jane Pattie:

"Lightning Bar had enormous flat knees, which is just what horsemen like. When he was born, I was green as grass, and he was very buck-kneed. I was entertaining the thought of doing away with him when he was about 5 days old. Dink came by, and I told him, 'Dink, I've got a crooked-legged colt, and I guess I ought to just knock him in the head.' He suggested that we go take a look at him, so we went to the pasture. There stood Lightning Bar with his little bucked knees.

"Dink just looked at me and shook his head. 'Ain't you ever gonna learn nothing? That colt's just what you're looking for. You only worry if a colt's calf-kneed with his knees bent the other way. Hell, in 2 or 3 weeks he'll be straight as a string!' And of course, he was."

Phee Pollard named all of the ranch's foals, and she chose the name of Lightning Bar for the promising youngster. It proved

Cactus Comet, a good-looking son of Lightning Bar who was AAA and an AQHA Champion. He was out of Black Beauty Pollard, by Fleeting Time (TB).

Photo by Orren Mixer

145

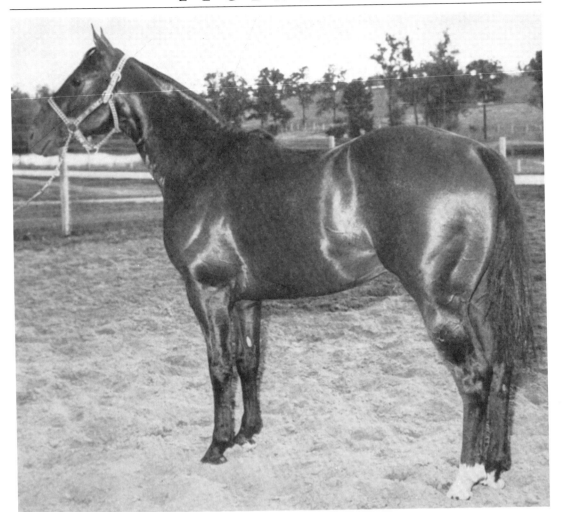

Pana Bar, AAA+ and an AQHA Champion, was by Lightning Bar and out of Miss Panama AAAT. Pana Bar was Co-Champion Quarter Running 2-Year-Old Colt in 1958. An all-around horse, Pana Bar earned 51 points in racing, 52 in halter, and 41 in performance, including 26 in reining, 14 in western pleasure, and 1 in trail.

prophetic in more ways than one, for just like a flash of lightning, the chestnut colt would flash across the Quarter Horse short tracks, then through the breeding shed, and then be gone.

Lightning Bar raced only in 1953, as a 2-year-old. In between bouts of pneumonia, distemper, cut coronet bands, and an injured knee, he managed to win his time trials in the Southwestern, Ruidoso, and Pomona futurities. At Pomona, he equalled the 2-year-old track record when he covered 330 yards in 17.2 seconds. From 10 career starts, he had 4 firsts, 3 seconds, and 1 third. His total track earnings came to a modest $1,491. But he achieved a AAA rating, and earned 26 points and a racing Register of Merit.

After retiring him from racing, Pollard began showing Lightning Bar. He had matured into a very good-looking, 15.2, 1,250-pound horse. And he was good enough to earn one grand championship and one reserve championship, eighteen halter points, and his AQHA Championship.

Even though Lightning Bar had not set the world on fire as a race horse, Pollard had never doubted his talents or his potential. He knew the horse could run, and he was convinced he was sire material. He had decided, even before Lightning Bar was born, that the only way he'd have a quality stallion to stand was to raise his own. He couldn't afford to buy a proven stallion such as Three Bars (TB) or Depth Charge (TB).

Pollard also knew that it was up to him to prove Lightning Bar as a sire. For a time, it seemed as if that might take awhile. Initially, in 1954, he set the stallion's stud fee at $250. He attracted only nine outside mares that year and none of them "resembled racing stock." Eleven outside mares went to Lightning Bar the second year; but one hundred two mares were booked the third year, when his stud fee was $500.

There's a humorous story of one attempt

146

to attract some attention to Lightning Bar the first year Pollard stood him. Evidently Frankie Figueroa, Pollard's right-hand man, suggested that he haul the stallion to the Garrigan Bros. Sunday jackpot roping at their eastside (Tucson) arena. Pollard thought that Frankie would just ride the stallion around so people could see what a good-looking horse he was.

"I should have been suspicious when he returned with Lightning Bar that afternoon, with a sheepish grin on his face," remembers Pollard. "I asked him how the horse was received and he said, 'The stud did good and I won the jackpot!' After congratulating him, I asked which rope horse he had used. He replied, 'The stud.'"

Even though there were few outside bookings to Lightning Bar the first 2 years, Pollard did have a few mares of his own to breed. The early production records of Hula Girl P. and Della P had convinced him that top-notch mares were the key to a successful race breeding program. By the time he retired Lightning Bar to stud, he had already assembled one of the most select, small broodmare bands in the country.

By 1954, several top ex-race mares— Black Beauty Pollard, Silhouette, Miss Pinkie, Miss Banks, and Miss Panama— all called Pollard's Lightning A Ranch home. With mares like this, Lightning Bar quickly began proving that he could sire offspring that could excel both on the track and in the show arena.

Fantasy and Hula Baby, 1955 mares out of Miss Bank and Hula Girl respectively, were his first AAA runners. Pana Bar, a 1956 stallion out of Miss Panama, was the Co-Champion Quarter Running 2-Year-Old Colt in 1958. He also went on to become a AAA AQHA Champion with a Superior in halter.

Another outstanding colt from the 1956 crop was Cactus Comet, out of Black Beauty Pollard, by Fleeting Time (TB). This good-looking son of Lightning Bar earned a AAA rating on the track and his AQHA Championship, and went on to sire a number of top colts himself, including several AQHA Champions.

Still another Lightning Bar son hit the ground in 1956 who would make quite an

Light Bar AAA, by Lightning Bar and out of Ariel Lady, by Little Joe Jr., was Co-Champion Quarter Running 3-Year-old Colt in 1960.

Lightnin Bar Jr. was out of Joe's Watch, by Monsieur Joe. Foaled in 1961, "Junior" was the top halter point-earning son of Lightning Bar with 88 points.

Three Bars (TB), the sire of Lightning Bar as well as many other great horses. This photograph was taken in the early 1950s when Sid Vail was standing him in Douglas, Arizona.

impact on the cutting horse world in the years to come. His name was Doc Bar (who is featured in *Legends 1*).

Light Bar was a 1957 stallion out of Ariel Lady, by Little Joe Jr. Rated AAA, he was the 1960 Co-Champion Quarter Running 3-Year-Old Colt. Explosive, also foaled in 1957, and out of Miss Pinkie, by Blob (TB), was a AAA speedster and a grand champion halter horse. Lightning Rey, a 1958 stallion out of Reina Rey, went on to become an AQHA Supreme Champion and was also a Superior halter horse. Crash Bang, a 1959 mare out of Red Cent, also became a AAA AQHA Champion and a Superior halter horse.

In 1960, Lightning Bar sired Glamour Bars—the dam of Impressive, who established his own dynasty in the halter-horse world.

Lightning Belle, a 1960 mare out of Bella St. Mary, was Lightning Bar's top money winner on the track. Rated AAAT, she ran out over $60,000 and just missed being named Champion Quarter Running 2-Year-Old Filly in 1962.

Manor Born, a 1960 stallion out of Chinchilla, won the Southwestern Futurity in 1962. Relampago Bar, a 1960 stallion out of Miss Jo Bain, became a AAA AQHA Champion. Lightnin Bar Jr., a 1961 stallion out of Joe's Watch, became a Superior halter horse and Lightning Bar's top halter point-earner with 88 points.

By 1960, Art Pollard and Lightning Bar were names that were known throughout the Quarter Horse world. Pollard had decided to build a new place 50 miles or so southeast of Tucson, near Sonoita. "I wanted to get both the horses and me off of the lower desert," he recalls. "I had found 500 acres at about 5,000 feet of elevation, with plenty of room for the mares and colts to run, so I bought it and put the Lightning A up for sale."

Roy Gill purchased the ranch and wanted to move in immediately. In order to accommodate Gill, Pollard and his new bride, Harriet, moved out. The new ranch, Sonoita Stallion Manor, was not completely ready, but Pollard turned the mares into pasture there. He put his stallions and young horses at the fairgrounds, where he had entered Lightning Bar in the local show. In retrospect, Pollard always figured that's where Lightning Bar must have picked up the Colitis-X virus that would result in his death one month later, in June 1960.

Pollard's other horses, including Hula Girl, Chinchilla, Little Nellie Bars, Manor Man, and all of the yearling racing prospects, also began "dropping like flies." Only three of the ones who contracted the virus lived, and they suffered from lasting effects.

Pollard was heart-broken and discouraged. He couldn't think of rebuilding, so he simply sold off his remaining horses. He eventually did regroup, but it was nearly 15 years later.

Even today, Pollard speaks of Lightning Bar as if the stallion were still in a pasture just outside the door. "I've owned a lot of horses," he says, "but Lightning Bar was the most brilliant of all of them— even smarter than Hula Girl, and she was unbelievable.

"Lightning Bar was a 4-year-old when my top hand, Bill Wilson, and I decided to ride from my old Lightning A Ranch high into the Catalina Mountains. It was just before breeding season and I thought Lightning Bar would benefit from the exercise.

"It was a long day's ride, and it was dusk when we were returning to the ranch. We were coming down a steep trail called Rattlesnake Ridge. It was a narrow path with cholla and prickly pear cactus along the sides. All of a sudden, Lightning Bar stopped dead in his tracks. He refused to go forward. I never wore spurs when I rode him—they weren't necessary. I kicked him with my boot heels and slapped the reins on him—I was really irritated.

"I turned to Bill and said, 'What the hell is this? This horse has gone nuts on me.' Finally, in desperation, I got him to sidle down the side of the ridge. Wilson and his horse started down the trail that Lightning Bar refused to follow and, all of a sudden,

Art Pollard with Lightning Bar, circa 1954.

Bill heard the sing-song of a big rattler. Lightning Bar was a lot smarter than we were and his nose was much keener, too.

"I always had to be careful about the kind of latch I used on a gate with that horse," Pollard continued. "He could figure them out faster than I could. He would open a gate, and go for a stroll. He was the best horse to ride I'd ever been on. He never tired and was easy to handle. Lightning Bar was a joy in all respects.

"Our interest was always more in breeding than anything else—more than it was in racing. We were lucky to have had a sire like Lightning Bar and lucky to own the mares that we did. But it was a nightmare when they were wiped out. Even now, we can still feel the sadness of losing those horses."

Fortunately for the Quarter Horse industry, the lasting effects of both Lightning Bar and the Art Pollard program will never truly be lost.

19 SUGAR BARS

By Diane Simmons

SUGAR BARS was one of the more influential and versatile sires in the history of the Quarter Horse breed. Sired by Three Bars (TB) and out of Frontera Sugar, Sugar Bars was foaled in 1951 on the El Paso,

This is the most widely recognized photo of Sugar Bars. It shows his beautiful head and excellent conformation. **Photo by Orren Mixer, Courtesy of Reba Warren**

Tex., ranch of his breeder, George Wood.

Wood had purchased Sugar Bars' dam, Frontera Sugar, in 1944, as a yearling, from Pete Reynolds, who was ranching in Chihuahua, Mexico, at the time. Frontera Sugar is listed in AQHA Studbook No. 4 as being sired by Rey, by Captains Courageous (TB). Her dam is listed as a dun mare, sired by Ben Hur. The dam of the dun mare is listed simply as a Reynolds mare.

However, there is some controversy regarding the distaff portion of Frontera Sugar's pedigree.

In an interview for the November 1986 issue of *Speedhorse* magazine, Pete Reynolds stated that the real dam of Frontera Sugar was a palomino mare named Palomino D.O. Bred by O.C. Dowe of Marfa, Tex., Palomino D.O. was sired by a son of Ben Hur, not Ben Hur himself. Her dam is listed correctly as a Reynolds mare.

Apparently Reynolds registered Frontera Sugar with the AQHA in 1945, 2 years before he registered her dam, Palomino D.O. Somehow, Frontera Sugar's dam was listed as a dun mare by Ben Hur. Although the records were never set straight, according to Reynolds, Palomino D.O. should be given credit as being the granddam of Sugar Bars.

The year Sugar Bars was foaled, Wood sold a half-sister to him, Sugar Reedie, by Joe Reed II, to Ken Fratis of Lemoore, California. Fratis raced the filly with some success and, in early 1953, expressed an interest in attempting to do the same with Sugar Bars.

The two men worked out a lease agreement whereby Fratis took possession of Sugar Bars and turned him over to his

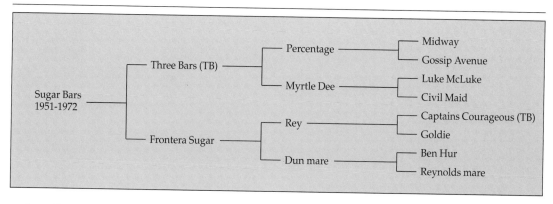

Sugar Bars
1951-1972
├── Three Bars (TB)
│   ├── Percentage
│   │   ├── Midway
│   │   └── Gossip Avenue
│   └── Myrtle Dee
│   ├── Luke McLuke
│   └── Civil Maid
└── Frontera Sugar
    ├── Rey
    │   ├── Captains Courageous (TB)
    │   └── Goldie
    └── Dun mare
        ├── Ben Hur
        └── Reynolds mare

trainer, Lee Dooley, for conditioning.

The 2-year-old stallion had been at the Fratis ranch for only a few days when he was spotted by Bud Warren of Perry, Oklahoma. In an article on Sugar Bars written by Sam Ed Spence in the April 1969 issue of *The Quarter Horse Journal*, Warren recalled the event.

"I had walked down to the arena where they were working some cutting horses," he said. "One of the boys was holding herd on a good looking sorrel stallion which I judged to be about a 4- or 5-year-old horse, although I could tell he was awfully green. He had a good flat hip about a mile and a half long sticking out from under that stock saddle. And what a beautiful head. In fact, he was pure quality from head to tail."

When Warren asked about the horse, he was surprised to find that he was a 2-year-old son of Three Bars. He had been trying to find a son of Three Bars to cross on his Leo mares but, until he saw Sugar Bars, he hadn't found one that he felt would work.

Sugar Bars was just what he had been looking for, but the colt was not for sale at the time, so Warren temporarily forgot about him.

In his freshman year on the track, Sugar Bars ran well enough for Fratis and Dooley, making six starts with three firsts, one second, and two thirds. There was nothing spectacular in his performances, however,

and, as a result, Wood decided to sell him, and Roy Hittson of Imperial, Calif., bought him. Sugar Bars started 23 races for Hittson as a 3-year-old, with 4 firsts, 2 seconds, and 6 thirds. In his final race in 1954, at Phoenix, he qualified for his AAA rating when he covered 350 yards in :18.1.

When Bud Warren found out that Sugar Bars had been sold, he was somewhat upset. He decided not to give up, however, and called Van Smelker, a friend who lived in Tucson, and asked him to try to either buy or lease Sugar Bars from Hittson. Hitt-

Out of every conceivable kind of mare, Sugar Bars sired speedy, good-looking, athletic horses who could and would do whatever was asked of them.

Frontera Sugar, the dam of Sugar Bars. Frontera Sugar was reportly a top show mare prior to the establishment of the AQHA performance department. Although the date and place of this photograph are unknown, information on the back of it states that Frontera Sugar earned grand champion honors that day.

Photo by John Stryker, Courtesy of Pete Reynolds

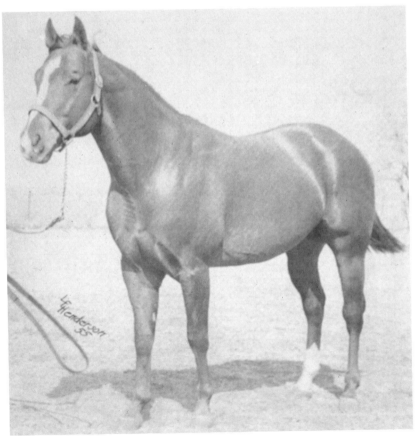

Here is another good shot of Sugar Bars, taken when he was a 4-year-old. Sugar Bars was only shown once at halter, in the fall of 1956, at Enid, Oklahoma. He placed second in the aged stallion class and then stood reserve champion, earning two halter points.
Photo by L.F. Henderson

son wasn't ready to turn loose of Sugars Bars, though. He indicated that he wanted to continue racing him and then stand him at stud.

Warren had also asked another friend of his, AQHA inspector Bob Weimer, to let him know if he should ever hear that Sugar Bars was for sale. In January 1955, Weimer placed a late evening call to Warren from the race barn in Tucson with the word that Sugar Bars was available.

"It was the middle of the night," recalled Warren years later. "Hittson was in need of some cash and had instructed his trainer to sell Sugar Bars to the first person to show up with $2,500 in cash. I didn't have $2,500 in cash, and there were no banks open. To make things worse, it was Saturday night and nothing would be available until Monday.

"Bob told me Hank Wiescamp was interested in the horse, but wanted to come down and look at him. John Hazelwood, who trained Leota W for me, was there in Tucson with Bob. He got on the phone and told me he had $2,500 stashed in his sock! He went over, bought Sugar Bars, and took him to his barn. I drove down with a trailer the next day and got him."

Warren immediately retired Sugar Bars from the track and set him on a career at

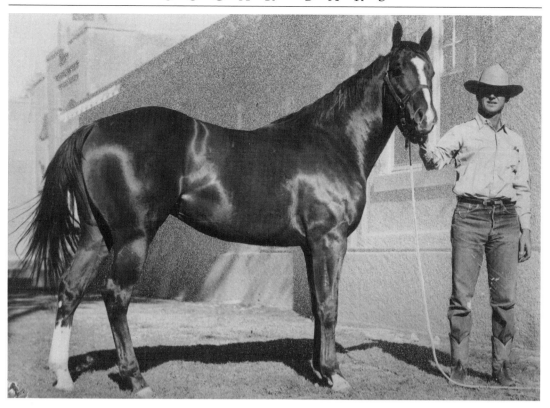

Rey, the maternal grand-sire of Sugar Bars. Rey was bred by Plunk Fields of Aeala, Tex., and foaled in 1939. He is shown here as a 2-year-old at the old El Paso stockyards with Pete Reynolds at the halter. Rey was well-known at one time in the Southwest as a sire of roping and bulldogging horses, but his greatest claim to fame would come as the maternal grandsire of Sugar Bars.

Photo by Nye Wilson Publications, Courtesy of Pete Reynolds

stud that would wind up having few equals within the Quarter Horse world.

As a sire of race horses, Sugar Bars had 324 starters who earned $378,081. Some 139 of his sons and daughters earned their Registers of Merit on the track, with 52 of those having speed indexes of 90 or higher and 14 having speed indexes of 100 or higher. Bar Face, a 1961 son of Sugar Bars, was his high-point race money-earner, with $77,726 in earnings.

As a sire of show horses, Sugar Bars proved even more successful. He sired 148 halter point-earners, who garnered 2,574 points. Sugar Leda, a 1966 daughter of Sugar Bars, was the 1968 Honor Roll Halter Horse, earning 379 points that year. In addition, Bar Flit, Otoe, Counterplay, Bit O' Sugar, Mr. Cabin Bar, Judge Sulena, Sugar Capri, and Little Bit A Sugar all earned their Superiors in halter.

In performance, Sugar Bars sired 147 horses who earned 4,465 points. Ninety-three of his get earned performance Registers of Merit and, beginning with Bar Gal in 1966, 30 of his get achieved their AQHA Championships. As a testimony

Classy Bar, a sorrel stallion foaled in 1956, was by Sugar Bars and out of Mokey, by Leo. Unraced and lightly shown, Classy Bar went on to become one of the leading sires in the Northwest. He was owned by Doug and Nancy Dear of Simms, Montana. He sired a number of AQHA Champions and ROM performance horses, and was also known as an excellent broodmare sire. **Photo Courtesy of Reba Warren**

Here is an action shot of Connie Reba, a 1959 daughter of Sugar Bars, who was out of Connie Leo, by Leo. Connie Reba was the stakes-placed earner of $16,773. She achieved a speed index of 100 and was an AQHA Champion as well.

Photo Courtesy of Reba Warren

Bars Bailey, a 1957 son of Sugar Bars, out of Beauty Bailey II, by Hank H. Bars Bailey was an AQHA Champion with 47 halter points and 27.5 performance points. He sired six AQHA Champions and numerous ROM qualifiers.

Photo by Orren Mixer, Courtesy of Reba Warren

to Sugar Bars' versatility as a sire, 22 of his get earned 27 Superiors in performance in racing, reining, western pleasure, hunter under saddle, western riding, cutting, and trail.

Sugar Bars sired 12 AAA AQHA Champions: Sugaree Bars, Albar, Connie Reba, Sugar Leo, Vanna Bar, Dan's Sugar Bars, Otoe, Figure 8 Bars, Gofar Bar, Justice Bars, Quick Henry, and Sugar Joe Reed. Of these 12 horses, 8 were out of Leo daughters.

Jay's Sugar Bars, a 1963 son of Sugar Bars, was the 1970 Honor Roll Reining Horse; and Sugar Line, a 1972 daughter of Sugar Bars, was the 1976 Honor Roll Reining Horse.

Judge Sulena, a 1969 gelding, earned 11 Superiors in performance and a total of 1,348 youth and open performance points.

Nice N Sweet, a 1970 daughter, earned four Superiors in performance, two high point amateur performance awards, and 527 open, youth, and amateur performance points.

Clink Chugie, a 1970 stallion, was the 1974 World Champion Junior Heeling Horse; and Sugar Select, a 1971 stallion, earned a Superior in cutting with 103 points.

Sugar Bars Junior, foaled in 1973 and Sugar Bars' last recorded performer, earned his Superior in western pleasure in 1976.

Sugar Bars sired a total of 867 foals during his lifetime and, during each season that Bud Warren stood him, as many outside mares had to be turned away as were booked.

Over the years, Warren turned down many offers to sell Sugar Bars, including one from E. Paul Waggoner of Vernon, Tex., that reportedly had $50,000 attached to it. Finally, in 1968, he agreed to sell the sorrel stallion to Dean Parker and Sid Huntley of California.

As Warren explained in the April 1969 *Journal* feature, there were several reasons behind his decision to sell.

"I had about 15 Sugar Bars fillies, and a number of Sugar Bars' daughters who were in my broodmare band. I also had several Leo daughters who were out of Sugar Bars mares. This left me with only a half-dozen mares which I could breed to Sugar Bars without going to line-breeding.

"I felt I had stayed with the horse long

Dan's Sugar Bars was a 1960 son of Sugar Bars, and was out of Lena Leo, by Leo. A AAA AQHA Champion, Dan's Sugar Bars was owned at one time by Bill and Dusty Rhoades of Kit Carson, Colorado. Among the top foals sired by Dan's Sugar Bars was the AQHA Supreme Champion Sugar Sabre.

Photo by Orren Mixer, Courtesy of Reba Warren

enough. I figured Sugar Bars would have the opportunity to be crossed on a lot of good mares on the West Coast that would not have come to him in Oklahoma."

Sugar Bars was moved to his new home at the Huntley ranch in Madera, Calif., in the fall of 1968 and was promptly booked full for 1969. He continued to stand to a full book for the next 3 years.

In June 1972, at the age of 21, Sugar Bars suffered an attack of colic. He was moved to the University of California-Davis where he underwent surgery. A tumor, which had blocked his colon, was removed, but Sugar Bars was unable to recover, and he died of heart failure on June 6, 1972.

"One of Sugar Bars' greatest assets was that he could sire anything," said Hugh Huntley. "He was what a Quarter Horse was supposed to be. His offspring won wherever their owners put them—the race track, halter ring, or performance arena—it didn't matter."

As to what kind of personality the famous sire had, both Reba Warren and Hugh Huntley can recall incidents that would

Connie Reb, a chestnut stallion foaled in 1963, was another successful result of the Sugar Bars-Connie Leo cross. Connie Reb was a stakes winner of $18,066 with an SI of 100.

Photo by Orren Mixer, Courtesy of Reba Warren

Otoe, one of the greatest sons of Sugar Bars. Foaled in 1960, Otoe was out of Juleo, by Leo. Owned by Dr. Jack Donald of Sulphur, Okla., Otoe was one of the first great horses shown by Jerry Wells. He was a AAA AQHA Champion and a Superior halter horse, standing grand at such shows as Chicago, Kansas City, and Fort Worth. Like his sire, he also enjoyed enormous success at stud, being the sire of 22 AQHA Champions, 26 Superior event earners, and 89 ROM earners.

Photo by Orren Mixer, Courtesy of Reba Warren

Here is the elegant Sugar Leda, a 1966 daughter of Sugar Bars, and out of Pesky's Peggy, by Pesky Britches. Owned by Edward Crowell of South Dennis, Mass., Sugar Leda was the 1968 Honor Roll Halter Horse. She earned 379 halter points that year, 106 more than her closest competitor, who was Hard To Beat, a son of Otoe.

Photo by Esler

point to a certain air of independence.

"I remember the night we unloaded him," said Mrs. Warren. "He and Bud had an argument about manners right there on the spot. He was a hot-headed horse, but he learned some manners from Bud. Most of our horses would walk up to Bud and put their heads on his shoulder as soon as they saw him. Not Sugar though. He just wasn't the type to use anybody's shoulder."

Huntley's observations of Sugar Bars were in the same vein.

"Sugar Bars was a smart horse, but he was also mischievous. Many times I can remember putting a halter on him. He'd look me straight in the eye while I was doing it, acting as if he were so glad to see me. Then, quick as can be, he'd nip me."

Foaled just a decade after the formation of the AQHA, Sugar Bars helped usher in a new era in the evolution of the Quarter Horse. Sugar Bars was an extremely consistent sire. Out of every conceivable kind of mare, he sired speedy, good-looking, athletic horses who could and would do whatever was asked of them.

And when his sons and daughters were placed into production, they proved that they could reproduce both their type and versatility.

Such Sugar Bars sons as Classy Bar, Flit Bar, Jule Bar, Sucaryl, Bar Flit, Bars Bailey, Sugar Band, Bar Pistol, Double Sugar, Albar, Flying Bar Fly, Sugar Leo, Vanna Bar, Bar's Bert, Dan's Sugar Bars, Otoe, Pacific Bars, Gofar Bar, Justice Bars, Sugar Bull, Quick Henry, Connie Reb, Counterplay, Mr. Cabin Bar, and others all proved to be superior sires.

Jewel's Leo Bar (best known as Freckles), a 1962 son of Sugar Bars who was out of Leo Pan, by Leo, headed a great family of cutting horses for Marion Flynt of Midland, Texas. His well-known get included, among others, Colonel Freckles, Freckles Playboy, and Mia Freckles.

And the daughters of Sugar Bars were every bit as potent as the sons. They produced 462 Register of Merit race horses who earned $2,490,028. They also produced 140 halter point-earners of 2,714.5 points and 300 performance point-earners of 6,279.5 points. Some 116 of their produce earned performance ROMs and 24 achieved their AQHA Championships.

When Sugar Bars came on the scene in the early 1950s, there was considerable controversy over the number of half-Thoroughbreds that were being admitted into the Quarter Horse registry. There was concern that, once these horses were put into breeding production, Quarter type conformation would be gradually lost.

At the beginning of the Sugar Bars era, it remained to be proved what a half-Thoroughbred could offer the Quarter Horse world as a sire. Sugar Bars established, beyond a shadow of a doubt, that with the right type of Thoroughbred blood and conformation it was something very positive, and his descendants are still proving it today.

Jewel's Leo Bar, a 1962 son of Sugar Bars, and out of Leo Pan, by Leo. Better known as Freckles, Jewel's Leo Bar was owned by Marion Flynt of Midland, Texas. Freckles sired only 101 foals, partially due to the fact that he died at the relatively young age of 16. Among the horses he sired, however, were Colonel Freckles, the 1976 NCHA Futurity Champion; Freckles Playboy, Co-Reserve Champion of the 1976 NCHA Futurity; Mia Freckles, 1976 Non-Pro Futurity Champion; and Jay Freckles, the 1976 NCHA Open Reserve Champion. He also sired a number of other great horses.
Photo by Dalco

20   MOON DECK

By Diane Simmons

**Moon Deck was
a very strong link
in the chain of the
Top Deck (TB) line.**

MOON DECK is responsible for one of the most important dynasties in the Quarter Horse racing industry. He sired the great Jet Deck, who, in turn, sired the incomparable Easy Jet; and he also sired Top Moon, who sired the renowned Lady Bug's Moon.

Moon Deck was sired by Top Deck (TB), who is featured in the first *Legends* book. Top Deck was foaled on the King Ranch in 1945. He was injured at an early age and never made it to the racetrack. However, one report says he did show some sizzling early speed before he was injured. He was either given or sold to Ernest Lane in Odom, Tex., and was later purchased by J.B. Ferguson, a well-known race-horse man from Wharton, Texas.

Moon Deck's dam was a sorrel mare initially named just Moonlight. Like so many other horses of that era, Moonlight's background cannot be documented completely. But, according to many records and reports, she was bred by David Colligan of Church Point, La., and her dam was Colligan's fine race mare Mae. This exceptional runner was sired by The Dun Horse (better known in Louisiana as Le Bye des Trahan), one of the greatest sons of Dewey.

Colligan bred Mae to a Thoroughbred stallion named Peace Pipe, who had been injured in training at the Fair Grounds, New Orleans' famous track. The result was the sorrel filly Moonlight, foaled in 1938. When she was a long yearling,

Moon Deck, with James Carter, circa 1964, in Clovis, California. A brown horse, Moon Deck stood about 16.2 hands and weighed approximately 1,100 pounds.

**Photo by
Darol Dickinson**

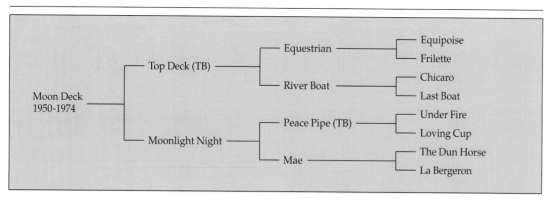

			Equipoise
		Equestrian	Frilette
	Top Deck (TB)		Chicaro
		River Boat	Last Boat
Moon Deck 1950-1974			Under Fire
		Peace Pipe (TB)	Loving Cup
	Moonlight Night		The Dun Horse
		Mae	La Bergeron

Colligan turned her over to Gabriel Strauss for training.

Moonlight, who began racing at the age of 22 months, had blazing speed, and whipped anyone who challenged her on the Louisiana straightaways.

J.B. Ferguson, meanwhile, was often in Cajun country. According to his daughter, Joan Ferguson Attaway, J.B. and a gentleman named Claude Morien owned a dinner club in Lafayette, La., called the Southern Club, which had a racetrack behind it. Says Joan, "Claude was always looking for mares for Daddy." Joan adds that it was through Morien that Ferguson bought Moonlight, for $300 cash.

About the only thing Ferguson changed for Moonlight was her name. He lengthened it to Moonlight Night since, when he applied for her registration, he found out the name Moonlight was already recorded. He continued racing the sorrel throughout Louisiana and south Texas. She became such a respected figure that an AQHA inspector reportedly wrote the following about her: "This mare was a great race mare prior to the AQRA, and won at least one race against Shue Fly."

In 1949, Ferguson bred Moonlight Night to Top Deck, who, at that time, was still at Ernest Lane's in Odom. On March 28, 1950, Moon Deck was foaled at Ferguson's Wharton ranch.

Ferguson watched the brown colt grow, and while the colt looked good as a youngster, he looked even better as he matured. Says Joan Attaway: "There was never a question in Daddy's mind about Moon Deck being a race horse."

When Moon Deck was a 2-year-old, Ferguson gave him to Paul Simar for training (the same Simar who trained Miss Princess) and jockey Pat Castille (the same Castille who rode Miss Princess when she defeated

Shue Fly at Del Rio, Texas). According to Joan, "Pat couldn't wait to ride him."

Moon Deck's first official out came on April 26, 1952, at Del Rio, Texas. It was a 3½-furlong contest, and the brown colt won by 4 lengths in :41.4. Adds Joan, "He was the only horse in the finish-line picture." Moon Deck followed that maiden victory with a win the following month in the 440-yard division of the Texas Futurity at San Angelo.

Like his more famous paternal half-brother, Go Man Go (also by Top Deck and bred by Ferguson), Moon Deck was a bit of a rogue as a race horse. "In fact, I always called Moon Deck an outlaw," recalls Joan. "He was the only horse we ever owned who had to be scratched from a race because he flipped over in the starting gates; this happened at Ruidoso Downs. He was also a handful to handle in the barn, although he wasn't as bad as Go Man Go in that respect.

"Moon Deck did enjoy people, though. He enjoyed being touched . . . he wanted

to be a part of the world, but he wanted it on his own terms. He also wanted to run, and I can remember a lot of match races in Louisiana where we cleaned a lot of Cajuns of their money."

Attaway also says that Moon Deck never sired anything that was easy to control, a sentiment echoed by top trainer Bubba Cascio. "They were all rank and hard to break," he said, "even if they were two or three generations down the line. And they can be a handful even after you think you have them completely broke and under control."

Moon Deck ran for 6 years. When he was retired, he had 62 outs to his credit with 11 firsts, 11 seconds, and 6 thirds. His list of wins included, among others, the 1955 Los Alamitos Quarter Horse Championship and the Albuquerque Derby. His bank account reflected $22,087. That's not much money by today's standards, but at the time, no more than two dozen Quarter Horses had won that much on the track.

In October 1955, Ferguson held his annual sale at his Bar JF Ranch, and Moon Deck was a feature offering. Among those attending the sale was James V.A. Carter, a noted horseman and breeder who was, at that time, ranching in southeastern Oregon. He later moved to Clovis, California. Evidently when Moon Deck was racing in California, Carter had seen him and liked what he saw.

Remembers Joan, "Carter called us before that sale to ask what horses would be in it. We told him Moon Deck would be there. He drove to the sale with only one thought on his mind—to buy Moon Deck. And, as far as we were concerned, he was the kind of man whom we wanted to buy Moon Deck." And he did, for $9,000.

Carter was no stranger to quality horses. In 1944, he had purchased four yearling fillies from H.S. Bissell of Las Cruces, New

Moon Deck ran away from the rest of the field in this race at Del Rio, Texas.

Mexico. Three of the fillies were sired by Midnight Jr. and the fourth was by Nassak (TB). As the story goes, Carter had initially selected just two Midnight Jr. fillies, but when it came time to load them, the third one raised such a ruckus over being separated from her buddies that she was loaded, too. Eventually registered as Belle of Midnight, that third filly would eventually become a key contributor to the Moon Deck story.

In 1946, Carter had purchased the good

Three Bars (TB) son, Barred, sight unseen, from Melville Haskell of Tucson. He wanted this horse to head his breeding program. By 1955, he had an outstanding set of Barred daughters in his broodmare band, and he had a hunch that Moon Deck would cross well with them—a hunch that proved to be right on target.

For the next 2 years, Carter continued to

Miss Moon Bar (No. 4) winning a race at Los Alamitos, circa early 1960s. This AAAT mare was by Moon Deck and out of Miss Capri Bar, and was foaled in 1958.

Photo Courtesy of *Speedhorse* **magazine**

Bar Deck AAA, by Moon Deck and out of Miss Night Bar, was foaled in 1958.
Photo by Darol Dickinson; Courtesy of *Speedhorse* **Magazine**

race Moon Deck as well as breed him. Moon Deck's first foals were yearlings when he was retired from the track in 1958.

One of Carter's Barred daughters was Miss Night Bar, foaled in 1950. A solid AAA race mare, she was the first foal of Belle of Midnight, that third filly by Midnight Jr. mentioned earlier. When bred to Moon Deck, Miss Night Bar produced an incredible eight AAA runners: Miss Jet Deck, Bar Deck, Clovis Deck, Limelite, Lightning Jet, Jet Too, Miss Prissy Jet, and Jet Deck. The Moon Deck-Miss Night Bar cross remains, to this day, one of the most successful in the history of horse racing.

Another of the Barred daughters bred to Moon Deck was Rica Bar. Her dam was Caprica, the Nassak (TB) filly that Carter had purchased from Bissell. Rica Bar produced only one foal before dying at an early age, but that foal was Top Moon, by Moon Deck. Top Moon, a AAAT stakes winner, became the founder of another great family of speed horses.

Three other Barred daughters out of Caprica distinguished themselves when bred to Moon Deck. They were Miss Capri Bar AA, who became a leading dam of ROM race colts (including Miss Caprideck AAAT); Barica, a AAA stakes winner; and Prica Bar.

When Caprica herself was bred to Moon Deck, she produced Caprideck AAAT, foaled in 1957, who won nearly $31,000 and was named the 1962 Champion Quarter Running Gelding.

By 1962, Carter had raised Moon Deck's stud fee to $2,000. In addition to those horses already mentioned, such hard-

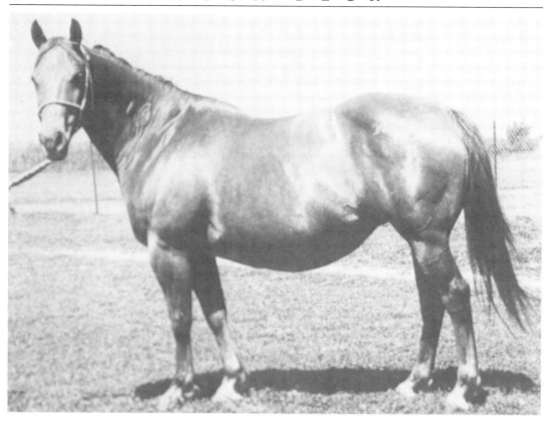

Miss Night Bar, foaled in 1950, produced eight AAA or AAAT running horses when bred to Moon Deck.

Photo Courtesy of Darol Dickinson

knocking race horses as Miss Moon Deck, Miss Moon Bar, Miss Bar Moon, Rica Moon, Cue Deck, and JVAC had firmly established Moon Deck as a leading sire of race horses. All of those horses were either AAA or AAAT. And there were many more to come, such as Cheque Deck, Harlequin, Mr Jet Deck, Van Moon, Van Deck, Moon's Copy, Moon O Sugar, Moon Request, and Moon Lad—all AAA.

In August 1966, Carter sold Moon Deck to Don Keith and J. Ralph Bell of the Keith-Bell Ranch in Visalia, California. A few months later, Keith and Bell sold half-interest in the horse to Lowell Dillingham of Honolulu. Per Dillingham's request, they agreed to no longer stand the stallion to outside mares.

Moon Deck remained at the Keith-Bell Ranch until his death on January 13, 1974, caused by an impacted intestine.

Although he never gained as much fame as a breeding horse as his sire did, Moon Deck played a key role in perpetuating the Top Deck line. If it were not for Moon Deck, there would have been no Top Moon, Jet Deck, Easy Jet, or Lady Bug's Moon. Moon Deck was indeed a very strong link in the chain of the Top Deck (TB) line.

Top Moon AAAT, one of Moon Deck's most influential sons. Foaled in 1960, he was out of Rica Bar, by Barred. Among his 799 sons and daughters who earned a Register of Merit in racing were 2 sons who won the All American Futurity: Bugs Alive In 75, and Moon Lark in 1978. He also sired Lady Bug's Moon, who won $191,573, and ran second in the 1968 All American Futurity.

Photo by Joseph P. Wilson; Courtesy of *Quarter Horse Track* magazine

21

JET DECK

By Diane Simmons

Jet Deck was the first Quarter Horse to win in excess of $200,000.

JET DECK, who was a champion race horse and champion sire, figures into some of Quarter racing's brightest moments . . . and one of its darkest.

Jet Deck was foaled April 19, 1960, on the Clovis, Calif., ranch of his breeders, William H. and James V.A. Carter. With Moon Deck as his sire and Miss Night Bar as his dam, Jet Deck was a product of one of the most successful crosses in Quarter racing history. In all, the Moon Deck—Miss Night Bar cross accounted for 10 Register of Merit race horses, 8 of whom were AAA.

Wilbur Stuchal, a race-horse trainer from Atlanta, Kan., purchased Jet Deck as a long yearling from the Carters for J.B. Chambers of Littleton, Colorado. Chambers had never seen the bay colt, but he had seen his full sister, Miss Jet Deck, run and thought enough of her to give the $6,500 asking price for Jet Deck.

Jet Deck arrived in Colorado in the fall of 1961, during the time that the Centennial race meet was being held in Denver. One evening Chambers invited a few friends who were attending the meet

Jet Deck was shown by Jerry Wells as a 4-year-old during the summer, and earned 5 halter points. A bay, Jet Deck stood 15.3 hands and weighed about 1,100 pounds.

Photo Courtesy of Reba Warren

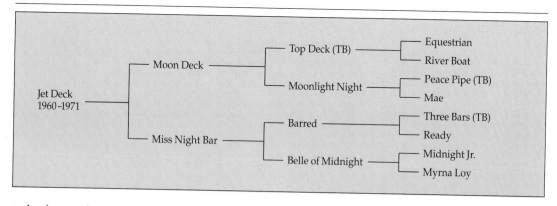

Jet Deck
1960–1971

- Moon Deck
  - Top Deck (TB)
    - Equestrian
    - River Boat
  - Moonlight Night
    - Peace Pipe (TB)
    - Mae
- Miss Night Bar
  - Barred
    - Three Bars (TB)
    - Ready
  - Belle of Midnight
    - Midnight Jr.
    - Myrna Loy

to look over his new acquisition.

One of those invited was Bud Warren of Perry, Okla., and, in an article on Jet Deck by Jim Scarbrough that appeared in the April 1972 issue of *The Quarter Horse Journal*, Warren recalled the occasion.

"Jay (Chambers) had a little 40-watt bulb up the top of that barn and we couldn't see nothin', but I thought I had seen all I wanted to anyway. My exact words were, 'If that's a race horse, I'm gonna quit the business.'"

A phone call from Stuchal the following spring, before Jet Deck had even started a race, gave Warren his first clue that he might have missed the mark in his assessment of the colt.

"Remember now that he (Stuchal) had been there, and actually was the one I was talking to, the night we were up at Jay Chambers' and looked at Jet Deck," recalled Warren in the Scarbrough feature.

"And understand that I had nothing to do whatsoever with Jet Deck at that time, other than the fact that Wilbur had some of my colts in his stable along with Jet Deck.

"Charlie Smith, the only jockey to ever ride Jet Deck, was working the colt on the track that morning, and another jockey was putting a blow in Tee Beau, a tough AAA stakes horse. Here comes ol' Tee Beau down the track with the jockey a hoopin' and hollerin', and before Charlie knows it, Jet Deck grabs the bit and, from almost a standing start, runs up and eyeballs the ol' horse.

"It scared Charlie to death because he knew Wilbur didn't want to work Jet Deck that fast, afraid he would hurt him. But, Charlie and Wilbur knew what they had

Halter and Performance Record: 1963 World Champion Quarter Running Horse; 1963 Champion Quarter Running Stallion; 1963 Champion Quarter Running 3-Year-Old Colt; 1962 Champion Quarter Running Stallion; 1962 Champion Quarter Running 2-Year-Old Colt; Register of Merit Racing; Halter Points: 5.

Progeny Record:

AQHA Champions: 5	Performance Registers of Merit: 9
Foal Crops: 8	Race Money Earned: $6,804,289
Foals Registered: 580	Race Registers of Merit: 383
Halter Point-Earners: 15	Race Starters: 486
Halter Points Earned: 198	Superior Halter Awards: 1
Performance Point-Earners: 14	Superior Performance Awards: 1
Performance Points Earned: 269.5	Supreme Champions: 1 (Jet Threat)
Leading Race Money-Earner: Easy Jet ($445,723)	

after that little episode, and it was that night that Wilbur called me to let me know so he could rub it in about the statement I had made up at Jay's."

Jet Deck won his first start at Bay Meadows in northern California on February 27, 1962. From Bay Meadows he was hauled to Los Alamitos in the southern portion of the state, but shinbucked before the opening of the meet there. Under Stuchal's care, however, Jet Deck recovered quicker than expected, and went to the post on May 3 in a 350-yard allowance, which he won.

Five days later, he won the Juvenile Championship at Los Alamitos over Tiny

Jet Deck easily won the second division of the 1963 Pacific Coast Quarter Horse Racing Association Derby Trials, and went on to win the championship. The race was held at Los Alamitos in California. Tiny Charger finished second, and Moolah Bar, third.

Photo Courtesy of Phil Livingston

Charger and Flicka's Request. Stuchal then hauled Jet Deck to Ruidoso Downs, but the colt was still sore, so he was pin-fired and turned out to rest in a Colorado pasture for 45 days.

Jet Deck returned to work in the fall of 1962, fit and ready to race. He won the Juvenile Prep at Arizona Downs in Phoenix in October, covering the 400 yards in :20.3. In November, he won the Juvenile Championship at the same track over his three-quarter brother, Top Moon. His time of :20.1 for the 400 yards equalled the 2-year-old colt record of the day.

In December of 1962, Jet Deck set the straightaways on fire.

Within the space of that one month, he won the Pacific Coast Quarter Horse Racing Association (PCQHRA) Cal-Bred Futurity, Los Alamitos Futurity, and the Kindergarten Futurity. In the latter, he set a 2-year-old world record of :19.9 for 400 yards.

He finished the year with earnings of $138,341—the most money ever won by a 2-year-old up to that time. He was named the Champion Quarter Running Stallion and the Champion Quarter Running 2-Year-Old.

Jet Deck began his 3-year-old campaign on January 5, 1963, at Bay Meadows, and he wrapped it up on December 21 at Los Alamitos. In between he finished first in the PCQHRA Derby, the Los Alamitos Championship, the Ruidoso Champion-ship, the Rocky Mountain Quarter Horse Derby, and the Colorado Wonderland Championship.

He won eight of eleven starts as a 3-year-old, and became the first Quarter

A well-known painting of Jet Deck, by Orren Mixer, with Charlie Smith, his regular jockey, in the irons. Mixer did this painting in 1963.

Reproduced Courtesy of Orren Mixer

The legendary Easy Jet was the star of Jet Deck's third crop of foals, in 1967.

Horse to win in excess of $200,000. He was named the 1963 World Champion Quarter Running Horse, Champion Stallion, and Champion 3-Year-Old Colt.

During his career of two seasons, Jet Deck started thirty-one times with twenty-two firsts, four seconds, and two thirds. He failed to light the board only three times, and one of those was due to disqualification. He failed to run AAA or AAAT only twice.

Bud Warren had kept up with Jet Deck's highly successful racing career. Chambers and Stuchal had never let him forget his initial assessment of their runner and had kidded him unmercifully over it. One day at Ruidoso, however, Warren approached Chambers about leasing Jet Deck.

Chambers liked the idea of Jet Deck standing at the home of Leo and Sugar Bars, so the two men shook hands to seal the deal and Jet Deck went to Oklahoma to stand the 1964 season. Warren purchased one-half interest in him in 1967.

From his first crop of foals, in 1965,

came Jet Smooth, a AAA AQHA Champion, and Jolly Jet Deck, who won 22 feature events and was the 1971 Champion Quarter Running Aged Mare.

Jet Deck Junior, foaled in 1966, won $148,172 in 2 years of racing and was the 1968 Champion Quarter Running 2-Year-Old Colt and the 1969 Champion Quarter Running 3-Year-Old Colt.

The legendary Easy Jet was the star of Jet Deck's third crop of foals, in 1967. Also foaled that year were Jet Injun, the 1971 Champion Quarter Running Aged Stallion; Jet Threat, an AQHA Supreme Champion; and Phantom Jet, an AQHA Champion and Superior halter horse.

Jet Charger was a member of Jet Deck's

Jet Charger was a 1968 son of Jet Deck and Rosa Leo, by Leo. Rated AAAT, he was the 1972 Champion Quarter Running Aged Stallion. After Jet Deck died, Bud Warren replaced him with Jet Charger, and stood him for several years.

Photo Courtesy of Reba Warren

Jet Deck Junior was a good-looking son of a gun. Foaled in l966, he was out of Drift, a Leo daughter. Rated AAAT, he won seven major races and $148,173, and sired many top running horses. **Photo by Orren Mixer**

1968 foal crop. In 3 years of racing he earned $190,068 and he was the 1972 Champion Quarter Running Aged Stallion.

The star of Jet Deck's fifth foal crop was Mr. Jet Moore. In 2 years of racing, he won 10 feature events and earned $341,405. He was the 1972 World Champion Quarter Running Horse, Champion Stallion, and Champion 3-Year-Old Colt.

Three Jet Deck superstars were foaled in 1970. Elan Again earned $199,544 in 4 years of racing and was the 1975 Champion Quarter Running Aged Mare. Gallant Jet raced only as a 2-year-old, earning $98,952. He was the 1972 Champion Quarter Running 2-Year-Old Colt. Possumjet, Jet Deck's top money-earning daughter, bankrolled $406,810 in 2 years of campaigning. She earned $336,630 of it by virtue of her victory in the 1972 All-American Futurity.

Lanty's Jet was the star of Jet Deck's 1971 foal crop. In 3 years of racing, she earned $216,942. Flaming Jet, with earnings of $168,778, and Twin Jet, who earned $104,111, were also standouts of the class of 1971.

The stars of Jet Deck's eighth and final crop of foals were Showum Jet, Jet Commanche, and Sompin Lika Jet. Showum Jet won two futurities and earned $151,522 in his only year on the tracks. Jet Commanche raced for 5 years, earning $122,642. He was the 1975 Champion Quarter Running 3-Year-Old Gelding. Sompin Lika Jet, Jet Deck's final AAA offspring, earned $111,417 in 4 years of racing.

By 1971 Jet Deck was, at the relatively young age of 11, a leading race horse sire whose star was on the rise. In Warren's own words, he (Warren), Chambers, and everyone who was breeding to Jet Deck was making money.

Then, in the early morning hours of August 26, 1971, Jet Deck was found dead in his paddock at the Warren Ranch.

Dean Schultz, a long-time Warren employee, discovered Jet Deck around 7 a.m. as he arrived at the ranch to begin his morning chores. He immediately called Warren, who was at Ruidoso Downs for the All-American Futurity trials.

An extensive post-mortem examination revealed that Jet Deck died of a massive injection of barbiturates into the jugular vein. The responsible party (or parties) has never been apprehended, and the case has never been solved.

Reba Warren, Bud's widow, remembers the legendary stallion well. "He was one of the most gentle horses I'd ever been around," she recalled. "His gentleness was probably one of the reasons he was killed so easily. He probably gave the people who did it no trouble.

"He was extremely easy to handle as a stud, and he enjoyed as much attention as he could get. I can remember lots of times when people would come to the ranch to take pictures of him. He'd run and play for them, doing everything he could to help them get a good picture."

In November of 1972, just a little more than 1 year after Jet Deck's death, *The Quarter Horse Journal* interviewed several horsemen and asked them to express their feelings about the stallion. One of the best replies came from Stuchal, who said, "As a sire, he was the greatest. His colts and racing record will speak for themselves, as everyone knows. He had great conformation, great desire and determination, and the best coordination of any horse I've ever seen in my life.

"His loss to the horse breeding industry can't be evaluated. As far as I am con-

A visitor to Bud Warren's place took this photograph of Jet Deck just a few days before he was killed in August 1971. **Photo Courtesy of Reba Warren**

cerned, there aren't enough adjectives and words in our language to describe his loss to the horse breeding industry."

Few things have changed since Stuchal offered those words in 1972. Jet Deck's loss to the industry is still viewed as a major one, and the mystery surrounding his death has never gone away.

There is, however, no mystery about the lasting contributions that Jet Deck made to the Quarter Horse world, both as a race horse and as a sire.

22

LENA'S BAR

By Frank Holmes

Although she was a good race mare, Lena's Bar gained her greatest fame as the dam of Easy Jet.

IF LENA'S BAR had no other claim to fame than being the dam of Easy Jet, she would still have earned for herself a permanent niche in the annals of Quarter Horse racing history. There was, however, more to the mare than that.

The Lena's Bar story began in 1951 when Walter Merrick, then living near Crawford, Okla., bought a 5-year-old Thoroughbred mare named Lena Valenti from Eldon Cluck of Dumas, Texas. She was sired by the good sprinting Thoroughbred, Gray Dream, and was out of Perhobo, by Percentage (TB)—the same Percentage who sired Three Bars (TB).

Merrick had trained Lena Valenti for Cluck in 1950 and thought enough of her breeding and early speed to purchase her.

Lena's Bar, probably Walter Merrick's greatest producing mare, is shown here after winning a 1961 400-yard race at Sunland Park, New Mexico. Trainer Ted Wells Jr. is at her head, and Elbert Minchey is the jockey. A horse called Safety First finished second, and Easter Rose was third.

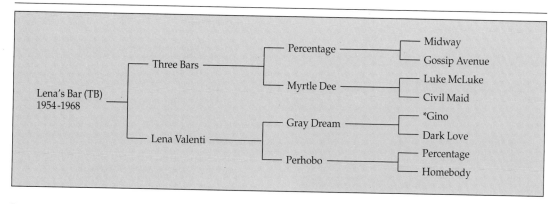

```
                                              ┌─── Midway
                              ┌─ Percentage ──┤
                              │               └─── Gossip Avenue
              ┌─ Three Bars ──┤
              │               │               ┌─── Luke McLuke
              │               └─ Myrtle Dee ──┤
Lena's Bar (TB)┤                              └─── Civil Maid
  1954-1968   │
              │                               ┌─── *Gino
              │               ┌─ Gray Dream ──┤
              └─ Lena Valenti ─┤              └─── Dark Love
                              │               ┌─── Percentage
                              └─ Perhobo ─────┤
                                              └─── Homebody
```

He continued racing her the following year, mostly at short Thoroughbred distances. In August of 1951, however, he did put her in a 440-yard sprint at Enid, Okla., to help fill the race. She responded by winning the race in wire-to-wire fashion and earning her AQHA racing Register of Merit in the process.

In 1952, Merrick leased the promising young Thoroughbred sire by the name of Three Bars from Sidney Vail of Tucson, Arizona. Merrick bred Lena Valenti to Three Bars, but she failed to get in foal.

Vail had agreed to lease Three Bars to Merrick for 2 years, but changed his mind after the first year and took the horse back to Tucson. Merrick was not to be deterred, however, and hauled Lena Valenti to Arizona to have her bred again. The resulting foal from this second try was Lena's Bar, foaled in 1954.

During the 1950s, New Mexico was the only state that allowed Thoroughbreds to compete in regular Quarter Horse races, but not in the Quarter Horse futurities for 2-year-olds. As a result, Merrick chose not to campaign Lena's Bar as a 2-year-old. As a 3-year-old, in 1957, she started eight times, winning four and equaling the track record for 400 yards at Albuquerque.

As a 4-year-old, she again started eight times and again won four races, including the Buttons and Bows Stakes and the Bright Eyes Handicap, both at Albuquerque. In 1959, she went to the post 22 times and earned a check in 21 races. On July 26, 1959, she won the 400-yard Bright Eyes Stakes at Ruidoso, and 3 weeks later

Halter and Performance Record: Racing Register of Merit.

Produce of Dam Record:

Double Dancer	1963 stallion by Double Bid Racing Register of Merit
Delta Rose	1964 mare by Tonto Bars Hank Racing Register of Merit
Jet Smooth	1965 stallion by Jet Deck Racing Register of Merit AQHA Champion
Mayflower Ann	1966 mare by Tonto Bars Hanks Racing Register of Merit
Easy Jet	1967 stallion by Jet Deck Racing Register of Merit 1969 World Champion Quarter Running Horse 1970 Champion Quarter Running Stallion

took the 400-yard Miller Motel Allowance at the same track.

The field that Lena's Bar went up against in the Miller Motel Allowance serves as a prime example of the fast company that she kept throughout her racing career. Finishing behind her that day were such world champion running horses as Go Man Go, Double Bid, War Chic, and Vanetta Dee.

In 5 years of racing, Lena's Bar started 76 times, winning 24, placing second 18 times, and third 10 times. Her total race winnings

Little Lena Bars, a full sister to Lena's Bar, set a world's record for 330 yards at La Mesa Park on July 19, 1964. This was one of several records she set. Bobby Harmon was the jockey. Although she was speedier on the track, Little Lena Bar did not match Lena's Bar as a producer.

Lena's Bar after winning the 1959 Miller Motel Allowance at Ruidoso Downs, New Mexico. Four current or past world champion running horses finished behind Lena's Bar in this race. Walter Merrick is on the left, holding the cooler, with his wife, Christien ("Tien") beside him. The jockey is E. Armstrong.

amounted to $28,311. She retired sound.

After foaling Lena's Bar, Lena Valenti continued to produce well for Merrick. In 1956, she foaled the filly, Clovis' Doll, by Clovis' Champ. Clovis' Doll went on to earn her AAA rating on the track and was the dam of the AAA AQHA Champion Clovis' Win. In 1958, Lena Valenti foaled Roman Bob, a colt by Bob's Folly, who was subsequently gelded and who also earned his AAA rating.

In 1960 Lena Valenti produced a full sister to Lena's Bar named Little Lena Bar, who as a race horse, turned the Quarter Horse world upside down.

From July 1963 to September 1964, Little Lena Bar tied or broke the existing world records for 220, 250, and 330 yards. In addition, she set new track records at 400 and 440 yards.

For a while it looked like all of the world records in Quarter Horse racing were going to belong to the diminutive Thoroughbred filly. Responding to this paradox,

Double Dancer was by Double Bid and out of Lena's Bar. The first foal of Lena's Bar, he is shown here after winning a 350-yard sprint at La Mesa Park on May 28, 1966. Merrick's famous "14" brand is on Double Dancer's left hip. Walter and Christien are at the far left.

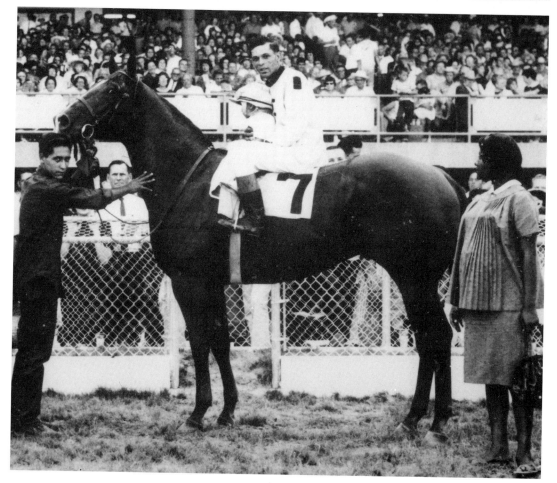

Tonto Bars Hank after setting a new track record for 400 yards at Albuquerque. Merrick trained Tonto Bars Hank for Milo and C.G. Whitcomb of Sterling, Colo., during this portion of his racing career. Merrick also stood Tonto Bars Hank at stud for several years, during which time he bred Lena's Bar to him twice to get the only two daughters she ever produced: Delta Rose and Mayflower Ann.

Delta Rose, a good-looking daughter of Tonto Bars Hank and Lena's Bar, shown here after winning the 1967 Kansas Quarter Horse Derby Trial at La Mesa Park on August 4, 1967. The trainer was Phil Garrett and the jockey, W. Lovell.

Byou Bird, a granddaughter of Lena's Bar. By Good Bird (TB) and out of Delta Rose, Byou Bird was one of Merrick's most consistent performers during the early 1970s. She earned over $300,000.

the AQHA deleted all mention, times, and records set by Thoroughbreds. From that date forward, the AQHA no longer recognized world's records; the only records that went into the books were track records. It should be mentioned that organized Quarter Horse racing was first sanctioned by the American Quarter Racing Association. The AQRA refused to recognize world's records because of the considerable variations in tracks. The AQRA went out of business in the late 1940s, and AQHA became the sanctioning body for Quarter racing.

Getting back to Lena's Bar, Merrick placed her in his broodmare band in 1962 and bred her to Double Bid, the 1959 Champion Quarter Running Stallion. The result of this cross was Double Dancer, a chestnut colt. The Oklahoma cowboy-turned-race-horse-man turned down $25,000 for him while the colt was still a weanling. A solid AAA runner, Double Dancer went on to enjoy a moderately successful career at stud.

Leased for several years by Hank Wiescamp of Alamosa, Colo., Double Dancer was instrumental in founding the St. Dancer-St. Limit line of horses featured by Wiescamp in the 1980s.

In 1963, Lena's Bar was bred to Tonto Bars Hank, winner of the 1960 All-American Futurity and Champion Quarter Running Stallion that year. Delta Rose, a good-looking sorrel filly, was foaled the following spring. In 16 starts as a 2- and 3-year-old, Delta Rose won 3 races, placed in 4 stakes, and earned $12,794. She also earned a solid AAA speed rating. Shown one time at halter, she took first in a class of seventeen 3-year-old mares at the 1967 Texas State Fair.

In 1968, Merrick bred Delta Rose to Good Bird (TB) and got Oh Johney, who earned a speed index of 94. Bred back to Good Bird in 1969, Delta Rose produced Byou Bird in 1970.

Byou Bird started 26 times for Merrick and won half of those races. She won four futurities as a 2-year-old and was named the 1972 World Champion 2-Year-Old-Filly. Her total track winnings were $309,643, and she earned a speed index of 113.

In 1964, Lena's Bar made the first of two visits to the court of Jet Deck, the 1963 World Champion Quarter Running

"MAYFLOWER ANN"

SUNLAND PARK, N.M.   FEB. 8, 1969   B. HARMON, UP
DONIS BE GOOD (2nd)   400 Yds 20.15   FAILA MAY DAY (3)
WALTER F. MERRICK, OWNER   ROBERT L. WILLOUGHBY, TR.

Mayflower Ann, the second of the two full sisters by Tonto Bars Hank and out of Lena's Bar. She is shown here winning a 400-yard race at Sunland Park on February 8, 1969. Robert Willoughby was her trainer for this event and Bobby Harmon was up.

Walter Merrick has often been quoted as saying that Lena's Bar was one of the greatest horses he had ever raised.

Horse. In 1965 she foaled a classy sorrel colt with white on his face and on all four legs. Named Jet Smooth, he became a stellar performer at both the track and in the show ring.

As a 2-year-old, he won the Kansas Futurity. The following year he won the All-American Congress Derby, and in 1968 the World's Championship Classic. In all, he started 25 times and earned $79,089.

As a show horse, he won his class and was reserve champion stallion at the 1967 All-American Quarter Horse Con-

gress; won his class at the 1967 Oklahoma State Fair; and won his class and was reserve champion stallion at the 1968 Texas State Fair. He was named an AQHA Champion in 1968.

Jet Smooth also enjoyed a highly successful career at stud. He sired 348 racing Register of Merit earners, 18 performance Register of Merit earners, and 23 halterpoint earners.

His get earned $2,546,842 on the tracks

Jet Smooth, by Jet Deck, was probably the best looking of the Lena's Bars and was her only AQHA Champion. After a successful career on the straightaway and in the show ring, Jet Smooth went on to achieve even greater fame as a sire. He proved equally adept at siring race horses, performance horses, and halter horses.
Photo by Peta-Anne, Courtesy of Roy Browning Ranches

and included Smooth Coin, the 1973 Champion Quarter Running 3-Year-Old-Filly, and A Smooth Request, the earner of $77,162.

Jet Smooth's arena-performing get earned 1,047.5 points. Among them was Smooth Herman, the 1977 AQHA Honor Roll High-Point Junior Cutting Horse.

In 1965, Lena's Bar returned to the court of Tonto Bars Hank, and produced a second filly, Mayflower Ann. From 23 starts, she garnered 10 wins and $18,947 in earnings. She achieved a speed index of 100 and was stakes-placed several times.

As a producer for Merrick, Mayflower Ann was the dam of three Register of Merit race horses. The best of the three was Talladega, a 1980 gelding by Hempen (TB). He earned $28,327 on the tracks, won the 1st Au Revoir Handicap (1st Div.), and achieved a speed index of 105.

In 1966, Lena's Bar was once again bred to Jet Deck for what was to be her last foal. Saving her best effort for last, she foaled Easy Jet in 1967.

Lena's Bar died in 1968 at the age of 14, after a 9-month bout with a bladder disease. No expense was spared to try to save her, but nothing worked.

Her final production record shows that she was the dam of five foals. All five were race winners with four attaining speed indexes of 100+, and one achieving a speed index of 90+. Race winnings of her offspring totaled $557,199. One of her foals, Jet Smooth, was shown to his AQHA Championship, and had Merrick been so inclined, several more surely could have.

Walter Merrick is, without a doubt, the dean of Quarter Horse race breeders. In Merrick's long and illustrious career as a breeder of sprinters, he has often been quoted as saying that Lena's Bar was one of the greatest horses he had ever raised.

And, after all, she was the dam of Easy Jet.

Smooth Coin, the 1973 Champion Quarter Running 3-Year-Old Filly. She was a paternal granddaughter of Lena's Bar . . . being by Jet Smooth and out of Scotch Coin, by Scottish. She was bred and owned by Larry and Charlotte Wilcox of Alamosa, Colorado.

Photo by Gloria Loose, Courtesy of Charlotte Wilcox

23 EASY JET

By Diane Simmons

Not only did Easy Jet burn up the racetracks, he was a sire extraordinaire.

FOR MORE than 60 years, Walter Merrick of Sayre, Okla., has been recognized as one of the leading kings of Quarter Horse racing. And, reigning right beside him, for some of those years was his stallion Easy Jet.

Easy Jet was foaled January 12, 1967, on a ranch Merrick was leasing at Quanah, Texas. At the end of the lease, Merrick loaded up and relocated to Sayre.

Merrick liked what he saw from the moment the sorrel colt with the white blaze hit the ground. And, if anyone had a practiced eye for recognizing quality horseflesh, it was Walter Merrick.

Merrick was born when the 20th century was still young. He grew up as a cowboy, tending cattle and riding the range for months at a time. He favored speed in his horses, and by the early 1930s, he was winning just about every match he could put together. Then, in 1936 he bought a

Easy Jet, easily one of the greatest.

Photo by Orren Mixer; Courtesy of Walter Merrick

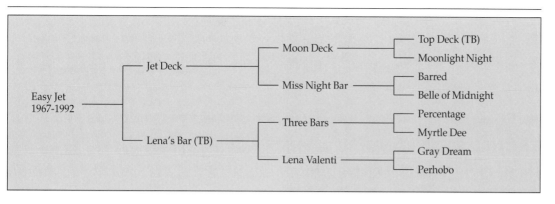

Easy Jet
1967-1992

- Jet Deck
  - Moon Deck
    - Top Deck (TB)
    - Moonlight Night
  - Miss Night Bar
    - Barred
    - Belle of Midnight
- Lena's Bar (TB)
  - Three Bars
    - Percentage
    - Myrtle Dee
  - Lena Valenti
    - Gray Dream
    - Perhobo

stallion named Midnight Jr.

That started Merrick on what would become one of the longest and most illustrious trails of any member of the Quarter Horse racing industry. His name was linked with Grey Badger II, Bob's Folly, Tonto Bars Hank, and many others. In 1951, he stood in the middle of a flurry of controversy when he leased Three Bars (TB) from Sid Vail. A large segment of the early QH world didn't believe in infusing Thoroughbred blood into their short-horse stock, but Merrick stood his ground. Not only did he breed to Three Bars, but he selected some of his best mares for the stallion. One of them was Lena Valenti.

A breeding between Lena Valenti and Three Bars resulted in Lena's Bar, discussed in the previous chapter. Lena's Bar, foaled in 1954, became an outstanding race horse and an equally outstanding producer.

When bred to Jet Deck, she foaled Easy Jet in January 1967. Lena's Bar died of a bladder infection soon after he was weaned.

Merrick definitely liked Easy Jet, but he also admitted he couldn't compare with his older full brother, Jet Smooth, in terms of prettiness. "He was never a refined horse," said Merrick, "but he was big, strong, and correct with tremendous bone structure. He looked as if he could take pressure."

The big colt began growing, getting bigger and stronger. Merrick watched him and, day by day, he could see something special in Easy Jet. "It was like an energy," he said. "He was never still. He was always doing something—even if it was just keeping the other colts in his pasture

in line. The only time he seemed to stop and rest was when he'd raise his head and just stand there, staring over a hill."

Merrick worked Easy Jet as a yearling against Jet Smooth at 350 yards, and Easy Jet won. He decided to try the big colt in a yearling race at Blue Ribbon Downs at Sallisaw, Oklahoma. He won by daylight. All that nervous energy had become pure speed.

There were some people who criticized Merrick as they stood on the sidelines and watched him take Easy Jet through his 2-year-old campaign. He was loaded into the starting gate for 26 races. He won 22 times, including the All-American,

Halter and Performance Record: 1969 Racing Register of Merit; 1969 World Champion Quarter Running Horse; 1969 and 1970 Champion Quarter Running Stallion; 1969 Champion Quarter Running 2-Year-Old Colt; 1970 Champion Quarter Running 3-Year-Old Colt; Superior Race Horse.

Progeny Record:

AQHA Champions: 1	Performance Registers of Merit: 11
Foal Crops: 24	Race Money Earned: $25,604,095
Foals Registered: 2,490	Race Registers of Merit: 1,517
Halter Point-Earners: 6	Race Starters: 1,968
Halter Points Earned: 74	Superior Performance Awards: 1
Performance Point-Earners: 27	World Champions: 9
Performance Points Earned: 440	

Leading Race Money-Earner (as of 1993): Mr Trucka Jet ($1,033,115)

179

A three-quarter front view of Easy Jet, one of the most durable race horses of all times. Note his good bone and short cannons. A sorrel, he stood 15.2 and weighed about 1,300-pounds. **Photo by Orren Mixer; Courtesy of Walter Merrick**

Kansas, Sunland Fall, Columbus Triple Crown, and the All American Quarter Horse Congress futurities. He was named World Champion Quarter Running Horse, Champion Stallion, and Champion 2-Year-Old Colt. He earned all of this success in a campaign that would have crippled almost any other 2-year-old. It's also worthwhile to note that, in most years, a 2-year-old is seldom even considered for world champion racing titles.

Merrick explained, however, that running was the best way to handle Easy Jet. "He had so much energy . . . the same energy that he'd had as a baby. He was a pain to hand-walk. All that energy had to go somewhere, and running him was the best way to handle it." And Merrick figured that if running was the best therapy for Easy Jet, he might as well be racing.

Merrick added that even though Easy Jet "didn't have a mean bone in his body, he was handful to ride. He was so quick, so fast, that he could unseat a rider who wasn't paying attention." Easy Jet returned to the tracks in 1970. He was named Champion Quarter Running Stallion and Champion Quarter Running 3-Year-Old Colt. When he retired, he took with him 38 official starts with 27 firsts, 7 seconds, 2 thirds and $445,721 in earnings. He failed to light the board only twice in his entire career. Every step the stallion took, Merrick was beside him.

In a 1971 article in *The Quarter Horse Journal*, Don Essary, AQHA director of racing at the time, wrote the following assessment of Easy Jet. ". . . Easy Jet has earned a permanent place in Quarter racing history and has done the Quarter Horse industry proud . . . If he proves himself as worthy at stud as he did on the track, he has a very, very bright future ahead of him."

In retrospect, those words formed the understatement of the century. Easy Jet did, indeed, become a truly outstanding sire, but he and his owners paid some high prices along the way.

In 1971, Merrick and Joe McDermott formed a partnership, with the latter purchasing one-half interest in both Easy Jet and Jet Smooth. Easy Jet's first foals were on the ground. By 1973, he was on the

This picture of Easy Jet was taken in 1981 when he was 14 years old.

Photo by Bill McNabb Jr.

"If he (Easy Jet) proves himself as worthy at stud as he did on the track, he has a very, very bright future ahead of him."

Walter Merrick with full brothers Easy Jet (left) and Jet Smooth.

Photo Courtesy of Diane Simmons

181

By 1973, as a 6-year-old, Easy Jet was on the AQHA Leading Sires list.

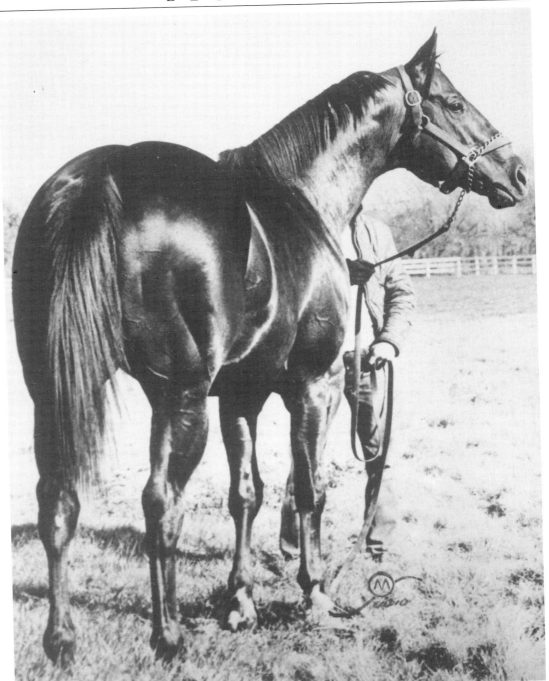

A three-quarter rear view of Easy Jet showing his powerful hindquarters.
Photo by Orren Mixer; Courtesy of Walter Merrick

AQHA Leading Sires list. His stud fee had risen from $2,000 to $5,000.

In 1976, Merrick and McDermott sold Easy Jet for $3.5 million to Buena Suerte Ranch in Roswell, New Mexico. Just a few months later, two of the ranch's principal partners were killed in an airplane crash. Merrick bought the controlling 51 percent interest in both the ranch and Easy Jet. He was partners with noted horsewoman Harriet Peckham and Leonard Blach, D.V.M.

In 1980, Easy Jet's stud fee was $30,000. The racing industry could handle it because that was the peak of the high-rolling wave that crested during the oil and gas boom. Easy Jet was then syndicated for an amazing $30,000,000. There were 50 shares at $600,000 each.

Looking back on it all, Merrick admits he was reluctant to consummate the deal. In the end, though, he agreed. He's also the first to admit that even he can "get dollar signs in my eyes just like everyone else."

Everything went fine for the first couple of years. Then, the oil bust replaced the oil boom. Some Easy Jet shareholders wanted out, and others simply ceased making their payments.

In 1982, Richard Wolfe and League Inc. stepped into the Easy Jet picture. Wolfe purchased 26 shares and threw a fistful of earnest money on the table. He wanted to move Easy Jet to his farm in Purcell, Oklahoma. Merrick refused, and hauled the stallion to Sayre, barely in time for the 1983 breeding season. Wolfe-League defaulted on their payments and filed bankruptcy. Easy Jet was moved to Belle Mere Farm in Lexington, Okla., and stood the 1985 season for $15,000.

There were some people who said Easy Jet was a "has been." They said he was overpriced and overrated. None of it was true, but Merrick was in financial trouble. So, in 1988 he sold the sorrel stallion to Roi Young of Hemet, California. Due to various problems, however, Easy Jet was in a van headed back for Oklahoma before a year had passed.

On September 28, 1989, AQHA records transferred the ownership of Easy Jet to Mark Allen and his father, Bill Allen, a

My Easy Credit, by Easy Jet and out of Kits Charge Acct, by Diamond Charge, was foaled in 1974. He had a Speed Index rating of 99, won $502,504, and was the 1977 Champion Quarter Running 3-Year-Old Colt. **Photo by Darol Dickinson**

Easy Date, a 1972 mare by Easy Jet and out of a Thoroughbred mare named Spot Cash, was the 1975 World Champion Quarter Running Horse. She had a Speed Index of 106, and earned $849,709. She was owned by Walter Merrick. Jockey Donald Knight is shown here.

prosperous businessman in Alaska. Less than 2 months later, the stallion's ownership became the Merrick-Allen Joint Venture. Then, on May 27, 1991, the name was changed to Mark Allen Inc. Easy Jet stood the 1992 breeding season at Lazy E Ranch in Guthrie, Oklahoma. He was humanely put down at the Lazy E on May 8, 1992, because of chronic laminitis (founder).

Easy Jet's first stakes winner was Our Jet in 1973. She was from his first crop in 1971. Also in that crop was Easy Mable, who won the West Texas Futurity. The

second crop included Easy Six and Easy Date. The latter was the stallion's first champion; she was named 1975 World Champion Quarter Running Horse, and when she was retired, she had nearly $850,000 in earnings. And, when she won the All-American Futurity in 1974, Easy Jet became the first All-American winner to sire an All-American winner.

Pie In The Sky was his second All-American winner, in 1979. His third All-American winner came in 1985 with Mr Trucka Jet. As of this writing, Easy Jet is still the only All-American winner to sire three All-American winners.

Easy Jet's direct offspring had earned

Real Easy Jet, by Easy Jet and out of Real Dish (TB), was foaled in 1975 and had a Speed Index of 101. He won $153,833 in two years of racing.

Photo Courtesy of Walter Merrick

more than $25,000,000 by the end of 1993. And he had sired more than 1,500 horses who earned their ROMs, with 143 of those having a 100-plus speed index. His sons and daughters have 14 championship titles and include 9 world champions. The champion names include Easy Date, Pie In The Sky, My Easy Credit, Easy Angel, Easily Smashed, Extra Easy, and Megahertz.

Easy Jet has headed the AQHA lists of All-Time Leading Sire of Sires, All-Time Leading Broodmare Sire, All-Time Leading Sire of ROM Qualifiers, All-Time Leading Sire of Stakes Winners, All-Time Leading Sire of Stakes Qualifiers, All-Time Leading Sire of Stakes Performers, and All-Time Leading Sire of AAA/AAAT Horses.

When it was decided in 1992 that Easy Jet should be put down because of his laminitis, it was necessary for a Merrick representative to travel to the Lazy E in Guthrie to look at the great old horse first.

"I couldn't go," said Walter Merrick. "I just couldn't see him like that. He was too good a friend."

Marty Powers, former Lazy E ranch manager, was there when Easy Jet was put down. Then Powers took Easy Jet back to Merrick's ranch for burial. Powers said later, "I can tell you it was the longest 3-hour trip I've ever made. This horse was the definition of greatness."

Merrick sums up his relationship with Easy Jet by saying, "I'll never be able to explain what Easy Jet did for me and my family. There's just no way. He had so much heart, so much class and pride. There can never be another one like him.

"He's buried on my place, right where I wanted to have him."

AUTHOR PROFILES

Jim Goodhue.

JIM GOODHUE is highly qualified to write on any subject dealing with the history of the American Quarter Horse.

Jim went to work for AQHA in 1958, immediately after receiving an advanced degree from Oklahoma State University. Originally hired to work for *The Quarter Horse Journal*, Jim went on to spend 11 years as head of the association's performance division and 22 years as AQHA registrar. For years, Jim wrote monthly columns for the *Quarter Running Horse Chart Book* and *Journal*. He also contributed feature material to the *Journal* on a regular basis.

A great deal of Jim's historical knowledge of the Quarter Horse breed was gained on a firsthand basis. He remembers, for instance, his first exposure to

Grey Badger II, one of the horses profiled in *Legends 2*.

"It was in the late 1940s, and Walter Merrick was match-racing Grey Badger II in Oklahoma," he recalls. "Walter was down on the track, getting the horse ready to go, and Tien, his wife, was up in the stands, taking bets. Tien had bills wrapped around every finger and she was sure doing her best to see that anybody who wanted to lay some money down on the race had the opportunity to do so."

Having retired from AQHA in 1991, Jim now lives with his wife, Robin, in Corrales, N.M., where he enjoys such retirement activities as reading, participating in the local community theater, and, by his own admission, "doing too much yard work."

Frank Holmes.

FRANK HOLMES has been writing historical articles involving the western horse for almost 30 years.

He sold his first feature article involving Quarter Horses to *Hoof and Horns* magazine in 1965. Frank is also considered one of the foremost historians of the Appaloosa breed and his historical articles have been a regular fixture in *The Appaloosa Journal* for years. He has also written a children's book with horses as its main theme.

After 18 years of working for the federal government, Frank pursued a career as a free-lance writer for several years. In addition to his work on *Legends 2*, he

wrote several historical articles involving Paint horses for *The Paint Horse Journal*, and several historical pieces involving the Appaloosa breed for *Western Horseman*.

"There is a common thread that is shared by the major stock horse breeds," he notes. "Often, while pursuing research on one breed, I find myself gaining insight into the history of another.

"It is interesting to take note of the common heritage shared by the different breeds and to observe how they branched off to form the separate and distinct breed registries that exist today."

Frank is now an assistant editor of *The Paint Horse Journal* in Fort Worth.

PHIL LIVINGSTON is well qualified to write about the stallions in this book who are remembered for their performance ability. A roper since his high school days, he has personally known many of the Texas, Arizona, and California ropers who rode the offspring of such horses as Driftwood and Lucky Blanton. And Phil roped lots of calves and steers from horses of those same bloodlines.

Phil has been acquainted with Matlock Rose for years. Matlock, of course, is the name most closely associated with the great cutting horse Jessie James. The late Jim Calhoun, who owned King's Pistol, was another friend of Phil's.

The son of an Army colonel who was in the horse cavalry, Phil spent his growing-up years in many locations, including China, where he graduated from junior high school. He says, "I've been crazy about horses ever since I was a little boy, and horses have always been the compelling interest in my life."

Today, Phil and his wife, Carol, live on a small ranch just outside Weatherford, Tex., where they raise a few Longhorn cattle. Phil always has a rope horse or two on hand, and Carol usually has a team penning horse.

Self-employed, Phil handles the advertising and public relations for several saddleries and western wear stores, and does some free-lance writing as well.

Phil Livingston.

DIANE SIMMONS authored the original *Western Horseman* book, *Legends.* Its overwhelming popularity has resulted in the publication of *Legends, Volume 2.*

Diane grew up in an agricultural area outside Memphis and began her career in journalism with the Scripps-Howard newspaper chain, while still working on her degree at Memphis State University.

She began her career as a free-lance writer in 1975, concentrating on horse-related subjects. By 1980, Diane's work had been carried in 12 publications, including *Western Horseman, American Horseman, Horse of Course, Horse & Rider, California Horse Review, Paint Horse Journal, Rodeo News, Horse Illustrated*, and *Speedhorse.*

She was one of the first equine journalists to begin working directly with veterinarians, providing medical and health articles in layman's terms for a number of magazines. She has also written feature material for *Art West* on equine and/or western artists.

Although Diane's writing accomplishments have involved almost every segment of the horse industry, she has concentrated on racing since 1978.

Now living in north Texas, she currently serves as editor for *Speedhorse/The Racing Report.* Her race-related editorials have won her several awards, including the American Quarter Horse Association Sprint Award twice, and her work was also reviewed in *The Best American Sports Writing of 1991.*

Diane C. Simmons

Photo by John R. Woodrum

PHOTO INDEX

REFERENCES

The following books and magazines were among those used for reference for this book:

That Special Breed, The American Quarter Horse, by Lyn Jank. Published in 1977 by Branch-Smith Inc., 120 St. Louis Ave., Fort Worth, TX 76104; 817-877-1314.

Outstanding Modern Quarter Horse Sires, by Nelson C. Nye. Published in 1948 by William Morrow & Company, New York City. (Out of print.)

The Great American Speedhorse, A Guide to Quarter Racing, by Walt Wiggins. Copyrighted in 1978 by Walt Wiggins. Published by Sovereign Books, a Simon & Schuster Division of Gulf & Western Corporation, New York City. (Out of print.)

The King Ranch Quarter Horses, by Robert Moorman Denhardt. Published in 1970 by the University of Oklahoma Press, 1005 Asp Ave., Norman, OK 73019; 1-800-627-7377 or 405-325-5111.

They Rode Good Horses, The First Fifty Years of the American Quarter Horse Association, by Don Hedgpeth. Published in 1990 by the American Quarter Horse Association, Box 200, Amarillo, TX 79104; 806-376-4811.

Speed and the Quarter Horse—A Payload of Sprinters, by Nelson C. Nye. Copyrighted in 1973 by Nelson C. Nye. Published by The Caxton Printers Ltd., Caldwell, ID 83605; sold through Premier Publishing, Box 137, Wamego, KS 66547; 913-456-2074.

The Quarter Running Horse, America's Oldest Breed, by Robert Moorman Denhardt. Published in 1979 by the University of Oklahoma Press, 1005 Asp Ave., Norman, OK 73019; 1-800-627-7377 or 405-325-5111.

The Quarter Running Horse 1947 and 1948 Year Books, published by the American Quarter Racing Association, Tucson, Arizona. (Out of print.)

The Quarter Horse, published by the National Quarter Horse Breeders Association, Knox City, Texas. (Out of print.)

The Most Influential Quarter Horse Sires, by Andrea Laycock Pitzer. Copyrighted in 1987 by Andrea Laycock Pitzer. Published by Premier Pedigrees, Puyallup, Wash.; sold through Premier Publishing, Box 137, Wamego, KS 66547; 913-456-2074.

Quarter Horse Reference, Volume I, by Don M. Wagoner. Published in 1972 by Quarter Horse Reference, Box 487, Grapevine, TX 76051. (We believe it is out of print.)

Great Horses of the Past, Volume I, by Bob Gray. Published in 1967 by Cordovan Corporation, Houston. (Out of print.)

Champions of the Quarter Track, by Nelson C. Nye. Published in 1950 by Coward-McCann Inc., New York City. (Out of print.)

Great Moments in Quarter Racing History, by Nelson C. Nye. Published in 1983 by Arco Publishing Inc., New York City. (Out of print.)

Speedhorse magazine, Box 1000, Norman, OK 73070.

The Quarter Horse Journal, Box 32470, Amarillo, TX 79120.

Western Horseman Magazine
Colorado Springs, Colorado

The Western Horseman, established in 1936, is the world's leading horse publication.
For subscription information and to order other Western Horseman books, contact:
Western Horseman, Box 7980, Colorado Springs, CO 80933-7980; 719-633-5524.

Books Published by Western Horseman Inc.

TEAM ROPING by Leo Camarillo
144 pages and 200 photographs covering every aspect of heading and heeling.

REINING, *Completely Revised* by Al Dunning
216 pages and over 300 photographs showing how to train horses for this popular event.

CALF ROPING by Roy Cooper
144 pages and 280 photographs covering the how-to of roping and tying.

BARREL RACING by Sharon Camarillo
144 pages and 200 photographs. Tells how to train and compete successfully.

HORSEMAN'S SCRAPBOOK by Randy Steffen
144 pages and 250 illustrations. A collection of popular handy hints.

WESTERN HORSEMANSHIP by Richard Shrake
144 pages and 150 photographs. Complete guide to riding western horses.

HEALTH PROBLEMS by Robert M. Miller, D.V.M.
144 pages on management, illness and injuries, lameness, mares and foals, and more.

CUTTING by Leon Harrel
144 pages and 200 photographs. Complete how-to guide on this popular sport.

WESTERN TRAINING by Jack Brainard
With Peter Phinny. 136 pages. Stresses the foundation for western training.

BACON & BEANS by Stella Hughes
136 pages and 200-plus recipes for popular western chow.

STARTING COLTS by Mike Kevil
168 pages and 400 photographs. Step-by-step process in starting colts.

IMPRINT TRAINING by Robert M. Miller, D.V.M.
144 pages and 250 photographs. Learn how to "program" newborn foals.

TEAM PENNING by Phil Livingston
144 pages and 200 photographs. Tells how to compete in this popular family sport.

NATURAL HORSE-MAN-SHIP by Pat Parelli
224 pages and 275 photographs. Parelli's six keys to a natural horse-human relationship.

LEGENDS by Diane C. Simmons
168 pages and 214 photographs. Includes these outstanding early-day Quarter Horse stallions and mares: Barbra B, Bert, Chicaro Bill, Cowboy P-12, Depth Charge (TB), Doc Bar, Go Man Go, Hard Twist, Hollywood Gold, Joe Hancock, Joe Reed P-3, Joe Reed II, King P-234, King Fritz, Leo, Peppy, Plaudit, Poco Bueno, Poco Tivio, Queenie, Quick M Silver, Shue Fly, Star Duster, Three Bars (TB), Top Deck (TB), and Wimpy P-1.

LEGENDS 2 by Jim Goodhue, Frank Holmes, Phil Livingston, Diane C. Simmons
192 pages and 224 photographs. Includes these outstanding Quarter Horses: Clabber, Driftwood, Easy Jet, Grey Badger II, Jessie James, Jet Deck, Joe Bailey P-4 (Gonzales), Joe Bailey (Weatherford), King's Pistol, Lena's Bar, Lightning Bar, Lucky Blanton, Midnight, Midnight Jr, Moon Deck, My Texas Dandy, Oklahoma Star, Oklahoma Star Jr., Peter McCue, Rocket Bar (TB), Skipper W, Sugar Bars, and Traveler.

ROOFS AND RAILS by Gavin Ehringer
144 pages, 128 black-and-white photographs plus drawings, charts, and floor plans. How to plan and build your ideal horse facility.

FIRST HORSE by Fran Devereux Smith
176 pages, 160 black-and-white photos, about 40 illustrations. Step-by-step, how-to information for the first-time horse owner and/or novice rider.

THE HANK WIESCAMP STORY by Frank Holmes
208 pages and over 260 photographs. The biography of the legendary breeder of Quarter Horses, Appaloosas, and Paints.